# PHP jQuery Cookbook

Over 60 simple but highly effective recipes to create
interactive web applications using PHP with jQuery

**Vijay Joshi**

[PACKT] open source *
PUBLISHING    community experience distilled

BIRMINGHAM - MUMBAI

# PHP jQuery Cookbook

First published: December 2010

Production Reference: 1081210

Published by Packt Publishing Ltd.
32 Lincoln Road
Olton
Birmingham, B27 6PA, UK.

ISBN 978-1-849512-74-9

www.packtpub.com

Cover Image by Vinayak Chittar (vinayak.chittar@gmail.com)

# Credits

**Author**

Vijay Joshi

**Reviewers**

Anis Ahmad

Md. Mahmud Ahsan

Joe Wu

Shameemah Kurzawa

**Acquisition Editor**

Chaitanya Apte

**Development Editor**

Neha Mallik

**Technical Editors**

Mohd. Sahil

Hithesh Uchil

**Editorial Team Leader**

Aanchal Kumar

**Project Team Leader**

Ashwin Shetty

**Project Coordinator**

Michelle Quadros

**Proofreader**

Mario Cecere

**Indexer**

Hemangini Bari

**Production Coordinator**

Aparna Bhagat

**Cover Work**

Aparna Bhagat

# About the Author

**Vijay Joshi** is a programmer with over six years of experience on various platforms. He discovered his passion for open source four years ago when he started playing with PHP on a hobby project after completing his Masters in Computer Applications. Vijay is a professional web developer now and prefers writing code ONLY in open source (but that does not always happen, unfortunately!). He switches hats as needed—he is full-time lead programmer at Philogy, independent consultant for a few selected companies where he advises them on a variety of Internet-based initiatives, and still remains an active blogger at http://vijayjoshi.org.

Besides his work, he enjoys reading, trekking, and sometimes getting obsessed with fitness.

Writing a book is a long and complicated task which requires the support and coordination of many people. I am thankful to the entire team at Packt, especially Michelle, Chaitanya, and Neha for being so cooperative and patient with me.

This book is dedicated to all open source developers, contributors, and enthusiasts around the world who have made PHP and jQuery the leading programming tools in their niche. A big thank you to you guys. I am feeling both proud and excited to be able to contribute to the community that gave me so much to learn.

On a personal note, I would like to thank my parents, my brother Ajay, and Sheethal for their support and encouragement.

A special thanks to Ravindra Vikram Singh for helping me get started on this project.

# About the Reviewers

**Md. Mahmud Ahsan** graduated in Computer Science & Engineering from the International Islamic University Chittagong (IIUC) in Bangladesh. He is a Zend Certified Engineer and expert in developing web applications, Facebook applications, Mashup applications, and iPhone-native applications. Besides his full time job, he blogs at `http://thinkdiff.net` and writes articles on different technologies, especially Facebook applications development. He lives in Bangladesh with his wife Jinat.

Currently, Mahmud works as a Software Engineer (remote developer) in i2we inc. (867 Avalon, Lafayette, CA) where he develops social web applications using PHP, MySQL, JavaScript, Zend Framework, CodeIgniter, jQuery, and Mashup APIs. He also leads various small to medium level projects.

Mahmud is also an Indie iPhone application developer and publishes his own applications at `http://ithinkdiff.net`.

He was a technical reviewer of the *Zend Framework 1.8 Web Application Development* book by Packt Publishing.

I'm very grateful to my father who bought a computer for me in 2001. Since then, I have loved programming and working with various technologies.

**Joe Wu** is a full-time Senior PHP Web Developer, and has been in the industry since 2005. He has worked on various projects of all sizes and is familiar with most of the open source technologies surrounding PHP web development.

Joe is always enthusiastic about new and upcoming technologies and is keen to learn and pick up new skill-sets wherever possible and utilize them in his current or future projects. He is also keen to learn about new opportunities and innovative ideas out there, and believes that the market is always wide open for new and upcoming innovations to improve our way of living.

Aside from all the technological computer work, Joe is a professional badminton player and manages to somehow fit a near full-time training schedule together with his full-time job. Joe's best ranking of 59th in the world in singles and the attendance of the Commonwealth Games Delhi 2010 means that he has equally as much experience in badminton and web developing.

Aside from all the endeavors, Joe also works for his own company (with his business partner) to put his skills and experience to good use and to help anyone who needs assistance with web development.

Wackyinnovation (www.wackyinnovation.com) promotes the concept of always moving forward and coming up with and utilizing new technologies and ideas. Their always enthusiastic and can-do attitude ensures jobs are done to perfection with an innovative edge on their competitors.

**Shameemah Kurzawa** has been programming since she was at high school. Being motivated to be a Systems Analyst, she pursued both undergraduate and postgraduate studies in Business Information System and Software Engineering, respectively.

She has been working as a Web Developer/Analyst for the past five years, for a renowned company SBS (Special Broadcasting Service) in Australia. Besides work, she enjoys spending her time with her family (she is the mum of a little two year old baby boy) and enjoys travelling as well as investigating new technologies.

I would like to thank my husband, my son, and the Packt Publishing team for their support and understanding in reviewing this book.

# www.PacktPub.com

## Support files, eBooks, discount offers, and more

You might want to visit www.PacktPub.com for support files and downloads related to your book.

Did you know that Packt offers eBook versions of every book published, with PDF and ePub files available? You can upgrade to the eBook version at www.PacktPub.com and as a print book customer, you are entitled to a discount on the eBook copy. Get in touch with us at service@packtpub.com for more details.

At www.PacktPub.com, you can also read a collection of free technical articles, sign up for a range of free newsletters and receive exclusive discounts and offers on Packt books and eBooks.

http://PacktLib.PacktPub.com

Do you need instant solutions to your IT questions? PacktLib is Packt's online digital book library. Here, you can access, read and search across Packt's entire library of books.

## Why Subscribe?

- ▶ Fully searchable across every book published by Packt
- ▶ Copy & paste, print and bookmark content
- ▶ On demand and accessible via web browser

## Free Access for Packt account holders

If you have an account with Packt at www.PacktPub.com, you can use this to access PacktLib today and view nine entirely free books. Simply use your login credentials for immediate access.

# Table of Contents

# Preface

Nowadays, web applications are behaving more and more like desktop applications with lesser page loads and more user interaction and effects. The Web has become faster and applications such as Gmail and Facebook have given a new meaning to web applications.

PHP on the server side and jQuery on the client side (browser) are a killer combination for developing interactive web applications. PHP is the leading language of choice among web developers and jQuery is now used on more than one-third of the top 1000 sites on the internet and is the most widely-used library.

One thing that PHP and jQuery have in common is that they are easy to learn. Once you know the basics, you can promote yourself to the next level easily.

And this is what the book will do for you. It is like a toolbox having a myriad of tools inside. It will allow you to write faster web applications, which feel like desktop applications, with the help of PHP and jQuery. Whether you want to learn live validations, create plugins, drag elements, create a menu, watch videos using YouTube API, or interact with the database, just jump to the respective recipe for the solution. AJAX, a key feature of rich internet applications, is also covered in detail.

You are not required to read this book from the beginning to the end. Each recipe is independent and is like a "how to" or a mini application in itself. You can directly look for a solution to a specific problem.

I hope you will find this book useful and that it will help you to take your skills to a higher level.

## What this book covers

*Chapter 1, Handling Events with jQuery,* helps you understand jQuery's cross-browser event handling methods. You will learn to work with keyboard and mouse events. Advance event handling topics, such as dragging and keyboard shortcuts are also discussed.

*Chapter 2, Combining PHP and jQuery,* lists several ways of sending AJAX requests using jQuery and also describes how PHP responds to such requests. This chapter also contains recipes that deal with caching of AJAX requests and error handling during AJAX requests.

*Chapter 3, Working with XML Documents*, explains working with XML files in PHP as well as jQuery. Recipes will describe how to read, write, and modify XMLs using DOM and SimpleXML extensions of PHP. Parsing XML with jQuery is also discussed.

*Chapter 4, Working with JSON*, discusses JSON in detail. You will be shown how to read and write JSON data in PHP, and also explore jQuery's inbuilt capabilities of parsing JSON.

*Chapter 5, Working with Forms*, deals with forms and form validations. You will learn how to validate forms for different types of data with jQuery. This will cover validating empty fields, numbers, e-mail addresses, web addresses, and much more. Server-side validation methods will also be discussed to make validations more powerful.

*Chapter 6, Adding Visual Effects to Forms*, extends the previous chapter and provides recipes for adding visual effects to forms. Recipes in this chapter allow you to create user-friendly forms by adding effects, such as highlighting, fading, expandable boxes, and various others.

*Chapter 7, Creating Cool Navigation Menus*, describes the creation of different types of menus, such as animated menus, accordions, and tabbed menus. Advanced techniques for creating tabs are also covered that will guide you in adding and removing tabs on the fly.

*Chapter 8, Data Binding with PHP and jQuery*, explains, in detail, how a database can be used along with PHP and jQuery. Examples included in this chapter will explain how to fetch data from the database and use it in web forms.

*Chapter 9, Enhancing your Site with PHP and jQuery*, teaches you some advanced techniques of PHP and jQuery. It will show how to overcome browser restrictions like cross-domain requests. You will learn to create a jQuery plugin for custom use and an endless scrolling page among other things.

*Appendix, Firebug*, explains the use of Firebug for debugging HTML and JavaScript in web pages. You will learn how to edit HTML and change the appearance of pages on the browser itself without switching to actual code files. You will be able to execute JavaScript directly from Firebug and further understand debugging JavaScript using this add-on.

# What you need for this book

You should have Apache (or another web server), PHP (version 5.0 or above), and MySQL installed on your system to be able to run the examples in this book. You can install them all at once using software such as WampServer or you can install them separately. jQuery (version 1.3.2 or higher) will also be required.

In terms of technical proficiency, this book assumes that you have working knowledge of PHP, jQuery, HTML, and CSS. You need to know only the basics of these, leave the rest to this book.

# Who this book is for

This book is for PHP and jQuery developers who just know the basics of these two and want to use PHP and jQuery together to create rich internet applications. It provides a large number of examples in each chapter that will take you from being a basic developer to a pro by giving step-by-step instructions for each task in developing web applications using PHP and jQuery.

# Conventions

In this book, you will find a number of styles of text that distinguish between different kinds of information. Here are some examples of these styles, and an explanation of their meaning.

Code words in text are shown as follows: "The `input` button has also been attached to a `click` event."

A block of code is set as follows:

```
$('input:text').bind(
{
  focus: function()
  {
   $(this).val('');
  },
  blur: function()
  {
    $(this).val('Enter some text');
  }
});
```

New terms and important words are shown in bold. Words that you see on the screen, in menus or dialog boxes for example, appear in the text like this: "Now click on the **Create New Element** button a few times to create some DIV elements".

 Warnings or important notes appear in a box like this.

 Tips and tricks appear like this.

# Reader feedback

Feedback from our readers is always welcome. Let us know what you think about this book—what you liked or may have disliked. Reader feedback is important for us to develop titles that you really get the most out of.

To send us general feedback, simply send an e-mail to feedback@packtpub.com, and mention the book title via the subject of your message.

If there is a book that you need and would like to see us publish, please send us a note in the **SUGGEST A TITLE** form on www.packtpub.com or e-mail suggest@packtpub.com.

If there is a topic that you have expertise in and you are interested in either writing or contributing to a book, see our author guide on www.packtpub.com/authors.

# Customer support

Now that you are the proud owner of a Packt book, we have a number of things to help you to get the most from your purchase.

**Downloading the example code for this book**

You can download the example code files for all Packt books you have purchased from your account at http://www.PacktPub.com. If you purchased this book elsewhere, you can visit http://www.PacktPub.com/support and register to have the files e-mailed directly to you.

## Errata

Although we have taken every care to ensure the accuracy of our content, mistakes do happen. If you find a mistake in one of our books—maybe a mistake in the text or the code—we would be grateful if you would report this to us. By doing so, you can save other readers from frustration and help us improve subsequent versions of this book. If you find any errata, please report them by visiting http://www.packtpub.com/support, selecting your book, clicking on the **errata submission form** link, and entering the details of your errata. Once your errata are verified, your submission will be accepted and the errata will be uploaded on our website, or added to any list of existing errata, under the Errata section of that title. Any existing errata can be viewed by selecting your title from http://www.packtpub.com/support.

# Piracy

Piracy of copyright material on the Internet is an ongoing problem across all media. At Packt, we take the protection of our copyright and licenses very seriously. If you come across any illegal copies of our works, in any form, on the Internet, please provide us with the location address or website name immediately so that we can pursue a remedy.

Please contact us at copyright@packtpub.com with a link to the suspected pirated material.

We appreciate your help in protecting our authors, and our ability to bring you valuable content.

# Questions

You can contact us at questions@packtpub.com if you are having a problem with any aspect of the book, and we will do our best to address it.

# 1
# Handling Events with jQuery

In this chapter, we will cover:

- ▶ Executing functions when a page has loaded
- ▶ Binding and unbinding elements
- ▶ Adding events to elements that will be created later
- ▶ Submitting a form using jQuery
- ▶ Checking for missing images
- ▶ Creating a select/unselect all checkbox functionality
- ▶ Capturing mouse movements
- ▶ Creating keyboard shortcuts
- ▶ Displaying user-selected text
- ▶ Dragging elements on a page

## Introduction

Events are actions that execute some JavaScript code for producing the desired result. They can be either some sort of manipulation of a document or some internal calculations.

Since different browsers handle events differently, it takes a lot of effort to write JavaScript code that is compatible with all browsers. This chapter will help you understand event handling and explore related methods of jQuery that can make scripts compatible on different browsers. You will learn to work with the keyboard and mouse events. Advanced event handling topics like dragging and keyboard shortcuts are also discussed.

# Executing functions when page has loaded

AJAX applications make extensive use of JavaScript to manipulate the content and the look and feel of web pages. Web pages should have the DOM loaded before any JavaScript code tries to perform any such modification on it.

This recipe will explain how to execute the JavaScript after the content has been loaded and the DOM is ready.

## Getting ready

Get a copy of the latest version of the jQuery library.

## How to do it...

1.  Create a file and name it as domReady.html.

2.  To run any JavaScript code only after the DOM has completely loaded, write it between the curly braces of .ready() method:

```
<script type="text/javascript">
    $(document).ready(function () {
        // code written here will run only after the DOM has loaded
    });
</script>
```

## How it works...

jQuery ensures that code written inside .ready() gets executed only after the DOM is fully loaded. This includes the complete document tree containing the HTML, stylesheets, and other scripts. You can, therefore, manipulate the page, attach events, and do other stuff. Note that .ready() does not wait for images to load. Images can be checked using the .load() method, which is explained in a separate recipe in this chapter.

If .ready() is not used, the jQuery code does not wait for the whole document to load. Instead it will execute as it is loaded in the browser. This can throw errors if the written code tries to manipulate any HTML or CSS that has not been loaded yet.

## Passing a handler to .ready()

In the previous example code we used an anonymous function with `.ready()`. You can also pass a handler instead of the anonymous function. It can be done as follows:

```
<script type="text/javascript">
    $(document).ready(doSomething);
    function doSomething()
    {
       // write code here
    }
</script>
```

## Another method of using .ready()

Instead of writing the code in the above mentioned format, we can also use one of the below described variations for finding out when the DOM is ready:

```
$(function ()
{
});
```

Or

```
$(doSomething);
function doSomething()
{
// DOM is ready now
}
```

## Multiple .ready() methods

If there are multiple script files in your application, you can have a `.ready()` for each of them. jQuery will run all of these after DOM loads. An example scenario may be when you are using some plugins on a page and each one of them has a separate `.js` file.

# Binding and unbinding elements

This recipe will demonstrate how you can attach events to DOM elements using the `.bind()` method and how to remove them using the `.unbind()` method.

## Getting ready

Get a latest copy of the jQuery library to use with this recipe.

## How to do it...

1. Create a new file, in a directory named `chapter1`, and name it as `binding.html`.

2. Write the HTML markup to create some HTML elements. Create an unordered list with the names of some countries. After that, create a select box containing names of continents as options. Finally, create a button that will be used to remove the event handler from the select box.

```html
<html>
  <head>
    <title>Binding Elements</title>
    <style type="text/css">
      ul { background-color:#DCDCDC; list-style:none; margin:0pt;
           padding:0pt; width:250px;}
      li { cursor:pointer; margin:10px 0px;}
    </style>
  </head>
  <body>
    <ul>
      <li>India</li>
      <li>USA</li>
      <li>UK</li>
      <li>France</li>
    </ul>

    <select>
      <option value="Africa">Africa</option>
      <option value="Antarctica">Antarctica</option>
      <option value="Asia">Asia</option>
      <option value="Australia">Australia</option>
      <option value="Europe">Europe</option>
      <option value="North America">North America</option>
      <option value="South America">South America</option>
    </select>

    <input type="button" value="Unbind select box"/>
  </body>
</html>
```

3.  It's time to add some jQuery magic. Attach a `click` event handler to list items using the `.bind()` method, which will set the background color of the clicked item to red. Attach the `change` event handler to the select box, which will display the value of the selected item. Finally, add a `click` handler to the button. Clicking on the button will remove the event handler from the select box.

```html
<script type="text/javascript" src="jquery.js"></script>
<script type="text/javascript">
  $(document).ready(function ()
  {
    $('input:text').bind(
    {
      focus: function()
      {
      $(this).val('');
      },
      blur: function()
      {
        $(this).val('Enter some text');
      }
    });

    $('li').bind('click', function()
    {
      $(this).css('background-color', 'red');
    });

    $('select').bind('change', function()
    {
      alert('You selected: '+ $(this).val());
    });

    $('input:button').bind('click', function()
    {
      $('select').unbind('change');
    });
  });
</script>
```

4. Run the `binding.html` file in your browser and click on some items in the list. The background color of each item clicked upon will change to red. Now select some value from the select box and you will see an alert box that displays the selected value as shown in the following screenshot:

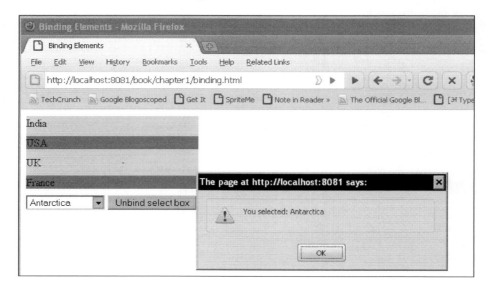

Clicking on the **Unbind select box** button will remove the `change` event handler here and the selection of a value from the combo box will now do nothing.

## How it works...

jQuery uses the `.bind()` method to attach standard JavaScript events to elements. `.bind()` takes two parameters. The first parameter is the event type to attach. It is passed in string format, and event types such as `click`, `change`, `keyup`, `keydown`, `focus`, `blur`, and so on can be passed to it. The second parameter is the callback function, which will be executed when the event fires.

In the previous code, we used `.bind()` for the list items to attach a `click` handler. In the callback function, `$(this)` refers to the element that fired the event. We then use the `.css()` method to change the background color of the element that is clicked upon.

Similarly, we attached the `change` event to the select box using the `.bind()` method. The callback function will be called each time the value of the select box is changed.

The `input` button has also been attached to a `click` event. Clicking on the button calls the `.unbind()` method. This method accepts an event type name and removes that event from the element. Our example code will remove the `change` event from the select box. Therefore, changing the value of the select box will not display any further alerts.

# There's more...

## Binding multiple events

Multiple events can also be attached using the .bind() method. The following code attaches two events focus and blur to a textbox. Focusing on a textbox will empty it, whereas taking the focus away from it will put some text in it.

```
$('input:text').bind(
{
  focus: function()
  {
    $(this).val('');
  },
  blur: function()
  {
    $(this).val('Enter some text');
  }
});
```

 Note that this functionality was added in Version 1.4 of jQuery. So, make sure that you have the correct version before running this code.

## Shortcut method for binding

Instead of using .bind(), events can be attached directly by using shortcut event names to elements. For example, $(element).click(function() {      }); can be written instead of using $(element).bind('click', function() {      });.

Other events can be attached similarly.

## Triggering events

Events can also be triggered from the code. For this we have to pass the event name without any parameter.

```
$(element1).click(function()
{
  $(element2).keydown();
});
```

The above code will execute the keydown event of element2 when element1 is clicked.

## Common event types

Here is a list of some common events that can be passed to the `bind()` and `unbind()` methods.

| | |
|---|---|
| blur | focus |
| load | unload |
| scroll | click |
| dblclick | mousedown |
| mouseup | mousemove |
| mouseover | mouseout |
| change | select |
| submit | keydown |
| keypress | keyup |

## Unbinding all events from an element

If no parameter is passed to the `.unbind()` method, it will remove all event handlers associated with the specified element.

```
$(element).unbind();
```

# Adding events to elements that will be created later

The `.bind()` method attaches events to only those elements that exist on a page. If any new elements are created that match the criteria for the `.bind()` method, they will not have any event handlers.

## How to do it...

1. Create a new file in the `chapter1` directory and name it as `live.html`.

2. Write the HTML, which creates a button and a DIV on the page and styles them a bit.

```
<html>
  <head>
    <title>Attaching events elements </title>
    <style type="text/css">
    div { border: 1px solid black;cursor:pointer;width:200px;margi
n:10px; }
    </style>
  </head>
  <body>
    <input type="button" id="button" value="Create New Element"/>
```

```
    <div class="future">Already on page</div>
  </body>
</html>
```

3. Time to spice things up with jQuery. Attach a `click` event to the button. This button will create the new DIV elements and will insert them into the page. Now attach a `click` event handler to the DIV using the `live()` method. Clicking on the DIV will change its CSS and HTML.

```
<script type="text/javascript" src="jquery.js"></script>
<script type="text/javascript">
  $(document).ready(function ()
  {
    $('#button').click(function()
    {
      $('body').append('<div class="future">I am a new
        div</div>');
    });

    $('div').live('click', function()
    {
      $(this).css({'color':'red','font-weight':'bold'})
        .html('You clicked me');
      });
    });
</script>
```

4. Run the `live.html` file and click on the DIV. You will see that its HTML and CSS has changed. Now click on the **Create New Element** button a few times to create some DIV elements. Clicking on any of these DIV elements will change their appearances. A typical screenshot after a few clicks will look similar to the following:

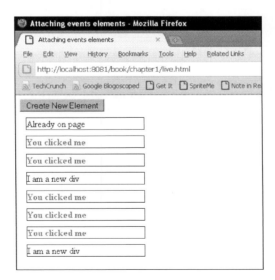

## How it works...

The `input` button creates the new DIV elements and appends them to the body of a document. The secret lies in the next function. We have used jQuery's `live()` method to attach an event on click of a DIV element. `live()` behaves exactly like `bind()` for attaching events with only one major difference. Where `bind()` can add events to only existing elements on a page, `live()` remembers the attached event for that selector and applies it to matching elements even if they are created later and then inserted into a page.

Therefore, all new DIV elements that are created as a result of clicking on the **Create New Element** button also respond to the `click` event handler.

### Removing event handlers with die()

The `die()` method is similar to the `unbind()` method. It is used to remove event handlers that were attached using the `live()` method. Similar to `unbind()`, `die()` also has two variations.

If it is called with no parameters, all event handlers will be removed. Another variation accepts an event type name that will remove that particular event:

```
$(element).die();
```

The following is the code for other variations that will remove only the specified event handler.

```
$(element).die('click');
```

If an element has more than one event handler attached to it, the above code will remove only the `click` event handler and will leave the others intact.

## See also

 ▶  *Binding and unbinding elements* provides basic information about adding and removing events from elements.

# Submitting a form with jQuery

We know that `submit` buttons are used in HTML forms to submit data to a server. Apart from `submit` buttons, JavaScript also provides a submit method that can be used to submit forms.

In this recipe, you will learn how to submit forms the jQuery way and will also learn how the form submission can be controlled using the `submit` button.

## Getting ready

Get the jQuery library to use with this recipe.

## How to do it...

1. Create a new file, name it as `formSubmit.html` and save it in the `chapter1` directory.

2. Write the following code, which creates a form with an `input` button (not `submit` button). Add some jQuery code that will be triggered on clicking the button and will submit the form.

```html
<html>
  <head>
    <title>Submitting forms</title>
  </head>
  <body>
    <form id="myForm">
      <input type="button" value="Submit Form" />
    </form>
    <script type="text/javascript" src="jquery.js"></script>
    <script type="text/javascript">
      $(document).ready(function ()
      {
        $('input:button').click(function()
        {
          $('#myForm').submit();
        });
      });
    </script>
  </body>
</html>
```

3. Run the `formSubmit.html` file and click on the `input` button. It will submit the form.

## How it works...

In this example we attached the `click` event handler to the `input` button. The event handler function will execute when the button is clicked. On clicking the button, jQuery's `submit()` method is called on the form, which submits the form. All browsers have a native submit method to submit the form programmatically. jQuery has wrapped this functionality into its own `submit()` method.

## There's more...

### Controlling form submission

If a form has a `submit` button then we can control whether to submit the form or not. In this case we will have to attach an event handler to the form. This event handler will be executed when a `submit` button on that particular form is clicked.

```
$('#myForm').submit(function()
{
  return false;
});
```

The above code will execute when a `submit` button on the form with ID `myForm` is clicked. If `false` is returned by the handler function, the form will not be submitted. This can be pretty handy for validating forms. The code for validating form values can be placed in the handler function. If values are validated, true can be returned, which will submit the form. In case the validation fails, false can be returned, which will not allow the form to be submitted.

Another option is to use `preventDefault()`. As the name indicates, `preventDefault()` prevents the default event from being executed. It is a property of the `event` object.

```
$('#myForm').submit(function(event)
{
  event.preventDefault()
});
```

## See also

 ▶   *Binding and unbinding elements* explains how to add and remove events
     from elements.

# Checking for missing images

If you are displaying some images in the browser and unfortunately some of the images are missing, the browser will either display a blank space or will display a placeholder with a cross symbol. This surely looks ugly and you would definitely want to avoid it. Wouldn't it be good if you had a method with which you could find missing images or those that failed to load?

After going through this recipe you will be able to detect missing images and replace them with an image of your choice.

## Getting ready

Get three or four images from your computer. You will need these with this recipe. Also keep the jQuery file handy. Create another image using a program like paint with text "Could not load image" written on it. This will be the default placeholder for images that fail to load.

## How to do it...

1. Create a new file in the `chapter1` directory and name it as `error.html`.

2. Place a DIV in the page, which will be filled with images. Also, write some CSS to style the DIV and the images.

```html
<html>
  <head>
    <title>Check missing images</title>
    <style type="text/css">
    div
    {
      border:1px solid black;
      float:left;
    }
    img
    {
      width:180px;
      height:200px;
      margin:10px;
    }
    </style>

  </head>
  <body>
    <div id="imageContainer"></div>
  </body>
</html>
```

3. Write the jQuery code that creates an array of image names. Intentionally put some random names of images that do not exist. Then fill the DIV by creating image tags from this array. Next, bind the `error()` event handler to the image elements.

```javascript
<script type="text/javascript" src="jquery.js"></script>
<script type="text/javascript">
  $(document).ready(function ()
  {
    var images= ['himalaya.png', 'chaukori.png', 'tree.png',
      'noSuchimage.png',   'anotheNonExistentImage.png'];
    var html = '';
    $.each(images,function(key, value)
    {
```

```
    html+= '<img src="'+value+'" />';
  });
  $('#imageContainer').html(html);

  $('img').error(function()
  {
    $(this).replaceWith('<img src="missing.png"
      alt="Could not load image">');
  });
});
</script>
```

4.  Run the `error.html` file in a browser. You will see that the last two images, which do not exist, have been replaced by another image that says **Could not load image**.

## How it works...

First we use jQuery's `$.each()` method to iterate in the array that holds image names and fills the DIV by creating `image` tags.

Then there is an `error()` event handler attached to `image` tags. This gets executed when the image fails to load or has a broken `src` attribute. The event handler for the `error()` method replaces the nonexistent image with another image of our choice. In our case we replace it with an image that we have created and that says **Could not load image**.

## See also

> ▸ *Binding and unbinding elements*, which explains the basics of adding events.

# Creating the select/unselect all checkboxes functionality

This is a frequently-used feature of web applications. A group of checkboxes exists on a page, which can be controlled by a single checkbox. Clicking on the master checkbox selects all checkboxes and unchecking it deselects all.

We will create the functionality to toggle checkboxes in this recipe. We will also learn how to get values for checked elements using jQuery's selectors.

## Getting ready

Make sure you have the jQuery library ready to be used.

## How to do it...

1. Create a new file in the `chapter1` directory and name it as `checkbox.html`.

2. Let us design the page first. Create an unordered list and apply some CSS to it. The first item in this list will be a checkbox that will work as a handle to toggle other checkboxes. Then create other items in the list: names of books each having a checkbox before it. All these checkboxes have the same class name `toggle`. Create another list item consisting of a button that will be used to display the selected books. Finally, create a last list item and assign an ID to it. We will use it to display selected book names.

```html
<html>
  <head>
    <title>Select/Unselect Checkboxes</title>
    <style type="text/css">
    ul { background-color:#DCDCDC; list-style:none; margin:0pt;
        padding:0pt; width:350px;}
    li { padding:10px; }
    </style>
  </head>
  <body>
    <ul>
      <li>
        <input type="checkbox" id="handle">
        <label for="handle">
```

```
                  <strong>Toggle All</strong></label>
      </li>
      <li>
        <input type="checkbox" class="toggle"/>
        <label>A Study in Scarlet</label>
      </li>
      <li>
        <input type="checkbox" class="toggle"/>
        <label>The Sign of the Four</label>
      </li>
      <li>
        <input type="checkbox" class="toggle"/>
        <label>The Adventures of Sherlock Holmes</label>
      </li>
      <li>
        <input type="checkbox" class="toggle"/>
        <label>The Valley of Fear</label>
      </li>
      <li>
        <input type="checkbox" class="toggle"/>
        <label>His Last Bow</label>
      </li>
      <li><input type="button" id="getValue"
                value="Get Selected Values"/></li>
      <li id="selected"></li>
    </ul>
  </body>
</html>
```

3. Running the `checkbox.html` file in browser will display the following screen:

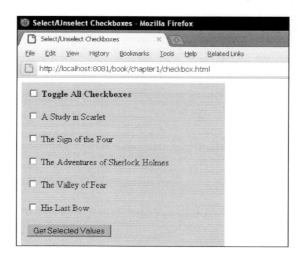

4. To bring this page to life include the jQuery library and attach event handlers to the checkboxes. The first event handler will be attached to the first checkbox, which will take care of selecting and deselecting all other checkboxes. The second one will be attached to individual checkboxes. It will select/deselect the main handle depending on whether all checkboxes are checked or not. The last event handler is for the `input` button that will display the selected values beneath it.

```
<script type="text/javascript" src="jquery.js"></script>
<script type="text/javascript">
  $(document).ready(function()
  {
    $('#handle').click(function(){
      if($(this).attr('checked') == true)
        $('.toggle').attr('checked', 'true');
      else
        $('.toggle').removeAttr('checked');
    });

    $('.toggle').click(function(){
      if($('.toggle:checked').length == $('.toggle').length)
        $('#handle').attr('checked', 'true');

      if($('.toggle:checked').length < $('.toggle').length)
        $('#handle').removeAttr('checked');

    });

    $('#getValue').click(function(){
      var values = '';
      if($('.toggle:checked').length)
      {
        $('.toggle:checked').each(function(){
          values+= $(this).next('label').html() + ' ,';
        });
        $('#selected').html('Selected values are: ' + values);
      }
      else
        $('#selected').html('Nothing selected');
    });
  });
</script>
```

5. Now, refresh your browser and start playing with the checkboxes. Clicking on the **Toggle All** checkbox will select and deselect all the checkboxes alternatively. Click on the **Get Selected Values** button and a comma-separated list will appear below the button displaying names of all selected books.

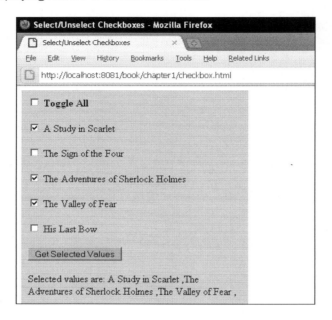

## How it works...

On clicking the **Toggle All** checkbox we check if it is selected or not. If it is selected, we select all the other checkboxes having the class `toggle` using the class selector and set their `checked` attribute to true, which selects all the checkboxes. On the other hand, if it is not selected we remove the `checked` attribute from all checkboxes that makes all of these deselected.

We will have to take care of another issue here. If all the checkboxes are selected and any one of them is deselected, the handler checkbox should also get deselected. Similarly, if all checkboxes are selected one by one, the handler checkbox should also get checked. For this we attach another event handler to all the checkboxes having class `toggle`. The `.toggle:checked` selector selects all those elements that have class `toggle` and those which are also selected. If the length of the selected elements is equal to the total number of checkboxes, we can conclude that all are selected and hence we select the handler checkbox too.

If the number of selected elements is less than the total number of checkboxes then we remove the `checked` attribute of the handler checkbox to deselect it.

## There's more...

### Using selectors

In the previous example we used `.toggle:checked` to select all the checkboxes that have class `toggle` and are checked. `:` is a selector that is used to filter a set of elements. Listed below are examples that demonstrate how it can be used to filter elements.

```
$('div:first').click(function()
{
  //do something
});
```

The above code will select the first DIV on the page and will add a `click` event handler to it.

```
$(p:gt(2)').hide();
```

`gt` stands for greater than. It accepts a 0-based index and matches elements that have an index greater than the one specified. If a page has 5 p elements, the above example will hide p numbers 3 and 4. Remember that the index is 0-based.

You can read about all the selectors on the jQuery site at this URL: `http://api.jquery.com/category/selectors/`.

# Capturing mouse events

jQuery can be used to determine the position of the mouse pointer on screen. This recipe explains the technique for getting the mouse pointer position on screen. You will learn how to create a tooltip that will appear at current mouse pointer position on a particular element.

## Getting ready

Keep the jQuery file ready to use with this recipe.

## How to do it...

1. Open a new file in your text editor and save it in `chapter1` directory as `mouse.html`.

2. Create a DIV with the ID `tip` and `display` set to `none`. This DIV will be displayed as tooltip. Create three more DIV elements and assign class `hoverMe` to the first and the last DIV. Write CSS styles for the DIV elements. The DIV that will be displayed as the tooltip must have `position` set to `absolute`.

```
<html>
  <head>
    <title>Mouse Movements</title>
```

```css
<style type="text/css">
  div
  {
    border:1px solid black;
    float:left;
    width:200px;
    height:200px;
    margin:10px;
    font-family:verdana,arial;
    font-size:14px;
  }

  div#tip
  {
    position:absolute;
    width:100px;
    height:auto;
  }
</style>
</head>
<body>

<div id="tip" style="display:none;">YaY! I am a tooltip</div>

<div class="hoverMe">Hover me for a tooltip.</div>
<div>This div will not display a tooltip</div>
<div class="hoverMe">Hover me for a tooltip.</div>

</body>
</html>
```

3. Write the jQuery code that will display the tooltip when hovering over the DIV with class hoverMe. Two functions will be required for this. The first one will take care of showing and hiding the tooltip on hover with fade effect. The second function will actually set the position of tooltip and will move it as the mouse pointer moves.

```javascript
<script type="text/javascript" src="jquery.js"></script>
<script type="text/javascript">
  $(document).ready(function ()
  {
    $('.hoverMe').hover(
    function()
    {
      $('#tip').fadeIn('slow');
    },
    function()
    {
```

```
    $('#tip').fadeOut('slow');
  });

  $('.hoverMe').mousemove(function(e)
  {
    var topPosition = e.pageY+5;
    var leftPosition = e.pageX+5;
    $('#tip').css(
    {
      'top' :  topPosition+ 'px',
      'left' : leftPosition +'px'
    });
  });
});
</script>
```

4. Open your browser and run the `mouse.html` file. Hovering over the first and last DIV elements will display a tooltip with fade effect. The tooltip will also follow the mouse pointer as it moves.

## How it works...

We have used the `hover()` method on the DIV elements to show and hide the tooltip. This method attaches two event handlers to the specified element. The first event handler gets executed when the mouse pointer enters the element and the second one executes when the mouse pointer leaves that element. We have used the `fadeIn()` method to display the tooltip when a mouse pointer enters a DIV and the `fadeout()` method to hide the DIV as soon as the mouse pointer leaves it.

The most important thing now is to position the tooltip where the mouse pointer is. For this we attached an event handler `mousemove` on the DIV. As the name indicates, the handler function will execute when the mouse pointer is moving over the DIV. jQuery makes an event object available to the handler function, using which we can get the current mouse pointer position. The `pageX` property of the event gives us the cursor position relative to the left corner of the document. Similarly, the `pageY` property gets the mouse pointer position relative to the top of the window.

We have the mouse pointer coordinates with us now. We then assign the value of `pageX` and `pageY` to the CSS properties `left` and `top` of the tooltip DIV respectively.The value 5 has been added to each value to avoid the cursor from hiding part of the tooltip.

# Creating keyboard shortcuts

Keyboard navigation is common in window-based applications. This is very handy for those who prefer keyboard controls over mouse controls. Keyboard shortcuts can also be created in web applications but they are difficult to implement due to inconsistency among browsers.

We will create a simple example in this recipe that will give you the basic understanding of implementing shortcut keys. You will be able to create your own shortcut keys for use in your web applications.

## Getting ready

Get the jQuery library to use with this recipe.

## How to do it...

1. Create a new file named `keyboard.html` and save it in the `chapter1` directory.

2. In the body of HTML create two DIV elements and in the `<head>` section write some CSS to apply styles to these DIV elements.

```
<html>
  <head>
    <title>Keyboard Shortcuts</title>
    <style type="text/css">
    div{ border : 1px solid black;float:left;height:200px;
            margin:10px; width:220px;}
    </style>
  </head>
  <body>
    <div>You can toggle this div using Alt+S</div>
```

```
      <div>You can toggle this div using Alt+G </div>

      <p style="clear:both;"> </p>
      <p>Press Alt+B to toggle both divs</p>
    </body>
</html>
```

3. Write the jQuery code that will create keyboard shortcuts to toggle these DIV elements. The `keydown` event handler will be used to implement this behaviour. It will check for the keys that are pressed and then take actions accordingly. Three shortcuts will be created. Pressing *Alt + S* will toggle the first DIV. *Alt + G* will toggle the second DIV. Pressing *Alt + B* will toggle both the DIV elements together.

Another handler `keyup` will be used to reset the required variables.

```
<script type="text/javascript" src="jquery.js"></script>
<script type="text/javascript">
  $(document).ready(function ()
  {
    //remember that this is a global variable
    var altPressed = false;
    $(document).keydown(function (event)
    {
      if(event.which == 18)
        altPressed = true;
      if(altPressed)
      {
        switch(event.which)
        {
          case 83:
              $('div:first').slideToggle('slow');
              return false;
              break;
          case 71:
              $('div:last').slideToggle('slow');
              return false;
              break;
          case 66:
              $('div').slideToggle('slow');
              return false;
              break;
        }
      }
    });
```

```
$(document).keyup(function (event) {
  if(event.which == 18)
    altPressed = false;
});
});
</script>
```

4.  Open your browser and run the `keyboard.html` file. Try pressing the shortcuts that we have just created. You will see that the DIV elements will toggle with a slide effect.

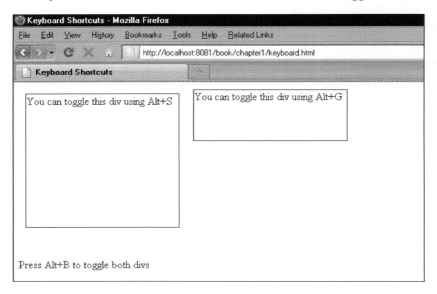

## How it works...

In order to be able to create shortcut keys, first we need to find out which key was pressed. Different browsers have their own methods of determining the value of the pressed key. jQuery normalizes the way this information can be retrieved across browsers. An `event` object is available to handler functions. This `event` object has a property `which` that gives the code of the pressed key. *Alt* key has the value 18.

The keyboard shortcuts in this recipe use the combination of *Alt* and the other keys. We begin by declaring a global variable `altPressed` with the value set to `false`. Then there are two events attached to the page. `keydown` will execute when a key is in a pressed state and `keyup` when a key is released. Whenever *Alt* is pressed the `keydown` event will set its value to true. When released, it will be reset to `false` again by the `keyup` handler function.

Next comes the `if` statement, which will evaluate to a `true` value if the *Alt* key is pressed. If *Alt* is pressed and another key is pressed along with it, the `switch` case will check the key's value and will execute the corresponding `switch` case.

The value for the *S* key is 83. So, pressing *S* along with *Alt* will select the first DIV and will apply the `slideToggle` effect to it. Similarly, *Alt + G* will toggle the second DIV and *Alt + B* will toggle both DIVs.

 Note the return of false in each case of switch statement. Returning false is necessary to override a browser's default behavior. If false is not returned, pressing the *Alt* key will activate the browser's menu.

## There's more...

### List of common key codes

A list of key codes can be found at `http://goo.gl/v2Fk`

## See also

▶  *Binding and unbinding elements* in this chapter explains how to attach events to elements.

# Displaying user selected text

You must have seen the **WYSIWYG (What You See Is What You Get)** editors in web applications, which allow you to select some text using the mouse or keyboard and then format it (like making it bold, changing its color, and so on).

This recipe will teach you how to retrieve the text that is selected by a user and perform some basic formatting on it.

## Getting ready

Get the jQuery library ready.

## How to do it...

1.  Create a file named `textSelect.html` in your `chapter1` directory.
2.  Create four buttons out of which the first three will be used to make the text bold, italic, and underlined respectively. Then create a textarea with some text in it. And finally, enter a paragraph that will be used to display the formatted HTML.

The last button will get the value of textarea and will insert it in the paragraph.

```html
<html>
  <head>
    <title>Manipulating user selected text</title>
    <style type="text/css">
      p { color:red;font-size:17px;width:670px;}
    </style>
  </head>
  <body>
    <input type="button" value="b" id="bold" class="button">
    <input type="button" value="i" id="italics" class="button">
    <input type="button" value="u" id="underline" class="button">
    <input type="button" id="apply" value="Apply HTML">
    <div>
    <textarea id="selectable" rows="20" cols="80">I consider that
      a man's brain originally is like a little empty attic, and
      you have to stock it with such furniture as you choose. A
      fool takes in all the lumber of every sort that he comes
      cross, so that the knowledge which might be useful to him
      gets crowded out, or at best is jumbled up with a lot of
      other things, so that he has a difficulty in laying his
      hands upon it.</textarea>
    </div>
    <p id="container"></p>
  </body>
</html>
```

3. Include the jQuery library and write the JavaScript function that will get the start and end positions of the selected text.

```javascript
<script type="text/javascript" src="jquery.js"></script>
<script type="text/javascript">
function getPositions()
{
  var startPosition = endPosition = 0;
  var element = document.getElementById('selectable');
  if (document.selection)
  {
    //for Internet Explorer
    var range = document.selection.createRange();
    var drange = range.duplicate();
    drange.moveToElementText(element);
    drange.setEndPoint("EndToEnd", range);
    startPosition = drange.text.length - range.text.length;
    endPosition = startPosition + range.text.length;
  }
```

```
   else if (window.getSelection)
   {
     //For Firefox, Chrome, Safari etc
     startPosition = element.selectionStart;
     endPosition = element.selectionEnd;

   }
   return {'start': startPosition, 'end': endPosition};
}
```

4. Next, write the code for the **Apply HTML** button that will simply get the text from the textarea and insert it in the paragraph.

```
$('#apply').click(function()
{
    var html = $('#container').html($('#selectable').val());
});
```

5. Let's code the first three buttons now. We will bind the click event with the three buttons. On the click of each button, the position of the selected text will be retrieved and it will be enclosed within HTML tags depending on which button is clicked.

```
$('.button').click(function()
{
  var positions = getPositions();
  if(positions.start == positions.end)
  {
    return false;
  }
  var tag = $(this).val();
  var textOnPage = $('#selectable').val();

  var startString = textOnPage.substr(0, positions.start);

  var targetString = textOnPage.substr(positions.start,
     positions.end - positions.start);
  var formattedString = "<" + tag +">" + targetString +
    "</" +  tag +">";
  var endString = textOnPage.substr(positions.end);
  $('#selectable').text(startString + formattedString +
     endString);
});
```

6.  Save the code, start your browser and point it to the file. Select some text with your mouse and click on any of the buttons. You will see that the selected text has been enclosed with the corresponding HTML tags. If you click on the second button (**u**), the selected text will be enclosed in `<u>` and `</u>` HTML tags.

    Now click on the **Apply HTML** button. You will be able to see the formatted text of the textarea in HTML format inside the paragraph, as seen in the following screenshot:

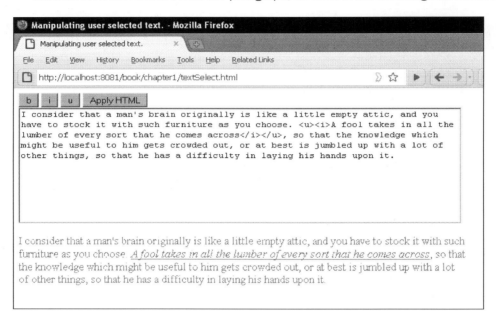

## How it works...

On click of a button, we first get the start and end positions of selected text using the `getPositions()` function. Determining this value is a bit complex as different browsers have different methods for handling selections. Internet Explorer uses `document.selection`, which represents a subset of documents, whereas Mozilla and similar browsers use `window.getSelection`.

IE has a range of objects using which we can determine what text was selected, and the start and end positions of selection in original text. First we create a range object from the selection. Then we create a clone of it using the `duplicate` method. After this, two functions `moveToElementText()` and `setEndPoint()` are used on the duplicated range. These methods align the values of original text and the selection.

Once this is done, we compare the values of the original and the duplicated range to find out the start position. Then we add the length of the selection to the start position, which gives us the end position marker.

For other browsers, getting positions is relatively simple. Start and end positions of selections in textarea can be retrieved using `.selectionStart` and `.selectionEnd` properties.

Once we get both these values, we create an object in which we put both of these and return the object to the calling function.

If the values of both these positions are equal, it means that no text is selected. In this case we simply return from the function and do nothing.

Then we determine which button was clicked. The clicked button's value will be used to format the selected text. After that, we store the value of textarea in a local variable `textOnPage`.

Now comes the part where the actual manipulation takes place. We break the `textOnPage` variable into three parts. The first part contains the string from the beginning to the starting position of the selection. The second part of the string is the actual selected text of textarea that has to be formatted. We now enclose it in HTML tags (`<b>`, `<i>`, or `<u>`) according to the button clicked. The third and final part is from where the selection ends to the end of the string.

To get the resulting string we can now simply concatenate these three strings and place it back into the textarea. The textarea will now have text that has the selected text enclosed in HTML tags. To verify this, click on the **Apply HTML** button. This will take the text from the textarea and insert it as HTML into the paragraph with ID `container`.

## There's more...

### Short method for getting selected text

Another method can be used to get the selected text from other elements, such as `<div>`, `<p>`, and so on. This will not give any positions but simply the selected text. Note that this method will not work for textareas for Mozilla and similar browsers but it will work in Internet Explorer for textareas as well as other controls.

Use the following function to get the selected text:

```
function getSelectedText()
{
  var selectedText = '';
  if (document.selection)
  {
  var range = document.selection.createRange();
    selectedText = range.text;
    }
    else if (window.getSelection)
    {
      selectedText = window.getSelection();
    }
  return selectedText;
}
```

# Dragging elements on a page

There are many plugins based on JavaScript, jQuery, and other libraries, which let users implement the dragging functionality. A user presses the mouse button on an element and moves it without releasing it. The element gets dragged along with the mouse pointer. The dragging stops once the mouse key is released.

After finishing this recipe, you will be able to implement a dragging feature for elements on your own. This recipe will show you how to make elements on a page draggable.

## Getting ready

Get the jQuery library to use with this recipe.

## How to do it...

1.  Create a new file in the `chapter1` directory and name it as `drag.html`.

2.  Create some DIV elements and assign the `dragMe` class to customize their appearance. This class will also be used to attach event handlers to the DIV.

```html
<html>
  <head>
    <title>Dragging</title>
    <style type="text/css">
      .dragMe
      {
        background-color:#8FBC8F;
        border:1px solid black;
        color: #fff;
        float:left;
        font-family:verdana,arial;
        font-size:14px;
        font-weight:bold;
        height:100px;
        margin:10px;
        text-align:center;
        width:100px;
      }
    </style>
  </head>
  <body>
```

```
    <div class="dragMe">Drag Me</div>
    <div class="dragMe">Drag Me too</div>
  </body>
</html>
```

3.  In the jQuery code, declare variables that will hold the coordinates of DIV being dragged and the mouse pointer. Proceed to `attach` event handlers for mouse movement to elements with the `dragMe` class.

    We have attached two event handlers. The first is `mousedown`, which will execute while the mouse button is in a pressed state on the target DIV. This will get the current left and top coordinates of the DIV being dragged and the mouse pointer. Now bind the `mousemove` element to the current DIV. The `dragElement` function will be called when the mouse moves while its button is pressed.

    The function `dragElement` calculates new values for the top and left of the DIV by determining mouse movements and the DIV's current position and applies these properties to the DIV. This results in the movement of the DIV.

    Finally, bind the `mouseup` event to the document, which will stop the dragging after the mouse has been released.

```
<script type="text/javascript" src="jquery.js"></script>
<script type="text/javascript">
  $(document).ready(function ()
  {
    var mousex = 0, mousey = 0;
    var divLeft, divTop;
    $('.dragMe').mousedown(function(e)
    {
```

```
      var offset = $(this).offset();
      divLeft = parseInt(offset.left,10);
      divTop = parseInt(offset.top,10);
      mousey = e.pageY;
      mousex = e.pageX;
      $(this).bind('mousemove',dragElement);
    });

    function dragElement(event)
    {
      var left = divLeft + (event.pageX - mousex);
      var top = divTop + (event.pageY - mousey);
      $(this).css(
      {
        'top' :  top + 'px',
        'left' : left + 'px',
        'position' : 'absolute'
      });
      return false;
    }
    $(document).mouseup(function()
    {
      $('.dragMe').unbind('mousemove');
    });

  });
</script>
```

4. Open the browser and run the `drag.html` file. Both DIV elements would be draggable by now. You will now be able to drag any of these DIV elements by pressing the mouse button over them and moving them around.

## How it works...

Global variables `mousex` and `mousey` will be used to store the left and top positions for the mouse pointer, and the `divLeft` and `divTop` variable will store the left and top coordinates of the DIV. Then we attached two event handlers to the DIV with class `dragMe`. First is `mousedown`, which will execute when the mouse button is in a pressed state on the target DIV. In this function get the left and top positions of the DIV being dragged and store them in the `divLeft` and `divTop` variables respectively. Secondly, get the left and top values for the current mouse pointer position from the event object and save them in the `mousex` and `mousey` variables. Now when the button is pressed, bind the `mousemove` element to current DIV. The `dragElement` function will be called when the mouse pointer moves while its button is pressed.

The `dragElement` function now calculates the new left and top values for the DIV being dragged. To calculate the new value for left, take the left value for the DIV (`divLeft`) and add the difference in the mouse position to it. The difference in mouse position can be calculated by subtracting the previous left value for mouse pointer from the current left value. Similarly calculate the new value for top.

After both these values are calculated, use the `css()` method to apply these values to the DIV being dragged. Don't forget to set the position as `absolute`. Without absolute positioning the DIV will not be able to move.

## See also

 ▸ *Capturing mouse movements* in this chapter explains the method of retrieving mouse coordinates.

 ▸ *Binding and unbinding elements* in this chapter teaches the basics of event handling.

# 2
# Combining PHP and jQuery

In this chapter, we will cover:

- ▶ Fetching data from PHP using jQuery
- ▶ Creating a query string automatically for all form elements
- ▶ Detecting an AJAX request in PHP
- ▶ Sending data to PHP
- ▶ Aborting AJAX requests
- ▶ Creating an empty page and loading it in parts
- ▶ Handling errors in AJAX requests
- ▶ Preventing a browser from caching AJAX request
- ▶ Loading JavaScript on demand to reduce page load time

## Introduction

You surely know how typical web applications work. You enter a URL in your browser and the browser loads that page for you. If you are required to submit a form, you will fill it and the browser sends the filled data to the server side for processing. During this time you wait for the entire page to load. If you are on a slow connection, the wait is even longer.

Let me describe another typical scenario, a web page has two select boxes. The first select box asks you to select the name of a country. You make your selection and the whole page loads to populate the second select box with the names of the cities in that country. If by mistake you made a wrong selection, fixing your mistake means another page load. Irritating isn't it?

The point I am trying to make here is: why load the complete page every time? Why can't you just select the country name and using some magic in the background be provided with the city list without loading the complete page? Maybe you can fill some other fields if the request is taking longer.

This is where AJAX fits. AJAX is short for Asynchronous JavaScript and XML. AJAX is a technique through which client-side scripts can interact with the server-side scripts using standard HTTP protocols. Data can be moved back and forth between a client and a server script without full page reloads.

Let's find out the meaning of AJAX word by word.

▶ **Asynchronous**: Asynchronous means that requests are made in the background eliminating the need for a full page load. They can also be sent in parallel, and in the meantime the user can continue interacting with other elements on the page. Users do not have to wait for AJAX requests to complete. Remember the previous country-city example? Yes it can be done.

▶ **JavaScript**: JavaScript means that the request to the server originates from JavaScript. Browsers have their own implementation of what is called an XMLHttpRequest object. It is not a standard but different browsers have their own implementation for it.

▶ **XML**: AJAX requests can be made to any platform be it a PHP page or a Java page. Therefore, to exchange any data between a client and server, there arises the need for a common format that can be understood by both JavaScript and server-side language. One such format is XML. Data can be transferred between both client and server using XML format.

▶ The XML in AJAX does not necessarily mean XML only. Data can be exchanged in other formats as well. It can be your custom format, text, HTML, or JSON too. Most common formats today are HTML and JSON.

Since the XMLHttpRequest implementation of browsers vary, jQuery has wrapped this functionality providing us with an array of cross-browser methods to work with AJAX requests.

In this chapter, you will get to know multiple AJAX methods of jQuery to transfer data between JavaScript and PHP. You will learn to create AJAX requests, send data to the PHP script, and perform actions on the received data.

We will also go through error handling mechanisms provided by jQuery.

In this chapter, we will primarily work with HTML or text response. Since JSON and XML are topics that need to be looked upon in detail, we will discuss both of these in separate chapters.

In all the recipes, we will add the jQuery file and other jQuery code just before the body tag closes and not in the head section as you might have seen so far. Placing the files in the head section blocks the rendering of a page until all JavaScript files have been loaded. By putting them at the end of page, the HTML will be rendered without the browser blocking anything and DOM will be ready. After the page is loaded, we can then add the JavaScript or jQuery files. This will make your pages faster.

# Fetching data from PHP using jQuery

This recipe will teach you the usage of jQuery's get method to retrieve data from a PHP script. We will see a simple example where data will be fetched from the server using the get method based on user selection from a form.

## Getting ready

Create a directory named chapter2 in your web root. Put the jQuery library file in this directory. Now create another folder inside and name it as Recipe1. As a recipe can have more than one file, it is better to keep them separate.

## How to do it...

1. Create a file index.html in the Recipe1 folder. Write the HTML code in it that will create a combo box with some options.

```
<html>
  <head>
    <title>jQuery.get()</title>
    <style type="text/css">
      ul{border:1px solid black; list-style:none;
          margin:0pt;padding:0pt;float:left;
          font-family:Verdana, Arial, Helvetica, sans-serif;
          font-size:12px;width:300px;}
      li{padding:10px 5px;border-bottom:1px solid black;}
    </style>
  </head>
  <body>
    <form>
      <p>
        Show list of:
        <select id="choice">
          <option value="">select</option>
          <option value="good">Good Guys</option>
```

```
              <option value="bad">Bad Guys</option>
          </select>
        </p>
        <p id="result"></p>
      </form>
    </body>
  </html>
```

2. Just before the `body` tag closes, include the jQuery file and write the code that will attach a `change` event handler on the combo box. The handler function will get the selected value from the combo box and will send an AJAX request to PHP using the `get` method. On successful completion of the request, the response HTML will be inserted into a paragraph present on the page.

```
<script type="text/javascript" src="../jquery.js"></script>
<script type="text/javascript">
  $(document).ready(function ()
  {
    $('#choice').change(function()
    {
      if($(this).val() != '')
      {
        $.get(
          'data.php',
          { what: $(this).val() },
          function(data)
          {
            $('#result').html(data);
          });
      }
    });
  });
</script>
```

3. Let's code some PHP and respond to the AJAX request. Create a file called `data.php` in the same directory. Write the code that will determine the parameter received from the AJAX request. Depending on that parameter, PHP will create some HTML using an array and will echo that HTML back to the browser.

```
<?php
  if($_GET['what'] == 'good')
  {
    $names = array('Sherlock Holmes', 'John Watson',
                   'Hercule Poirot', 'Jane Marple');
    echo getHTML($names);
  }
```

```
    else if($_GET['what'] == 'bad')
    {
      $names = array('Professor Moriarty', 'Sebastian Moran',
                'Charles Milverton', 'Von Bork', 'Count Sylvius');
      echo getHTML($names);
    }
    function getHTML($names)
    {
      $strResult = '<ul>';
      for($i=0; $i<count($names); $i++)
      {
        $strResult.= '<li>'.$names[$i].'</li>';
      }
      $strResult.= '</ul>';

      return $strResult;
    }
?>
```

4.  Run the `index.html` file in your browser and select a value from the combo box.
    jQuery will send the AJAX request, which will get the formatted HTML from PHP and
    will display it in the browser.

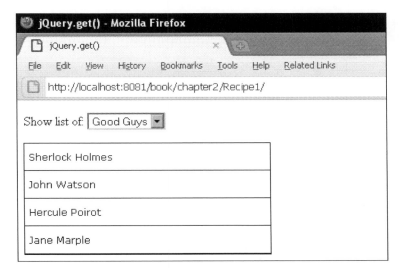

## How it works...

When a value is selected from the combo box, the corresponding event handler executes. After validating that the selected value is not blank, we send an AJAX request using the $.get() method of jQuery.

This method sends an HTTP GET request to the PHP script. $.get() accepts four parameters, which are described below. All parameters except the first one are optional:

- ▶ **URL**: This is the file name on the server where the request will be sent. It can be the name of either a PHP file or an HTML page.

- ▶ **Data**: This parameter defines what data will be sent to the server. It can be either in the form of a query string or a set of key-value pairs.

- ▶ **Handler function**: This handler function is executed when the request is successful, that is, when the server roundtrip is complete.

- ▶ **Data type**: It can be HTML, XML, JSON, or script. If none is provided, jQuery tries to make a guess itself.

Note that the URL should be from the same domain on which the application is currently running. This is because browsers do not allow cross-domain AJAX requests due to security reasons.

For example, if the page that is sending the request is http://abc.com/, it can send AJAX requests only to files located on http://abc.com/ or on its subdomains. Sending a request to other domains like http://someothersite.com/ is not allowed.

We specified the URL as data.php. We sent a key what and set its value to a selected value of the combo box. Finally the callback function was defined. Since the method is GET, the data that will be sent to the server will be appended to the URL.

Now the request is fired and reaches the PHP file data.php. Since it is a GET request, PHP's Superglobal array $_GET will be populated with the received data. Depending on the value of key what (which can be either good or bad), PHP creates an array $names that is passed to the getHTML() function. This function creates an unordered list using the names from the array and returns it to the browser.

Note the use of echo here. echo is used to output strings on a page. In this case the page has been called through an AJAX request. Hence, the result is sent back to the function that called it. jQuery receives the response and this is available to us as a parameter of the success event handler. We insert the received HTML in a <p> element with the ID result.

▸  *Sending data to PHP* later in this chapter

▸  *Creating an empty page and loading it in parts*

# Creating a query string automatically for all form elements

## Getting ready

Create a new folder `Recipe2` inside the `chapter2` directory. Now create a file `index.html` in the newly created directory.

## How to do it...

1.  Open the `index.html` file for editing and create a form with some HTML elements, such as textboxes, radio buttons, and check boxes.

```
<html>
<head>
    <title>Serializing form values</title>
    <style type="text/css">
      ul{ border:1px solid black; list-style: none;
          margin:0pt;padding:0pt;float:left;font-family:Verdana,
          Arial, Helvetica, sans-serif;font-size:12px;width:400px;
          }
      li{   padding:10px 5px;border-bottom:1px solid black;}
      label{width:100px;text-align:right;
            margin-right:10px;float:left;}
    </style>
</head>
<body>
  <form>
    <ul>
      <li><label>Email:</label>
          <input type="text" name="email"/></li>
      <li><label>Full Name</label>
          <input type="text" name="fullName"/></li>
      <li>
        <label>Sex</label>
        <input type="radio" name="sex" value="M"/>Male
        <input type="radio" name="sex" value="F"/>Female
```

```
        </li>
        <li>
          <label>Country</label>
          <select name="country">
            <option value="IN">India</option>
            <option value="UK">UK</option>
            <option value="US">USA</option>
          </select>
        </li>
        <li>
          <label>Newsletter</label>
          <input type="checkbox" name="letter"/>Send me more
              information</li>
        <li>
          <input type="button" value="GO"/>
        </li>
      </ul>
    </form>
  </body>
</html>
```

2.  Once again include the link to the jQuery file. After that add an event handler for the input button that we have placed on the form. This button will use the `serialize()` method on the form and will alert the resulting query string.

```
<script type="text/javascript" src="../jquery.js"></script>
<script type="text/javascript">
  $(document).ready(function ()
  {
    $('input:button').click(function()
    {
      alert($('form:first').serialize());

    });
  });
</script>
```

3.  Open your browser and run the `index.html` file. Fill the form and click on the **GO** button. The browser will display the values of form elements in a query string format, as shown in the following screenshot:

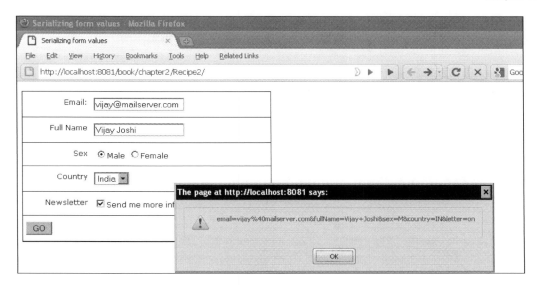

## How it works...

The serialize() method of jQuery turns form elements into query string format. Rather than getting each value manually and creating a query string, this function can be very handy when you want to send the values of all form elements as a part of AJAX requests. You can use any of the methods like GET or POST to send this data to the server.

## There's more...

### serializeArray() method

Another useful function for getting values of form elements is serializeArray(). This function turns all the elements into a JavaScript object.

```
var data = $('form:first').serializeArray();
```

If the form has two textboxes named input1 and input2 and their values are value1 and value2 respectively then the object will be created as shown below:

```
[
    { input1: 'value1'  },
    { input2: 'value2'  },
]
```

## Not all values are serialized

Remember that **Submit** buttons and File select elements are not serialized.

## Name should be provided to elements

In order to successfully serialize elements do not forget to assign a `name` attribute to them. If an element has been assigned an ID but not a name, it will not get serialized.

## See also

▶ *Fetching data from PHP using jQuery*

▶ *Sending data to PHP*

# Detecting an AJAX request in PHP

After going through this recipe you will be able to distinguish between AJAX requests and simple HTTP requests in your PHP code.

## Getting ready

Create a new directory named `Recipe3` in the `chapter2` directory. Inside it create an HTML file named `index.html` and another PHP file `check.php`.

## How to do it...

1. Open the `index.html` file and create a button that will load a string from a PHP file using the `$.get()` method.

```html
<html>
  <head>
    <title>Detecting AJAX Requests</title>
  </head>
  <body>
    <form>
      <p>
        <input type="button" value="Load Some data"/>
      </p>
    </form>
  </body>
</html>
```

2. Next, include jQuery and write the code for a `click` event of the button. Clicking on the button will simply send an AJAX request to `check.php`, which will return a string. The response string will be appended to the page after the input button.

```
<script type="text/javascript" src="../jquery.js"></script>
<script type="text/javascript">
  $(document).ready(function ()
  {
    $('input:button').click(function()
    {
      $.get(
        'check.php',
        function(data)
        {
          $('input:button').after(data);
        });
    });
  });
</script>
```

3. To validate that the request is indeed an AJAX request and not a direct one from the browser, open the `check.php` file and write the following code:

```
<?php
  if(isset($_SERVER['HTTP_X_REQUESTED_WITH']) && $_SERVER['HTTP_X_REQUESTED_WITH'] == 'XMLHttpRequest')
  {
    echo 'YaY!!! Request successful.';
  }
  else
  {
    echo 'This is not an AJAX request. This page cannot be accessed directly.';
  }
?>
```

4. Run the `index.html` file in a browser and click on the **Load Some Data** button. You will see the text **YaY!!! Request successful.** inserted after the button. Now in another window enter the direct path to the `check.php` file. You will see the following message:

   **This is not an AJAX request. This page cannot be accessed directly.**

## How it works...

Browsers send HTTP headers with every request that goes to a server. To distinguish between normal requests and AJAX requests, modern libraries send an additional header with AJAX request. The header's name is `X-Requested-With` and its value is `XMLHttpRequest`.

Superglobal `$_SERVER` contains the headers sent with the request. In the example, we have checked whether the `$_SERVER` array has an entry for the `HTTP_X_REQUESTED_WITH` key or not. If an entry is found and its value is `XMLHttpRequest`, we can assume it is an AJAX request. Depending upon the result of the `if` expression we display the resulting string to the user.

## There's more...

### Don't rely on X-Requested-With alone

jQuery and most of the other modern libraries (such as Prototype and Dojo) send an `X-Requested-With` header for the ease of the server. However, relying on this header alone is not recommended.

This is due to the reason that HTTP headers can be easily spoofed. So a user can send a request with this header that the code will assume to be an AJAX request but that won't be.

There are other ways through which you can ensure the request is legitimate but that is beyond the scope of this book.

# Sending data to PHP

GET and POST are the two most frequently used methods for accessing pages. In the first recipe you learned to make requests using GET method.

This recipe will make use of jQuery's `$.post()` method to retrieve data from a PHP script. We will see a simple example where we will fill some data in a form and the data will be sent to PHP using the POST method. Sent data will be processed by PHP and then displayed in the browser.

## Getting ready

Create a new directory named `Recipe4` under the `chapter2` directory.

## How to do it...

1. Create a file named `index.html` in the newly created `Recipe4` directory. In this recipe, we will use the same form that we created in the second recipe (Creating query string automatically for all form elements) of this chapter. So write the HTML that will create a form with multiple controls.

```html
<html>
  <head>
    <title>Sending data through post</title>
    <style type="text/css">
      ul{ border:1px solid black; list-style:none;
        margin:0pt;padding:0pt;float:left;
          font-family:Verdana, Arial, Helvetica,
          sans-serif;font-size:12px;width:400px;   }
      li{padding:10px 5px;border-bottom:1px solid black;}
      label{width:100px;text-align:right;margin-right:10px;
          float:left;}
      #response {display:none;}
    </style>
  </head>
  <body>
    <form>
      <ul id="information">
        <li><label>Email:</label>
          <input type="text" name="email"/></li>
        <li><label>Full Name</label>
          <input type="text" name="fullName"/></li>
        <li>
          <label>Sex</label>
          <input type="radio" name="sex" value="Male"
            checked="checked"/>Male
          <input type="radio" name="sex" value="Female"/>Female
        </li>
        <li>
          <label>Country</label>
          <select name="country">
            <option value="India">India</option>
            <option value="UK">UK</option>
            <option value="US">USA</option>
          </select>
        </li>
        <li>
          <input type="button" value="GO" name="submit"/>
        </li>
      </ul>
      <p id="response"></p>
    </form>
  </body>
</html>
```

2. Include jQuery and after that attach an event handler for the button. Clicking on the button will send an AJAX request to a PHP file using the HTTP POST method. Upon successful completion of the request, the form will be made hidden and the response received from PHP will be inserted into a paragraph.

```
<script type="text/javascript" src="../jquery.js"></script>
<script type="text/javascript">
  $(document).ready(function ()
  {
    $('input:button').click(function()
    {
      var data = $('form:first').serialize();
      $.post(
        'process.php',
        data,
        function(data)
        {
          $('#information').hide();
          $('#response').html(data).show();
        },
            'html'
      );
    });
  });
</script>
```

3. Since the request is made to a PHP file, first of all create a file named `process.php` in the same directory as `index.html`. The code in this file will create a string using the data filled in the form by the user. This string will be sent back to the browser to notify the user of the values they entered.

```
<?php
  $responseString = 'Dear '.$_POST['fullName'].', Your contact
information has been saved.';
  $responseString.= 'You entered the following information: ';
  $responseString.= '<br/>';
  $responseString.= '<strong>E-mail:</strong> '.$_POST['email'];
  $responseString.= '<br/>';
  $responseString.= '<strong>Sex:</strong> '.$_POST['sex'];
  $responseString.= '<br/>';
  $responseString.= '<strong>Country:</strong> '.$_
POST['country'];
  header('Content-type:text/html');
  echo $responseString;
?>'
```

4.  Run the file `index.html` in your browser and you will see the form with some fields. Fill the value in fields and click on the **GO** button. You will see that the form will be hidden and the entered values will be displayed in the form as follows:

**Dear Ajay Joshi, Your contact information has been saved.You entered the following information:**
**E-mail: test@test.com**
**Sex: Male**
**Country: India**

## How it works...

We have registered a `click` event handler for **GO** button. Clicking the button sends a POST request to server using jQuery's `$.post()` method.

`$.post()` is almost similar to `$.get()` except for a couple of differences. The first, and obvious difference, is the method used which is POST for `$.post()` and GET for `$.get()`. The second difference is that POST requests are not cached whereas GET requests are cached by the browser. Therefore, the use of the cache option with POST request will have no effect on the request.

Other than that, both `$.get()` and `$.post()` have the same signatures.

In our example the AJAX request goes to the `process.php` file with the serialized data from the form. Since it is a POST request, PHP's `$_POST` Superglobal is populated with form data. We then extract the fields from this array and put them in a formatted string. After we have built the string we echo it back to the browser.

On receiving a successful response, we hide the form and insert the received HTML in a paragraph.

## There's more...

### Alternative method for $.post()

`$.post()`, `$.get()`, and other shortcut methods can also be implemented using the `$.ajax()` method. Given below is the `$.post()` implementation using `$.ajax()`. We will see other usage of `$.ajax()` in the coming recipes.

```
$.ajax(
{
  url: 'process.php',
  method: 'post',
  data: $('form:first').serialize(),
   dataType: 'html',
  success: function(response)
```

```
  {
    $('#information').hide();
    $('#response').html(response);
  }
});
```

Since $.ajax() gives more flexibility than $.post(), you can use it when you want to have a specific error callback function for request.

## See also

▶ *Fetching data from PHP using jQuery* explains the $.get() method in detail

▶ *Creating a query string automatically for all form elements*

▶ *Handling errors in AJAX requests*, which shows how to handle errors encountered during AJAX requests

# Aborting AJAX requests

Consider a case where a user is allowed to select a date on a page and an AJAX request is made to the server to fetch some data against that date. If the request is under processing and in the meantime the user selects another date and a new request is sent, the server now has two requests pending.

Imagine what will happen to an application if there are multiple users repeating the same behavior. Desirable behavior in this case will be to cancel the pending request and allow only the current one.

This recipe will explain how to cancel any pending requests.

## Getting ready

Create a new folder in chapter2 directory and name it as Recipe5.

## How to do it...

1. We will use the same markup that we created in the first recipe of this chapter. So create a new file index.html and write the code to create an HTML page with a combo box and two options. Also create a paragraph element on the page that will display the received response.

```html
<html>
  <head>
    <title>Aborting ajax requests</title>
    <style type="text/css">
```

```
        ul{border:1px solid black; list-style:none;
            margin:0pt;padding:0pt;float:left;
            font-family:Verdana, Arial, Helvetica, sans-serif;
            font-size:12px;width:300px;}
        li{padding:10px 5px;border-bottom:1px solid black;}
      </style>

  </head>
  <body>
    <form>
      <p>
        Show list of:
        <select id="choice">
          <option value="">select</option>
          <option value="good">Good Guys</option>
          <option value="bad">Bad Guys</option>
        </select>
      </p>
      <p id="response"></p>
    </form>
  </body>
</html>
```

2. Now comes the jQuery code. Define a global variable and after that attach an event handler for the combo box. The handler function checks if an AJAX request to the server is already pending or not. On finding a pending request it will abort that request and a new request will be sent to the server.

```
<script type="text/javascript" src="../jquery.js"></script>
<script type="text/javascript">
  $(document).ready(function ()
  {
    var ajax;
    $('#choice').change(function()
    {
      if(ajax)
      {
        ajax.abort();
      }
      ajax = $.get(
        'wait.php',
        { what : $(this).val() },
        function(response)
        {
          $('#response').html(response);
        },
```

```
        'html'
      );
    });
  });
</script>
```

3.  Finally comes the PHP part. Create a PHP file and name it as `wait.php`. Write the same code from the recipe *Fetching data from PHP using jQuery*. The code will check for the values received from the browser and will send a response accordingly. For this example we will make PHP wait for 10 seconds before any response is sent to the browser so that we are able to send multiple requests within 10 seconds.

```php
<?php
  sleep(10);
  if($_GET['what'] == 'good')
  {
    $names = array('Sherlock Holmes', 'John Watson', 'Hercule
Poirot', 'Jane Marple');
    echo getHTML($names);
  }
  else if($_GET['what'] == 'bad')
  {
    $names = array('Professor Moriarty', 'Sebastian Moran',
              'Charles Milverton', 'Von Bork', 'Count Sylvius');
    echo getHTML($names);
  }
  function getHTML($names)
  {
    $strResult = '<ul>';
    for($i=0; $i<count($names); $i++)
    {
      $strResult.= '<li>'.$names[$i].'</li>';
    }
    $strResult.= '</ul>';

    return $strResult;
  }
?>
```

4.  Now run your browser and select a value from the combo box. PHP will send the response after 10 seconds. Now select another value from the combo box. The pending request will be aborted and the current request will be sent to the server. The response received will be according to the currently selected value. No response will be received for previous selection as the request was aborted.

## How it works...

All AJAX methods of jQuery return an XMLHttpRequest object when called. We have declared a global variable ajax that will store this object. When a value is selected from the combo box, the handler function checks if the variable ajax is defined or not. In case of the first selection it will be undefined, hence nothing happens and the request is sent to the wait.php file. The XMLHttpRequest object created for sending this request is stored in variable ajax.

Now when a value of combo box is changed ajax will be holding the XMLHttpRequest object that was used to send the previous request. XMLHttpRequest has an abort() method that cancels the current request. In our case the pending request to the server is cancelled and a new request is made, which is again stored in the ajax variable.

Now onwards, changing a value of combo box within 10 seconds will cancel out a pending request and will send a fresh one to the server.

## See also

▶  *Handling errors in AJAX requests*

# Creating an empty page and loading it in parts

The larger a web page the more time a browser will take to download it. This may degrade the user experience in case of slow connections or larger pages.

One approach that can be followed is to load only what is absolutely necessary for the user and load the rest of the content when required. There are some sections on a page which are rarely accessed. It will make page loads faster and user experience will improve.

In this recipe we will demonstrate this case with a simple example. We will create a single HTML page and will allow the user to load its one section when required.

## Getting ready

Create a folder named Recipe6 in chapter2 directory.

## How to do it...

1. Create a new file and save it as `index.html`. This page will have three sections: head, content, and footer. HTML for the footer will not be created; instead we will load it dynamically. We have also applied some CSS in the `head` section to customize the appearance of the page.

```html
<html>
  <head>
    <title>Load page in parts</title>
    <style type="text/css">
      body { border:1px solid black;margin:0 auto;text-align:
center;width:700px; }
      div { padding:10px;border:1px dotted black; }
      #footer > a { font-size:12px;margin:50px; }
    </style>
  </head>
  <body>
    <div>
      <div id="head"><h2>My new awesome page</h2></div>
      <div id="content">
        <span>
        Aliquam quis massa at elit fermentum vestibulum.
        Vestibulum id nunc et nulla placerat gravida. Praesent
        sed purus ante. Vestibulum pulvinar tortor sed odio
        accumsan a cursus magna pellentesque. In hac habitasse
        platea dictumst. Cras viverra sodales sem in facilisis.
        Nulla congue, risus eget gravida feugiat, nisi ante
        laoreet est, ullamcorper hendrerit lacus velit eget urna.
        Suspendisse rutrum lacus eget nulla semper sit amet
        egestas tellus scelerisque. Maecenas at vulputate enim.
        Etiam blandit magna iaculis tellus tincidunt vel ornare
        diam.
        </span>
      </div>
      <div id="footer">
        <a href="#" id="loadFooter">Show footer</a>
      </div>
    </div>
  </body>
</html>
```

2.  Next, we will need to create a file where we will write HTML for the footer. Open a new file and save it with the following markup as `footer.html`.

    ```
    <a href="#">Link1</a>
    <a href="#">Link2</a>
    <a href="#">Link3</a>
    <a href="#">Link4</a>
    <a href="#">Link5</a>
    ```

3.  To glue all the above things, switch back to `index.html` and write the jQuery code for the **Show footer** link.

    ```
    <script type="text/javascript" src="../jquery.js"></script>
    <script type="text/javascript">
      $(document).ready(function ()
      {
        $('#loadFooter').click(function()
        {
          $('#footer').load('footer.html');
        });
      });
    </script>
    ```

4.  Open your browser and run the `index.html` file. Click on the **Show footer** link. jQuery will load the HTML for the footer from the `footer.html` file and will insert it inside the footer section.

## How it works...

jQuery provides a method `load()` that acts on HTML elements. It gets the data from the server and inserts it into the HTML element or elements that called it. `load()` takes three parameters. The first parameter is the URL, from where data will be loaded, the second parameter is the data that can be sent to the server. The third parameter is a callback function which executes once data has loaded.

In the previous example, clicking the **Show footer** link calls the `load()` method on element with ID `footer`. It loads the `footer.html` file in which we wrote the markup for the footer. After the file has loaded successfully its HTML is inserted into the footer.

## There's more...

### Difference between load and get

Both these methods are similar except for the fact that `load` is a method, which means it acts on a set of elements specified by a selector. Once the request is complete, the HTML of elements specified by the selectors is set. On the other hand `$.get` is a global method that has an explicitly defined callback function.

- ▸ *Fetching data from PHP using jQuery*
- ▸ *Sending data to PHP* earlier in this chapter
- ▸ *Loading JavaScript on demand to reduce page load time*, in this chapter

# Handling errors in AJAX requests

Errors are inevitable. Period. Sometimes things are not in your control—like server failures—and in this case you must have an error handling mechanism in place, which can catch the errors and show them to the users. Throughout the recipes in this chapter we have implemented callback functions that execute when a request is successful. It may happen (and I promise you it will happen) that you typed a filename incorrectly or the server encounters an error and you get an error rather than a successful response.

This recipe will explain how to deal with such situations in AJAX requests.

## Getting ready

Create a folder `Recipe7` inside the `chapter2` folder.

## How to do it...

1. Create a file named `index.html` in the `Recipe7` folder. Define some CSS styles in it and create an input box that will ask for a filename to load and a button. Also create a paragraph where contents loaded in a file will be displayed.

```
<html>
  <head>
    <title>Error handling</title>
    <style type="text/css">
      ul{ border:1px solid black; list-style:none;margin:0pt;
          padding:0pt;float:left;font-family:Verdana,
          Arial, Helvetica, sans-serif;font-size:12px;width:300px;
        }
      li{  padding:10px 5px;border-bottom:1px solid black;}
      span{ color:red;}
    </style>
  </head>
  <body>
    <label for="fileName">Enter file name to load: </label>
    <input type="text" id="fileName"/>
    <input type="button" value="Load file"/>
    <p id="result"></p>
  </body>
</html>
```

2. Before the `body` tag closes, include jQuery and write code using the `$.ajax()` method that will fire an AJAX request to load the file specified by the user. Define both success and error callbacks here.

```
<script type="text/javascript" src="../jquery.js"></script>
<script type="text/javascript">
$(document).ready(function ()
{
  $('input:button').click(function()
  {
    if($('#fileName').val() == '')
    {
      $('#result').html('<span>Please provide a file
          name.</span>');
      return;
    }
    $.ajax({
    url: $('#fileName').val(),
    method: 'get',
    success: function(data)
      {
        $('#result').html(data);
      },
    error : function()
      {
        $('#result').html('<span>An error occured.</span>');
      }
    });
  });
});
</script>
```

3. Create another HTML file and name it as `books.html`. In this file create an unordered list of books, as follows:

```
<ul>
  <li>
    A Study in Scarlet
  </li>
  <li>
    The Sign of Four
  </li>
  <li>
    The Adventures of Sherlock Holmes
  </li>
  <li>
```

```
      The Memoirs of Sherlock Holmes
   </li>
   <li>
      The Hound of the Baskervilles
   </li>
   <li>
      The Return of Sherlock Holmes
   </li>
   <li>
      The Case-Book of Sherlock Holmes
   </li>
</ul>
```

4.  Launch your browser and run the `index.html` file. Enter **books.html** in the textbox and click on the **Load file** button. jQuery will send an AJAX request and you will see a nicely formatted list of books on your screen. Leaving the field blank and clicking on the **Load File** button will display an error.

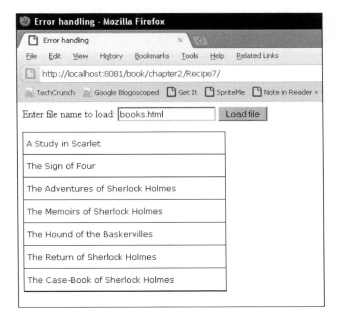

5.  Now enter the name of any non-existent file such as **none.html** or **nofile.html**. Clicking on the **Load file** button will display an error.

## How it works...

In this example we used the low level AJAX implementation of jQuery. Other methods like $.get(), $.post(), and so on are task-specific implementations of $.ajax(). As you just saw $.get() is specific to GET requests whereas another method $.getScript() is used only for loading scripts.

One of the many options of $.ajax() is the error callback. When a request fails due to some reason like a missing file, timeout on server, or a server error this callback executes, whereas higher-level implementations do not take any action in this case.

In the previous example, we have used the error callback to display an error message to the user. We intentionally typed a filename that does not exist and jQuery passed the control to the error callback.

## There's more...

### Parameters passed to error callback

jQuery makes three parameters available to the error callback. These are the XMLHttpRequest object that was used to send a request, a string indicating the type of error, and an exception (if any) from the JavaScript side.

The second parameter is a string that can be one of these: timeout, error, notmodified, parsererror, or null.

## The ajaxError() method

Another method `ajaxError()` is available that can be attached to HTML elements. This method will execute every time there is an error in AJAX request.

```
$('#result').ajaxError(function()
{
  $(this).html('<span>An error occured.</span>');
})
```

Place this code inside `document.ready()` and then remove the error callback from the function's definition. Now enter an incorrect filename and click on the button. You will still see an error.

This method can be pretty useful when you have AJAX requests originating from multiple places in a page and you want a single placeholder for error messages. The error message will be displayed each time because it will be executed regardless of where the request originated.

## See also

► *Fetching data from PHP using jQuery*

► *Sending data to PHP*

► *Creating an empty page and loading it in parts*

► *Loading JavaScript on demand to reduce page load time*

# Preventing browser from caching AJAX requests

In case of GET requests, browsers cache these requests and when the request is invoked again they do not send the request to the server and instead serve it from the cache.

This recipe will explain how to force browsers to send the request to a server instead of serving it from the cache.

## How to do it...

1. While sending an AJAX request use the `cache` option to force no caching by the browser. Setting the `cache` option to `false` does not let the browser cache any AJAX requests and the data is loaded from the server each time the request is made.

```
$.ajax({
  url : 'someurl.php',
  cache: false,
  success: function(data)
```

```
    {
        //do something with received data
    }
});
```

## How it works...

On an AJAX request, the browser checks if a request to that URL is already in the browser cache or not. If it is found in the cache, no request to the server is sent and response from the cache is served.

jQuery provides a cache option that can be used to override this browser behavior. By default, cache is set to `true`. When this option is set to `false`, jQuery appends an underscore key ( _ ) with a random numeric value to the URL. This makes the browser assume that each URL is unique even when only the value of the underscore key is different. Hence, the browser does not cache the request and it goes to the server each time.

## There's more...

### Only GET requests are cached

It is worth noting that only GET requests are cached by the browser and not POST requests. Therefore, using the cache option with POST requests will have no effect. Every POST request is a fresh request.

## See also

▶ *Fetching data from PHP using jQuery* explains `$.get()` method for making get requests

▶ *Sending data to PHP* explains the `$.post()` method for making POST requests

# Loading JavaScript on demand to reduce page load time

Think of a rich Internet application that makes heavy use of JavaScript to interact with the user. Such a page typically consists of more than one JavaScript files, such as a file for calendar control, another file for special effects, yet another plugin for your cool accordion, and so on.

This results in the increase of the page load time as browsers cannot download all of these files simultaneously. The best solution for this is to load only absolutely necessary files at the time of loading the page and load the other files when required.

This recipe will explain how JavaScript files can be loaded on demand.

## Getting ready

Create a directory named Recipe9 in the chapter2 folder.

## How to do it...

1. Create a file index.html in the chapter2 folder. Write the HTML to create a page that will have a paragraph element and four buttons. The first button will be used to load another JavaScript file and rest of the buttons will manipulate the paragraph.

```
<html>
  <head>
    <title>getScript example</title>
  </head>
  <body>
    <p id="container">
      This text will be replaced with new text.
    </p>
    <input type="button" class="loader" value="Load Script"/>
    <input type="button" class="bold" value="Bold"/>
    <input type="button" class="color" value="Change color"/>
    <input type="button" class="change" value="Change text"/>
  </script>
  </body>
</html>
```

2. Before the body tag closes, include the jQuery library and add event handler for the first button. On click of the button, jQuery will load a JavaScript file. On successful loading of the JavaScript, a function named addEvents() will be called that will add event handlers for all other buttons.

```
<script type="text/javascript" src="../jquery.js"></script>
<script type="text/javascript">
$(document).ready(function ()
{
  $('input:button:first').click(function(aaa)
  {
    $.getScript('new.js', function()
    {
```

```
            alert('Script loaded');
            addEvents();
          });
        });
     });
     </script>
```

3. Now create a new file in the same directory as `index.html` and name it as `new.js`. Define the function `addEvents()` in it to add events for the four buttons.

```
function addEvents()
{
  $('.bold').click(function()
     {
       $('#container').css('font-weight', 'bold');
     });

  $('.color').click(function()
     {
       $('#container').css('color', 'red');
     });

  $('.change').click(function()
     {
       $('#container').html('<em>New html inserted</em>');
     });
}
```

4. Open your browser and run the `index.html` file. Click on any of the buttons except **Load Script**. You will find that nothing happens to the paragraph's content. Now click on the **Load Script** button. An alert will appear notifying that script has been loaded. Clicking on any of the last three buttons will now change the appearance of the paragraph.

## How it works...

Clicking on the **Load Script** button invokes the $.getScript() method of jQuery. This function has two parameters: the file name to be loaded and a callback function that executes when the file is successfully loaded.

It loads the specified JavaScript file asynchronously from the server. After a successful load, all the variables and functions of that file are available in the global context. This means they can be used by other JavaScript files too. A successful callback ensures that the file has been loaded and, therefore, we can safely work with the variables or functions of that file.

In the previous example the function addEvents() is defined in the new.js file. This function binds event handlers to our buttons. Since new.js is not available on the page, these buttons do nothing. After the file is loaded, we call the addEvents() function, which binds these buttons to respective events. Thus, these buttons become functional.

## There's more...

### Alternative method for getScript

The $.getScript() method is specifically for loading scripts only. It can be written using the $.ajax() method too.

```
$.ajax(
{
  url: 'new.js',
  dataType: 'script',
  success: function()
  {
    alert('Script loaded');
    addEvents();
  }
});
```

The above code will also load the new.js file and execute it. Use this method if you need the error callback too, which is not available with $.getScript().

Also note the use of the dataType option here. We have provided its value as script. The dataType parameter tells jQuery what type of data to expect from the server (which is script in this case).

## See also

- ▶ *Fetching data from PHP using jQuery* explains get method for fetching data
- ▶ *Sending data to PHP* explains how to send data to PHP through jQuery
- ▶ *Creating an empty page and load it in parts*

# 3
# Working with XML Documents

In this chapter, we will cover:

- ▶ Loading XML from files and strings using SimpleXML
- ▶ Accessing elements and attributes using SimpleXML
- ▶ Searching elements using XPath
- ▶ Reading an XML using DOM extension
- ▶ Creating an XML using DOM extension
- ▶ Modifying an XML using DOM extension
- ▶ Parsing XML with jQuery

## Introduction

Extensible Markup Language—also known as XML—is a structure for representation of data in human readable format. Contrary to its name, it's actually not a language but a markup which focuses on data and its structure. XML is a lot like HTML in syntax except that where HTML is used for presentation of data, XML is used for storing and data interchange.

Moreover, all the tags in an XML are user-defined and can be formatted according to one's will. But an XML must follow the specification recommended by W3C.

With a large increase in distributed applications over the Internet, XML is the most widely used method of data interchange between applications. Web services use XML to carry and exchange data between applications. Since XML is platform-independent and is stored in string format, applications using different server-side technologies can communicate with each other using XML.

Consider the following XML document:

```xml
<?xml version="1.0" encoding="UTF-8" ?>
<websites>
    <site>
        <name>Google</name>
        <url>http://google.com</url>
        <information>Google is a search engine</information>
    </site>
    <site>
        <name>Reddit</name>
        <url>http://reddit.com</url>
        <information>Reddit is a social news website</information>
    </site>
</websites>
```

From the above document, we can infer that it is a list of websites containing data about the name, URL, and some information about each website.

PHP has several classes and functions available for working with XML documents. You can read, write, modify, and query documents easily using these functions.

In this chapter, we will discuss **SimpleXML** functions and **DOMDocument** class of PHP for manipulating XML documents. You will learn how to read and modify XML files, using SimpleXML as well as DOM API. We will also explore the **XPath** method, which makes traversing documents a lot easier.

Note that an XML must be well-formed and valid before we can do anything with it. There are many rules that define well-formedness of XML out of which a few are given below:

- ▶ An XML document must have a single root element.
- ▶ There cannot be special characters like <, >, and soon.
- ▶ Each XML tag must have a corresponding closing tag.
- ▶ Tags are case sensitive

To know more about validity of an XML, you can refer to this link:
http://en.wikipedia.org/wiki/XML#Schemas_and_validation

For most of the recipes in this chapter, we will use an already created XML file. Create a new file, save it as `common.xml` in the `Chapter3` directory. Put the following contents in this file.

```xml
<?xml version="1.0"?>
<books>
  <book index="1">
    <name year="1892">The Adventures of Sherlock Holmes</name>
    <story>
      <title>A Scandal in Bohemia</title>
      <quote>You see, but you do not observe. The distinction
             is clear.</quote>
    </story>
    <story>
      <title>The Red-headed League</title>
      <quote>It is quite a three pipe problem, and I beg that you
             won't speak to me for fifty minutes.</quote>
    </story>
    <story>
      <title>The Man with the Twisted Lip</title>
      <quote>It is, of course, a trifle, but there is nothing so
             important as trifles.</quote>
    </story>
  </book>
  <book index="2">
    <name year="1927">The Case-book of Sherlock Holmes</name>
    <story>
      <title>The Adventure of the Three Gables</title>
      <quote>I am not the law, but I represent justice so far as
             my feeble powers go.</quote>
    </story>
    <story>
      <title>The Problem of Thor Bridge</title>
      <quote>We must look for consistency. Where there is a want
             of it we must suspect deception.</quote>
    </story>
    <story>
      <title>The Adventure of Shoscombe Old Place</title>
      <quote>Dogs don't make mistakes.</quote>
    </story>
  </book>
  <book index="3">
    <name year="1893">The Memoirs of Sherlock Holmes</name>
    <story>
      <title>The Yellow Face</title>
```

```
      <quote>Any truth is better than indefinite doubt.</quote>
    </story>
    <story>
      <title>The Stockbroker's Clerk</title>
      <quote>Results without causes are much more impressive. </quote>
    </story>
    <story>
      <title>The Final Problem</title>
      <quote>If I were assured of your eventual destruction I would,
             in the interests of the public, cheerfully accept my
             own.</quote>
    </story>
  </book>
</books>
```

# Loading XML from files and strings using SimpleXML

True to its name, SimpleXML functions provide an easy way to access data from XML documents. XML files or strings can be converted into objects, and data can be read from them.

We will see how to load an XML from a file or string using SimpleXML functions. You will also learn how to handle errors in XML documents.

## Getting ready

Create a new directory named `Chapter3`. This chapter will contain sub-folders for each recipe. So, create a folder named `Recipe1` inside it.

## How to do it...

1. Create a file named `index.php` in `Recipe1` folder. In this file, write the PHP code that will try to load the `common.xml` file. On loading it successfully, it will display a list of book names. We have also used the **libxml** functions that will detect any error and will show its detailed description on the screen.

```php
<?php
libxml_use_internal_errors(true);
$objXML = simplexml_load_file('../common.xml');

if (!$objXML)
{
  $errors = libxml_get_errors();
```

```
        foreach($errors as $error)
        {
            echo $error->message,'<br/>';
        }
    }
    else
    {
      foreach($objXML->book as $book)
      {
        echo $book->name.'<br/>';
      }
    }
    ?>
```

2. Open your browser and point it to the `index.php` file. Because we have already validated the XML file, you will see the following output on the screen:

   **The Adventures of Sherlock Holmes**

   **The Case-book of Sherlock Holmes**

   **The Memoirs of Sherlock Holmes**

3. Let us corrupt the XML file now. For this, open the `common.xml` file and delete any node name (like closing name tag of the first book). Save this file and reload `index.php` on your browser. You will see a detailed error description on your screen:

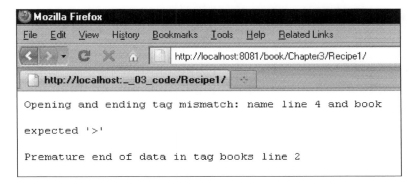

## How it works...

In the first line, passing a `true` value to the `libxml_use_internal_errors` function will suppress any XML errors and will allow us to handle errors from the code itself. The second line tries to load the specified XML using the `simplexml_load_file` function. If the XML is loaded successfully, it is converted into a **SimpleXMLElement** object otherwise a `false` value is returned.

We then check for the return value. If it is `false`, we use the `libxml_get_errors()` function to get all the errors in the form of an array. This array contains objects of type **LibXMLError**. Each of these objects has several properties. In the previous code, we iterated over the `errors` array and echoed the message property of each object that contains a detailed error message.

If there are no errors in XML, we get a SimpleXMLElement object that has all the XML data loaded in it. We iterate over each book element using `foreach` and print the name for each book.

## There's more...

### Parameters for simplexml_load_file

More parameters are available for the `simplexml_load_file` method, which are as follows:

- `filename`: This is the first parameter that is mandatory. It can be a path to a local XML file or a URL.
- `class_name`: You can extend the SimpleXMLElement class. In that case, you can specify that class name here and it will return the object of that class. This parameter is optional.
- `options`: This third parameter allows you to specify **libxml** parameters for more control over how the XML is handled while loading. This is also optional.

### simplexml_load_string

Similar to `simplexml_load_file` is `simplexml_load_string`, which also creates a SimpleXMLElement on successful execution. If a valid XML string is passed to it we get a SimpleXMLElement object or a `false` value otherwise.

```
$objXML = simplexml_load_string('<?xml version="1.0"?><book><name>My
favourite book</name></book>');
```

The above code will return a SimpleXMLElement object with data loaded from the XML string. The second and third parameters of this function are same as that of `simplexml_load_file`.

### Using SimpleXMLElement to create an object

You can also use the constructor of the **SimpleXMLElement** class to create a new object.

```
$objXML = new SimpleXMLElement('<?xml version="1.0"?><book><name>My
favourite book</name></book>');
```

### More info about SimpleXML and libxml

You can read about **SimpleXML** in more detail on the PHP site at http://php.net/manual/en/book.simplexml.php and about **libxml** at http://php.net/manual/en/book.libxml.php.

## See also

▶ *Accessing elements and attributes using SimpleXML*

▶ *Searching elements using XPath*

# Accessing elements and attributes using SimpleXML

This recipe will explain how we can get the values of the node and/or attributes from an XML file using SimpleXML methods. We will write an example using our `common.xml` file that will be used to get the publication year or list of stories in a selected book.

## Getting ready

Create a folder for this recipe in the `Chapter3` directory and name it as `Recipe2`.

## How to do it...

1. Create a new file named `index.php` in `Recipe2` folder. In this file, create a select box and create its options, which will be the names of books in the `common.xml` file. Next, create two buttons that will get the publication year and list of stories in the selected book. Each of these buttons has an ID attribute that will be used to distinguish between the clicked buttons. After that, create a paragraph element to display the result.

```html
<html>
<head><title>Accessing node and attribute values</title></head>
<body>
  <p>
  <select id="bookList">
    <option value="">select a book</option>
    <?php
      $objXML = simplexml_load_file('../common.xml');
      foreach($objXML->book as $book)
      {
        echo '<option value="'.$book['index'].'">'.$book->name.'
              </option>';
      }

    ?>
  </select>
  <input type="button" id="year" value="Get Year of publication"/>
  <input type="button" id="stories" value="Get story list"/>
```

```
      </p>
      <p id="result"></p>
    </body>
  </html>
```

2. We will use jQuery to get the selected values from the form and send an AJAX request to a file that will process the selected values and will send back the result accordingly. For this, we will write some jQuery code, just before closing of <body> tag. Include the jQuery library using the correct path, and then register event handlers for input buttons. On click of a button, handler function will send an AJAX request to a PHP file with values of the selected book and the clicked button. The received response will be inserted into the paragraph with ID result.

```
<script type="text/javascript" src="../jquery.js"></script>
<script type="text/javascript">
  $(document).ready(function ()
  {
    $('input:button').click(function()
    {
      if($('#bookList').val() != '')
      {
        $.get(
          'process.php',
          { id: $('#bookList').val() , action: $(this).attr('id')
          },
          function(data)
          {
            $('#result').html(data);
          });
      }
    });
  });
</script>
```

3. Now, create the process.php file in the same directory. This file gets the values of selected book and clicked button from the $_GET Superglobal. The common.xml file is loaded and depending on the value of action and ID variables in $_GET array, the books are iterated upon, and a response variable is created that is echoed to the browser.

```
<?php
  $bookId = $_GET['id'];
  $action = $_GET['action'];
  $strResponse;
  $objXML = simplexml_load_file('../common.xml');
  foreach($objXML->book as $book)
  {
```

```
if($book['index'] == $bookId)
{
  if($action == 'year')
  {
    $strResponse = 'This book was published in year:'.
                      $book->name['year'];
  }
  else if($action == 'stories')
  {
    $stories = $book->story;
    $strResponse = '<ul>';
    foreach($stories as $story)
    {
      $strResponse.= '<li>'. $story->title. '</li>';
    }
    $strResponse.= '</ul>';
  }
  else
  {
    $strResponse = 'Nothing to do';
  }
  break;
  }
}
echo $strResponse;
?>
```

4. Run your browser and point it to the index.php file. You will see a combo box and two buttons. Select a book from the combo box and click any of these buttons. The following image shows a list of stories that gets displayed after selecting a book and clicking on the **Get story list** button.

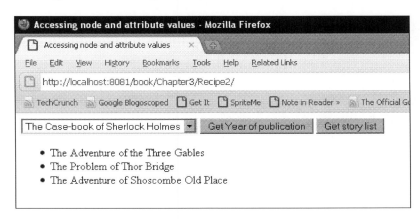

## How it works...

To get the value of a node we can refer it by its name as a property of the SimpleXMLElement object. In the index.php file, we created a SimpleXMLElement object from the common.xml file by loading it through the simplexml_load_file method. Since there are multiple book nodes, we get an array of these in our object on which we can loop like a normal array. Similarly, attributes of a node can be fetched like values from arrays, using the attribute name as an index of an associative array.

For each book, we created an option element with its value set to the index attribute and text set to the value of the name node. The way we selected these values shows us how easy it is to fetch values using SimpleXML methods.

The jQuery code registers event handlers for each of the two buttons as shown in the previous screenshot. Clicking on a button gets the value of the selected book and the clicked button and sends it to the process.php file, using jQuery's $.get() method.

The values sent by jQuery are available in $_GET Superglobal. These values are stored in PHP variables; $bookId and $action. Then we load the XML file and we have a SimpleXMLElement object available to us in the form of $objXML.

To determine the selected book, we can iterate over each book element and check if its index attribute matches the $bookId variable. When a match is found we check the value of $action variable. If $action is "year", we get the year attribute from the book's name that is stored in the $strResponse variable.

If $action is set to "stories", we get the array of the story object from the current $book object. Then we iterate over this array and create an unordered list for each story name and store it in $strResponse.

Finally, we echo the $strResponse variable to the browser where it is filled in a paragraph by jQuery.

## There's more...

### Modifying an XML with SimpleXML

The value of nodes in an existing XML can also be modified using SimpleXML functions. For example, if we have to change the name of the first book in our common.xml file, we can do so by using the following code:

```
$objXML->book[0]->name = 'New name for book';
$result = $objXML->asXML();
```

If no parameter is passed to `asXML()` method, it will return the modified XML in the form of a string, `false` in case of failure. A filename can also be passed to `asXML()` in which case it will write the resulting XML to that file.

### Adding elements to an XML

New elements can also be added to an XML as shown in the following code:

```
$objXML->book[0]->addChild('remark','Stories in this novel were
narrated by Sherlock Holmes himself');
$objXML->book[0]->remark->addAttribute('totalStories','13');
$result = $objXML->asXML();
```

This code will add a `remark` node as the first book element and also add a `totalStories` attribute to it.

Do not forget that the resulting XML will be stored in `$result` variable and not in the original XML file, though you can save it to the original XML also by specifying the filename to `asXML`, as explained in the previous section.

## See also

- ▶ *Loading XML from files and strings using SimpleXML*
- ▶ *Searching elements using XPath*
- ▶ *Fetching data from PHP using jQuery in Chapter 2*

# Searching elements using XPath

XPath or the XML Path is used to navigate an XML document. It is basically a query language that provides a standard set of expressions and functions for traversing a document tree. XPath operates on a document tree and can be used for functions, such as searching, comparing, and so on in a document.

PHP has built-in support for using XPath. This recipe will explain some concepts of XPath and how they can be used to get information from XML.

Using the `common.xml` file we will write a simple example that will demonstrate the capabilities of XPath.

## Getting ready

Like earlier recipes, create a separate folder named `Recipe3` inside the `Chapter3` directory.

## How to do it...

1. Create an HTML file and name it as `index.html`. Create four buttons that will be used to show different usage of XPath. Also, create an empty DIV element for displaying the result. Also, define some CSS in the `<head>` section for better display.

```html
<html>
  <head>
    <title>Using XPath</title>
    <style type="text/css">
      ul{border:1px solid black;padding:5px;
          list-style:none;width:550px;}
      label{font-weight:bold;}
      li{   padding:5px;}
    </style>
  </head>
  <body>
    <input type="button" value="Show all books" id="all"/>
    <input type="button" value="Show stories with quotes"
        id="total"/>
    <input type="button" value="Get last book" id="last"/>
    <input type="button" value="Books with year <1900" id="year"/>

    <div id="result"></div>
  </body>
</html>
```

2. Include the jQuery library and write the jQuery code that will send an AJAX request to a PHP file, `process.php`. The request will contain the ID of the clicked button for processing on the server side. Response from the PHP script will be inserted into the DIV element.

```javascript
<script type="text/javascript" src="../jquery.js"></script>
<script type="text/javascript">
  $(document).ready(function ()
  {
    $('input:button').click(function()
    {
      $.get(
        'process.php',
        { action: $(this).attr('id')},
        function(data)
        {
          $('#result').html(data);
        });
    });
  });
</script>
```

3. Switching to the server side now, create a PHP file, `process.php`, in the same directory. This file will load the XML file and will perform appropriate actions depending on the value of the clicked button. It will use the `xpath` method to search the document and echo the result back to the browser. This response will be inserted into a page by jQuery.

```php
<?php
    $objXML = simplexml_load_file('../common.xml');
    if (!$objXML)
    {
      echo 'Error loading xml';
    }
    else
    {
      $response = '';
      $action = $_GET['action'];
      switch($action)
    {
      case 'all':
        $book = $objXML->xpath('//book/name');
        $response.= '<ul>';
        foreach ($book as $item)
        {
          $response.= '<li>';
          $response.= $item[0].' ('.$item['year'].')';
          $response.= '</li>';
        }
        $response.= '</ul>';
      break;
      case 'total':
        $response.= '<ul>';
        $stories = $objXML->xpath('//story');
        foreach ($stories as $story)
        {
          $response.= '<li>';
          $response.= '<label>'.$story->title.'</label>
                      <br/><em>'.$story->quote.'</em>';
          $response.= '</li>';
        }
        $response.= '</ul>';
      break;

      case 'last':
        $lastElement = $objXML->xpath('//book[last()]');
```

```
        echo '<strong>'.$lastElement[0]->name.'
('.$lastElement[0]->name['year'].')</strong>';
        break;

    case 'year':
        $book = $objXML->xpath('//book/name[@year<1900]');
        $response.= '<ul>';
        foreach($book as $item)
        {
          $response.= '<li>';
          $response.= $item.' ('.$item['year'].')';
          $response.= '</li>';
        }
        $response.= '</ul>';
    break;
    }
    echo $response;
  }
?>
```

4. Run the `index.php` file and click on any buttons. The AJAX request will be fired, which will then go to the `process.php` file and the result will be displayed on the page. For example, clicking on the last button will show the books that have `year` value less than 1900.

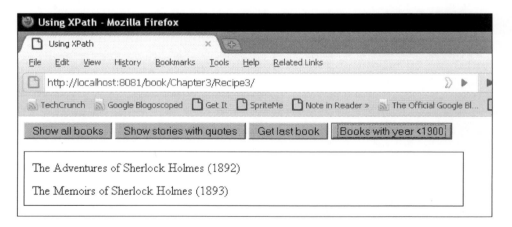

## How it works...

We have defined four buttons here. The first button for getting the names and years of all books, the second one for displaying list of all the stories and quotes regardless of book, the third one is for getting the name and year of the last book and the fourth button for displaying all those books that have the value of `year` attribute less than 1900.

We have also provided four different IDs to each of these buttons that include all, total, last, and year respectively.

Clicking a button sends that button's ID in an AJAX request to `process.php` file where ID of the clicked button is retrieved and stored in a variable called `$action`. We have already loaded the `common.xml` file in `$objXML` variable. Next is a **switch** statement that executes the case matching the ID.

SimpleXML provides the `xpath` method for running XPath queries on a loaded document. `xpath` method takes an XPath query as a parameter and returns an array of SimpleXML elements on successful execution, `false` on failure.

Expression `//book` will select all book elements in the document, regardless of their position.

Expression `//book/name` selects all name elements that are children of book elements in the whole document.

`//book[last()]` selects the last book element in the document.

Expression `//book/name[@year<1900]` looks like a complex one but is actually not the case. Just try breaking it in parts. `@` refers to an attribute. Hence, this expression will select all the name elements under book elements that have a name attribute with `year` value less than 1900. In this case, only two books qualify—the first and the last one. The second book has year 1927, hence it does not qualify for selection.

We then format the results by putting some HTML tags around them and return the result back to the browser.

## There's more...

### More info about XPath

Here are some online resources where you can learn more about the XPath syntax and its usage:

► http://www.w3schools.com/xpath/
► http://oreilly.com/catalog/xmlnut/chapter/ch09.html

## See also

► *Accessing elements and attributes using SimpleXML*
► *Reading an XML using DOM extension*

# Reading an XML using DOM extension

In this recipe, you will see the use of PHP's DOM extension to read an XML and extract information from it. We will create an example where we will display a list of books. Clicking a book name will reveal the list of stories in that book.

## Getting ready

Create a folder `Recipe4` in the `Chapter3` directory and make sure you have `common.xml` file accessible.

## How to do it...

1. Create an `index.php` file in the `Recipe4` folder. In the HTML markup, write the PHP code that will load the XML using DOM methods. From the loaded XML, create `h1` sections that will contain the book name and its publication year.

2. Under each `h1`, create an unordered list of stories in that book. Note that in the `<head>` section, we have hidden `ul` using `display` property. Therefore, on the page only book names will be visible.

```
<html>
  <head>
    <title>Using DOM</title>
    <style type="text/css">
      h1{ cursor:pointer;font-size:20px;}
      ul{ display:none; list-style:none;margin:0pt;padding:0pt;}
    </style>
  </head>
  <body>
<?php
  $objXML = new DOMDocument();
  $objXML->load('../common.xml', LIBXML_NOBLANKS);
  $books = $objXML->getElementsByTagName('book');
  foreach($books as $book)
  {
    echo '<h1>'.$book->firstChild->nodeValue.'
        ('.$book->firstChild->attributes->item(0)->value.')</h1>';
    $stories  = $book->getElementsByTagName('story');
    echo '<ul>';
    foreach($stories as $story)
    {
      echo '<li>'.$story->firstChild->nodeValue.'</li>';
    }
```

```
      echo '</ul>';
   }
?>
   </body>
</html>
```

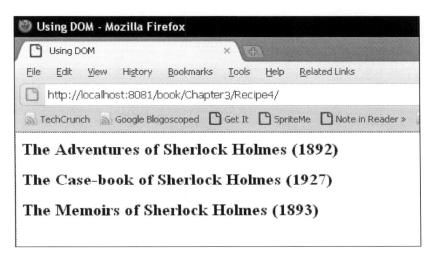

3. To spice up our example, we will write some jQuery code that will be used to show the list of stories in each book. An event handler will be attached to each book name that will show or hide stories.

```
<script type="text/javascript" src="../jquery.js"></script>
<script type="text/javascript">
  $(document).ready(function ()
  {
    $('h1').click(function()
    {
      $(this).next('ul').toggle('fast');
    });
  });
</script>
```

4. Run the `index.php` file in your browser and you will be presented with the list of books. Clicking a book name will toggle the list of stories in that book with animation.

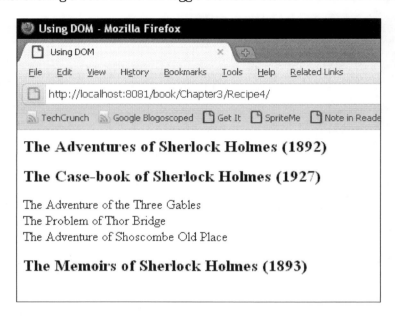

## How it works...

First, we create an object `$objXML` of the **DOMDocument** class. This class provides a number of properties and methods that can be used to manipulate an XML file. Names of nodes, their values, attributes, and so on, can be extracted from an XML file.

Then, we use the load method on the `$objXML. load()` method takes two parameters. First is the filename and the second parameter is **libxml** option constants. The second parameter is optional. We pass `common.xml` as the first parameter and `LIBXML_NOBLANKS` as the second one. We also pass `LIBXML_NOBLANKS` because we do not want any blank nodes to appear.

Because we want to access all the book nodes, we use the `getElementsByTagName` method and pass a book to it that returns a **DOMNodeList** object. A `foreach` loop has been used to iterate in this collection. There are several methods available to objects of the **DOMNode** class. We have used some of them here.

The `firstChild` property gives us the immediate first child which is the book node in our case. `nodeValue` gives us the value inside the book tag, which is the name of book. We wrap it in an `h1` element.

To access the attribute, we use the `attributes` property. Attributes gives a map of all the attributes. We can navigate in this attribute collection using the item property. We retrieved the value of attribute at 0th position and that gives us the value of the `year` attribute.

Similarly, to get the list of stories for a book, we use `getElementsByTagName` again and then iterated in it for the value of each book title.

Finally, we wrap it into an unordered list.

After the DOM is ready on the browser, the jQuery code attaches a `click` event handler to each `h1` element on the page. Clicking on an `h1` element toggles its next `ul` element.

## There's more...

### Getting child nodes

We can also check if a node has child nodes and can also fetch them. In the above example, to get the child nodes of a book use the following code:

```
if($book->hasChildNodes())
{
    $children = $book->childNodes;
}
```

### nodeType, nodeName, and nodeValue

When you are not familiar with the XML structure or if it is inconsistent, you can determine the name and values of nodes and attributes at run time itself.

```
$node->nodeType
$node->nodeName
$node->nodeValue
```

`nodeType` may return different values depending on node. These values are **libxml** constants. Some common values for `nodeType` are as follows:

▶   XML_ELEMENT_NODE

▶   XML_ATTRIBUTE_NODE

▶   XML_TEXT_NODE

▶   XML_CDATA_SECTION_NODE

## See also

▶   *Creating an XML using DOM extension*

▶   *Searching elements using xPath*

# Creating an XML using DOM extension

DOM extension gives us the ability to create whole new documents using its numerous functions. In this recipe you will learn how to create new XML documents using DOM functions. As you know we have multiple book elements in our `common.xml` file, we will create a similar book element with name and story elements using DOM methods.

## Getting ready

Create a new folder `Recipe5` in the `Chapter3` directory.

## How to do it...

1. Create a file and name it `index.php` in the `Recipe5` folder.

2. Write the PHP code that will create a new XML document, then create some elements and add these to the new document. Some of these elements will have text as well as attributes and their values. Finally, this XML will be saved on the disk.

```php
<?php
  $objXML = new DOMDocument('1.0', 'utf-8');  /* <?xml
version="1.0" encoding="UTF-8" ?> */
  $books = $objXML->createElement('books');//books

  $book = $objXML->createElement('book');
  $attrIndex = new DOMAttr("index", "4");
  $book->appendChild($attrIndex);
  $bookName = $objXML->createElement('name','The case book of
              sherlock holmes');
  $attrYear = new DOMAttr("year", "1894");
  $bookName->appendChild($attrYear);

  $book->appendChild($bookName);

  $story = $objXML->createElement('story');
  $title = $objXML->createElement('title', 'Tha case of ....');
  $quote = $objXML->createElement('quote', 'Yet another quote');

  $story->appendChild($title);
  $story->appendChild($quote);

  $book->appendChild($story);
```

```
    $books->appendChild($book);

    $objXML->appendChild($books);

    if($objXML->save('new.xml') != FALSE)
    {
      echo 'XML file generated successfully.';
    }
    else
    {
      echo 'An error occured.';
    }
?>
```

3.  Now run the index.php file in your browser. If the code executed successfully, you will see some text telling you that the XML file has been generated. Look up in the Recipe5 folder and you will find the newly generated XML file. This file will have the same structure as the common.xml file.

```
<?xml version="1.0" encoding="utf-8"?>
<books>
  <book index="4">
    <name year="1894">The case book of sherlock holmes</name>
    <story>
      <title>Tha case of ....</title>
      <quote>Yet another quote</quote>
    </story>
  </book>
</books>
```

## How it works...

The constructor of DOMDocument class creates a new DOMDocument object. There are two optional parameters that can be passed to it. The first parameter indicates the version of XML specification and its value is 1.0 by default and the second parameter denotes the encoding of the document.

To create a new node, createElement() method is used. It creates a new object of DOMElement class. createElement() accepts two parameters out of which the second is optional. The first parameter is the name of node and the second is the text value inside a node.

To create an attribute, we can create an object of **DOMAttr** class. Similar to createElement, it also has two parameters: attribute name and its value.

Elements and attributes thus created are standalone at this moment and are not a part of the document. To insert them into the document, we can call the `appendChild` method. This method takes an element as a parameter and appends it to the calling object.

In the previous example, we created new elements with `createElement` and appended them to the document according to the required format.

When we are done with creating elements, we saved the resulting XML to a file using the `save()` method.

## See also

▶ *Reading an XML using DOM extension*

▶ *Modifying an XML using DOM extension*

# Modifying an XML using DOM extension

Apart from creating a new XML from scratch as in the previous recipe, we can modify existing XML files too. We can add and remove elements from them.

In this recipe, we will create an example that will allow you to add new stories for a particular book. You will be able to add a title and quote for the selected book.

## Getting ready

Create a new folder `Recipe6` in the `Chapter3` directory.

## How to do it...

1. Create a new file named `index.php`. Next, create a form that has a list of books and two input fields for entering story name and a quote. Also, create a button that will be used to add the new story and the quote to the XML file.

```
<html>
  <head>
    <title>Modifying xml with</title>
  <style type="text/css">
    ul{border:1px solid black;padding:5px;
list-style:none;width:350px;}
    label{float:left;width:100px;}
```

```
    </style>
  </head>
  <body>
    <ul>
      <li>
        <label for="bookList">Book:</label>
        <select id="bookList">
          <option value="">select a book</option>
          <?php
            $objXML = new DOMDocument();
            $objXML->load('../common.xml', LIBXML_NOBLANKS);
            $books = $objXML->getElementsByTagName('book');
            foreach($books as $book)
            {
              echo '<option value="'.$book->attributes->
    item(0)->value.'">'.$book->firstChild->nodeValue.'</option>';
            }
          ?>
        </select>
      </li>
      <li>
        <label for="storyName">Story Name</label>
          <input type="text" id="storyName" value=""/>
      </li>
      <li>
        <label for="quote">Quote</label>
        <textarea id="quote"></textarea>
      </li>
      <li>
        <input type="button" id="add" value="Add new story"/>
      </li>
    </ul>
  </body>
</html>
```

2. Now write the jQuery code that will invoke on the click of the button. jQuery will collect the values filled in the form and will send them to a PHP file, `process.php`, through an AJAX post request for further processing. The response received from PHP file will be displayed next to the button.

```
<script type="text/javascript" src="../jquery.js"></script>
<script type="text/javascript">
  $(document).ready(function ()
  {
    $('#add').click(function()
    {
```

```
        $.post(
          'process.php',
          { bookId: $('#bookList').val() , storyTitle:
            $('#storyName').val(), quote: $('#quote').val() },
          function(data)
          {
            $('#add').after(data);
          });
      });
    });
</script>
```

3. We turn to the PHP script now where the actual magic will take place. Create a file in the same folder and name it `process.php`. This file will take the values out from `$_POST`. After that, it will load the `common.xml` file. The script will find the selected book. When the selected book has been found, it will create new elements, fill them with respective values, and then save them back to the XML.

```php
<?php
  $bookId = $_POST['bookId'];
  $title = $_POST['storyTitle'];
  $quote = $_POST['quote'];
  $objXML = new DOMDocument();
  $objXML->load('../common.xml', LIBXML_NOBLANKS);
  $books = $objXML->getElementsByTagName('book');
  foreach($books as $book)
  {
    if($book->attributes->item(0)->value == $bookId)
    {
      $story = $objXML->createElement('story');
      $title = $objXML->createElement('title', $title);
      $quote = $objXML->createElement('quote', $quote);
      $story->appendChild($title);
      $story->appendChild($quote);
      $book->appendChild($story);
          break;
    }
  }
  if($objXML->save('../common.xml') != FALSE)
  {
    echo 'New story added successfully.';
  }
  else
  {
    echo 'An error occured.';
  }
?>
```

4.  Run the `index.php` file and you will be presented with a form. Select a book from the select box, fill in the values for story name, and quote in the textboxes and click on **Add new story**. On successful submission, you will see a message next to the button. Open the XML file with an editor and you will see that a new story has been inserted into the appropriate book.

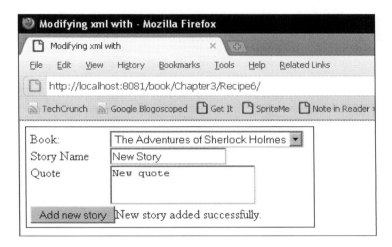

## How it works...

When the values are filled in the form and the button is clicked, jQuery sends the filled values to the `process.php` file. First, we get the values from `$_POST` array. Now **DOMDocument** class is used to load the XML file. We then use function `getElementsByTagName` to get all the book elements and then loop through them using `foreach` loop. Our main task here is to identify which book has been selected and also to modify that book node. Using the `attributes` property, we can compare the index attribute of a book with variable `$bookId` to find out the selected book. Once the book is found, we can break out of the loop.

Now that we have found the selected book, we can use DOM functions to add new elements. In the previous example we created three elements: story, title, and quote, and assigned the received values to title and quote.

To add these newly-created elements to the document tree, we use the `appendChild` method that we have used in the previous recipe. We appended the `$title` and `$quote` objects to `$story` objects and finally appended the `$story` object to `$book` object.

To change the modified object to a real XML string, we can use either of two methods: `save` and `saveXML`. `save()` method saves to a file whereas `saveXML()` returns XML as a string.

We can then echo the appropriate message that is displayed in the browser. Now, you can also check the value by opening the XML file that you have written.

## There's more...

### Deleting nodes

Opposite to `createElement()` method is the `removeChild()` method, which is used to remove elements from a document.

```
$objXML = new DOMDocument();
$objXML->load('new.xml');
$book = $objXML->getElementsByTagName('book')->item(0);
$book->parentNode->removeChild($book);
$objXML->save('new.xml');
```

The above code will remove the first book element (and all its children) from the document. If you wish to call the `removeChild` method from the root node itself, you can do this quite easily. You just need to replace the line:

```
$book->parentNode->removeChild($book);
```

with the following line:

```
$objXML->documentElement->removeChild($book);
```

## See also

- ▶ *Reading an XML using DOM extension*
- ▶ *Creating an XML using DOM extension*
- ▶ *Accessing elements and attributes using SimpleXML*

# Parsing XML with jQuery

jQuery itself can be used to parse an XML document on the client side. We can fetch an XML file using jQuery's AJAX methods and then process it on the browser itself and get data from it.

We will recreate the same example that we wrote in the recipe *Reading an XML using DOM extension*. Contrary to that recipe where we used DOM methods on the server side, we will use jQuery's selector functions to traverse through the XML.

## Getting ready

Create a new folder under `Chapter3` directory and name it as `Recipe7`. Also copy the `common.xml` file to this folder.

## How to do it...

1. Create a file named `index.html` in the `Recipe7` folder. In this file, simply declare some styles for `h1` and `ul` elements that will be created later through jQuery. Create a DIV element in which we will insert the HTML.

```html
<html>
  <head>
    <title>Reading xml through jQuery</title></head>
    <style type="text/css">
      h1{ cursor:pointer;font-size:20px;}
      ul{ display:none; list-style:none;margin:0pt;padding:0pt;}
    </style>
<body>
  <div id="result"></div>
</body>
</html>
```

2. Include the jQuery file. Next bind click handler for `h1` elements using `live` method. After that send an AJAX request to get the `common.xml` file. When the file is fetched, write success event handler to traverse through it and create HTML in the desired format. Finally, insert this HTML to the DIV element on the page.

```javascript
<script type="text/javascript" src="../jquery.js"></script>
<script type="text/javascript">
  $(document).ready(function ()
  {
    $('h1').live('click',function()
    {
      $(this).next('ul').toggle('fast');
  });

  $.ajax(
      {
        url: 'common.xml',
        type: 'GET',
        dataType: 'xml',
        success: function(xml)
        {
          var str = '';
          $(xml).find('book').each(function()
          {
            var book = $(this);
            str+= '<h1>' + book.find('name').text() + '</h1>';
            str+= '<ul>';
```

```
                        book.find('story').each(function()
                        {
                          str+= '<li>';
                          str+= $(this).find('title').text();
                          str+= '</li>';
                        });
                        str+= '</ul>';
                      });
                      $('#result').html(str);
                  }
                });
            });
    </script>
```

3.  Run the `index.html` file in the browser and you will see names of all the books in the XML file. Click on any of the titles to show or hide the story list for that book.

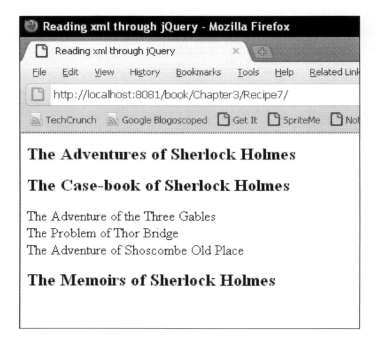

## How it works...

After the page has been loaded, the `common.xml` file is fetched through an AJAX GET request. Note the `dataType` property; we have set it to `xml`. Now jQuery knows that the response is going to be an XML file. So, when jQuery receives the XML string it converts it into a document object.

Now, we can apply all the jQuery's selector functions to it and extract the data. We used the `find` method to get all the book elements. Using `each()` we iterated in each book and again iterated for stories in each book. During this whole process, we also wrapped book names into `h1` elements and story names into list items.

When we are done looping, we have an HTML string that we insert into the page. Since we had already used live method for `h1` elements, clicking the book names will toggle the list of stories.

 Remember that the `live` method is used to attach event handlers to elements that will be created in future.

## There's more...

### The delegate() method

`delegate()` is another method similar to live—the difference being that it also takes selector elements as parameters and filters them against a set of elements that trigger the event.

```
$('div').delegate("span", "click", function(){
  $(this).toggleClass("hover");
});
```

If a DIV is clicked then the code will check whether this event has been fired by clicking on a span element inside the DIV. `toggleClass` will execute only when a span inside a DIV is clicked. `delegate()` has done the filtering in this case.

## See also

▸ *Reading an XML using DOM extension*

▸ *Accessing elements and attributes using SimpleXML*

▸ *Adding events to elements that will be created later in Chapter 1*

# 4
# Working with JSON

In this chapter, we will cover:

- ▶ Creating JSON in PHP
- ▶ Reading JSON in PHP
- ▶ Catching JSON parsing errors
- ▶ Accessing data from a JSON in jQuery

# Introduction

Recently, JSON (JavaScript Object Notation) has become a very popular data interchange format with more and more developers opting for it over XML. Even many web services nowadays provide JSON as the default output format.

JSON is a text format that is programming-language independent and is a native data form of JavaScript. It is lighter and faster than XML because it needs less markup compared to XML.

Because JSON is the native data form of JavaScript, it can be used on the client side in an AJAX application more easily than XML.

A JSON object starts with { and ends with }. According to the JSON specification, the following types are allowed in JSON:

- ▶ **Object**: An object is a collection of key-value pairs enclosed between { and } and separated by a comma. The key and the value themselves are separated using a colon (:). Think of objects as associative arrays or hash tables. Keys are simple strings and values can be an array, string, number, boolean, or null.
- ▶ **Array**: Like other languages, an array is an ordered pair of data. For representing an array, values are comma separated and enclosed between [ and ].
- ▶ **String**: A string must be enclosed in double quotes
- ▶ The last type is a number

A JSON can be as simple as:

```
{
   "name":"Superman", "address": "anywhere"
}
```

An example using an array is as follows:

```
{
   "name": "Superman", "phoneNumbers": ["8010367150", "9898989898",
   "1234567890" ]
}
```

A more complex example that demonstrates the use of objects, arrays, and values is as follows:

```
{
   "people":
   [
     {
       "name": "Vijay Joshi",
     "age": 28,
     "isAdult": true
     },
     {
       "name": "Charles Simms",
     "age": 13,
     "isAdult": false
     }
   ]
}
```

An important point to note:

```
{
    'name': 'Superman', 'address': 'anywhere'
}
```

Above is a valid JavaScript object but not a valid JSON. JSON requires that the name and value must be enclosed in double quotes; single quotes are not allowed.

Another important thing is to remember the proper charset of data.

Remember that JSON expects the data to be UTF-8 whereas PHP adheres to ISO-8859-1 encoding by default.

Also note that JSON is not a JavaScript; it is basically a specification or a subset derived from JavaScript.

Now that we are familiar with JSON, let us proceed towards the recipes where we will learn how we can use JSON along with PHP and jQuery.

Create a new folder and name it as Chapter4. We will put all the recipes of this chapter together in this folder. Also put the jquery.js file inside this folder.

 To be able to use PHP's built-in JSON functions, you should have PHP version 5.2 or higher installed.

# Creating JSON in PHP

This recipe will explain how JSON can be created from PHP arrays and objects.

## Getting ready

Create a new folder inside the Chapter4 directory and name it as Recipe1.

## How to do it...

1. Create a file and save it by the name index.php in the Recipe1 folder.

2. Write the PHP code that creates a JSON string from an array.

```php
<?php
  $travelDetails = array(
    'origin' => 'Delhi',
    'destination' => 'London',
    'passengers' => array
      (
        array('name' => 'Mr. Perry Mason', 'type' => 'Adult',
            'age'=> 28),
        array('name' => 'Miss Irene Adler', 'type' => 'Adult',
            'age'=> 28)
      ),
    'travelDate' => '17-Dec-2010'
  );
  echo json_encode($travelDetails);
?>
```

3.  Run the file in your browser. It will show a JSON string as output on screen. After indenting the result will look like the following:

```
{
"origin":"Delhi",
"destination":"London",
"passengers":
[
 {
   "name":"Mr. Perry Mason",
   "type":"Adult",
   "age":28
 },
 {
   "name":"Miss Irene Adler",
   "type":"Adult",
   "age":28
 }
],
"travelDate":"17-Dec-2010"
}
```

## How it works...

PHP provides the function `json_encode()` to create JSON strings from objects and arrays. This function accepts two parameters. First is the value to be encoded and the second parameter includes options that control how certain special characters are encoded. This parameter is optional.

In the previous code we created a somewhat complex associative array that contains travel information of two passengers. Passing this array to `json_encode()` creates a JSON string.

## There's more...

### Predefined constants

Any of the following constants can be passed as a second parameter to `json_encode()`.

  ▶   `JSON_HEX_TAG`: Converts < and > to \u003C and \u003E
  ▶   `JSON_HEX_AMP`: Converts &s to \u0026

- ▶ JSON_HEX_APOS: Converts ' to \u0027
- ▶ JSON_HEX_QUOT: Converts " to \u0022
- ▶ JSON_FORCE_OBJECT: Forces the return value in JSON string to be an object instead of an array

 These constants require PHP version 5.3 or higher.

## See also

- ▶ *Reading JSON in PHP*
- ▶ *Catching JSON parsing errors*

# Reading JSON in PHP

Opposite to the previous recipe, this recipe will explain how JSON strings can be read in PHP and converted to objects or arrays. Decoding JSON strings is very easy in PHP with its JSON functions.

## Getting ready

Create a new folder named Recipe2 in the Chapter4 directory.

## How to do it...

1. Create a file named index.php in Recipe2 folder.

2. Now try to convert a JSON string to object using json_decode() method. After that, print the resulting object on screen. For json_decode(), you can use the output from previous recipe which is a valid JSON string.

```php
<?php
$json = <<<JSON
{
  "origin":"Delhi",
  "destination":"London",
  "passengers":
  [
    {
      "name":"Mr. Perry Mason",
      "type":"Adult",
      "age":28
```

```
    },
    {
      "name":"Miss Irene Adler",
      "type":"Adult",
      "age":25
    }
  ],
  "travelDate":"17-Dec-2010"
}
JSON;
echo '<pre>';
$objJson = json_decode($json);
print_r ($objJson);
echo '</pre>';
?>
```

3.  Run the `index.php` file in the browser and you will see the structure of JSON string in the form of an object. To access the values from this object, you can query it just like any other object in PHP.

```
Mozilla Firefox
File  Edit  View  History  Bookmarks  Tools  Help  Related Links

               http://localhost:8081/book/Chapter4/Recipe2/

http://localhost:__04_code/Recipe2/

stdClass Object
(
    [origin] => Delhi
    [destination] => London
    [passengers] => Array
        (
            [0] => stdClass Object
                (
                    [name] => Mr. Perry Mason
                    [type] => Adult
                    [age] => 28
                )

            [1] => stdClass Object
                (
                    [name] => Miss Irene Adler
                    [type] => Adult
                    [age] => 25
                )

        )

    [travelDate] => 17-Dec-2010
)
```

## How it works...

`json_decode()` converts valid JSON strings into objects. It accepts three parameters each of which is described below:

- ▸ The JSON string itself
- ▸ Optional parameter `assoc`: By default this value is `false`. If changed to `true`, `json_decode` will convert objects to associative arrays
- ▸ Depth: Maximum allowed depth of a recursive structure in the JSON string. It used to be 128 before PHP 5.3. PHP 5.3 has this limit increased to 512 bytes default. This parameter is also optional.

In the previous code we used the HEREDOC syntax to define a JSON string. Then we passed this string to the `json_decode()` function which converted it to an object.

We can now access the values from this object using standard PHP operators. For example, to get the travel date from this object use:

```
$objJson->travelDate
```

Similarly,

```
$objJson->passengers[1]->name
```

will output the name of a second passenger, that is, **Miss Irene Adler**

## See also

- ▸ *Creating JSON in PHP*
- ▸ *Accessing data from a JSON in jQuery*
- ▸ *Catching JSON parsing errors*

# Catching JSON parsing errors

Errors are a part of application development. It depends on how the developer handles them to ease the life of users. While encoding or decoding JSON it may happen that the value passed to these JSON functions is erroneous or violates the JSON rules. In such cases you should always try to catch these errors and handle them.

This recipe deals specifically with error handling for JSON functions. We will use PHP's inbuilt JSON error handling methods to detect any errors in JSON.

 Please note that error handling in JSON is only available in PHP versions 5.3 and higher. So make sure you have the correct version of PHP installed to use this feature.

## Getting ready

Create a new folder inside the Chapter4 directory and name it Recipe3. Also make sure you have PHP version 5.3 or higher installed.

## How to do it...

1. Create a new PHP file index.php in the Recipe3 folder.
2. Using the same JSON string as present in the previous recipe, try to convert it into an object. Then write a switch case that will check for any errors in JSON and will output the result accordingly.

```php
<?php
$json = <<<JSON
{
  "origin":"Delhi",
  "destination":"London",
  "passengers":
  [
    {
      "name":"Mr. Perry Mason",
      "type":"Adult",
      "age":28
    },
    {
      "name":"Miss Irene Adler",
      "type":"Adult",
      "age":25
    }
  ],
  "travelDate":"17-Dec-2010"
}
JSON;
$objJson = json_decode($json);
switch(json_last_error())
{
```

```
    case JSON_ERROR_NONE:
      echo'Travel date is:' . $objJson->travelDate;
    break;
    case JSON_ERROR_DEPTH:
      echo 'The JSON string has exceeded maximum allowed stack
            depth';
    break;
    case JSON_ERROR_CTRL_CHAR:
      echo 'Control character error';
    break;
    case JSON_ERROR_SYNTAX:
      echo 'Incorrect JSON : Please check your JSON syntax';
    break;
  }
  ?>
```

3.  Now, run the `index.php` file. Since JSON is correct, you will see the output **Travel date is:17-Dec-2010** on your screen. Now remove the comma from the line `"destination":"London"`,. Save the file and reload it. You will see an error message : **Incorrect JSON : Please check your JSON syntax**

## How it works...

PHP version 5.3 onwards provides a function `json_last_error()`. This function takes no parameters and captures the last error through JSON parsing. It returns an integer value that can be checked to know the specific error. PHP has some predefined constants for these error values. These are:

▶  JSON_ERROR_NONE: It means the JSON was parsed successfully and there was no error

▶  JSON_ERROR_SYNTAX: Means there is a syntax error in the JSON string

▶  JSON_ERROR_CTRL_CHAR: Invalid control character encountered

▶  JSON_ERROR_DEPTH: The JSON string has exceeded maximum allowed stack depth

## See also

▶  *Reading JSON in PHP*

# Accessing data from a JSON in jQuery

So, now we know how to generate JSON using PHP. We can put this knowledge of ours to some real use. We will write an example that will request some JSON data from PHP (using jQuery of course) and then we will display it in the web page.

## Getting ready

Create a folder for this recipe inside the Chapter4 directory and name it Recipe4.

## How to do it...

1. Create a file named index.html in the newly created Recipe4 folder.

2. Write some HTML code in this file that will create and empty select box and an empty unordered list. Also define some CSS styles for these elements in the <head> section.

```
<?php
<html>
  <head>
  <title>Accessing data from a JSON</title>
  <style type="text/css">
  body,select,ul{ font-family:"trebuchet MS",verdana }
  ul{ list-style::none;margin:0pt;padding:0pt;}
  </style>
  </head>
  <body>
    <h3>Select a date to view Travel Details</h3>
    <p>
      <select id="travelDates">
      </select>
      <ul>
        <li id="origin"></li>
        <li id="destination"></li>
        <li id="travellers"></li>
      </ul>
    </p>
  </body>
</html>
?>
```

3. Time for some jQuery now. First, add a reference to the jQuery library, just before the closing of the `<body>` tag. Then, write the jQuery code that will request some JSON data from a PHP file `json.php`. On receiving the response, jQuery will fill the select box and will bind a `change` event handler for it. On selecting a value from this select box, another function will be called that will search for the JSON response for the selected date and will display relevant details on finding it.

```
<script type="text/javascript" src="../jquery.js"></script>
<script type="text/javascript">
  $(document).ready(function ()
  {
    var jsonResult;
    $.getJSON("json.php",displayData);
    function displayData(data)
    {
      jsonResult = data;
      var str = '<option value="">select a date</option>';
      for(var i=0; i<data.length;i++)
      {
        str+= '<option value="' + data[i].travelDate + '">' +
                data[i].travelDate + '</option>';
      }
      $('#travelDates').html(str);
      $('#travelDates').change(function()
      {
        if($(this).val() != '')
        {
          displayDetails($(this).val());
        }
      });
    }

    function displayDetails(selectedDate)
    {
      for(var i=0; i<jsonResult.length;i++)
      {
        var aResult = jsonResult[i];
        if(aResult.travelDate == selectedDate)
        {
          $('#origin').html('<strong>Origin : </strong>'+
            aResult.origin);
          $('#destination').html('<strong>Destination :
            </strong>'+ aResult.destination);
          var travellers = aResult.passengers;
          var strTraveller = '<ul>';
```

```
                    for(var j=0; j<travellers.length;j++)
            {
                strTraveller+= '<li>';
                strTraveller+= travellers[j].name;
                strTraveller+= '</li>';
            }
            strTraveller+= '</ul>';
            $('#travellers').html('<strong>Travellers : <br/>
                </strong>'+ strTraveller);
            break;
            }
        }
    }
  });
</script>
```

4.  Now let's get to the file that will receive the request for JSON. Create this new file and
    save it as json.php. In this file, create an array of travel details of some travellers,
    then convert it to JSON and send it to the browser.

```php
$travelDetails = array(
  array(

    'origin' => 'London',
    'destination' => 'Paris',
    'passengers' => array
      (
        array('name' => 'Mr. Sherlock Holmes', 'age'=> 34),
        array('name' => 'Mr. John H. Watson', 'age'=> 32)
      ),
    'travelDate' => '17-Dec-2010'
    ),
  array(
    'origin' => 'Delhi',
    'destination' => 'London',
    'passengers' => array
      (
        array('name' => 'Mr. Albert Einstein', 'age'=> 51),
        array('name' => 'Mr. Isaac Newton' ,'age'=> 43)
      ),
    'travelDate' => '25-Jan-2011'
    ),
  array(
    'origin' => 'Delhi',
    'destination' => 'London',
```

```
        'passengers' => array
          (
            array('name' => 'Prof. John Moriaty', 'age'=> 44),
            array('name' => 'Miss Irene Adler', 'age'=> 28)
          ),
        'travelDate' => '30-Mar-2011'
        )
);
header('Content-Type:text/json');
echo json_encode($travelDetails);
```

5.  All done now. Open your browser and run the `index.html` file. A select box will appear on screen with some dates filled in it. Select a date and you will see the details for that particular date.

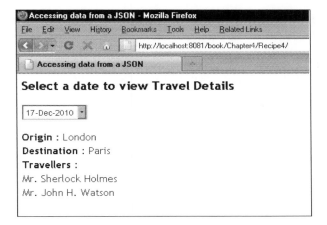

## How it works...

When the DOM is ready, we call the AJAX method `$.getJSON()`. Previously, you learnt about `$.get()` and `$.post()`. Similarly, this is a special method that is used when the expected data from the server is in JSON format. Here is the breakdown of parameters of `$.getJSON()`:

- ▶  **URL**: This is the URL where the request will be sent.
- ▶  **Data**: The data (if any) that has to be sent to the server.
- ▶  **Callback function**: This function is fired when the response is received from the server. In case of a JSON response, jQuery parses it and a JavaScript object of the parsed data is made available to the callback function.

In our example, the request is sent to the `json.php` file first, where an array with multiple records has been declared. We then use the `json_encode` method to convert this array to JSON and echo it to the browser.

On receiving the response jQuery parses it and an object is made available to the callback method, `displayData`. Here we store it in a global variable `$jsonResult` for future use.

Then we iterate in this object and fill the select box with all the travel dates in the array. Because the data is now a JavaScript object, JavaScript syntax will apply to it.

After the select box is filled with data, we attach a `change` event handler for it. When a value is selected from the select box, the `displayDetails()` function is called. This function searches the object for the selected date. When the date is found we retrieve the values for origin, destination, and passengers from the selected set and insert them into corresponding elements on the page.

## There's more...

### Other AJAX methods for requesting JSON data

As mentioned earlier, `$.getJSON()` is solely designed for conditions where we know in advance that the response from the server is going to be JSON. However, this behavior can be simulated with other high-level AJAX methods like `$.get()`, `$.post()` and the low level implementation `$.ajax()`.

```
$.get(
  'json.php',
   displayData,
  'json'
);
```

By specifying the last parameter as JSON, jQuery will try to assume the response as JSON string and will try to parse it. Same can be done with `$.post()` and `$.ajax()`.

### Handling errors while requesting JSON

The method that we have used above use AJAX methods such as `$.getJSON` or `$.get`. These methods do not have error-handling abilities by themselves. For example, if we have requested JSON using `$.getJSON` and the server sends malformed JSON, `$.getJSON` will fail silently. There are two ways to resolve this: either use the `ajaxError()` method, which gets executed when any AJAX request encounters an error, or use the low level `$.ajax` method, which provides both success and error callbacks. Both of these have been described in detail in the recipe *Handling errors in AJAX requests* in the previous chapter.

## Parsing a JSON

Other than using $.getJSON or specifying a data type in AJAX requests, you can also parse a valid JSON string to convert it to JSON object. jQuery provides a method parseJSON() to convert a JSON string to a JavaScript object.

```
var objJSON = jQuery.parseJSON('{"key":"value"}');
```

objJSON is now a JavaScript object.

Another method, which is not recommended, is to use eval() function of JavaScript.

```
var objJSON = eval('(' + '{"key":"value"}' + ')')
```

Using eval() may harm your site as the eval() will execute any data that is passed to it. Therefore, it is recommended to use either parseJSON or a specific AJAX method of jQuery that returns parsed JSON.

### See also

- ▶ *Creating JSON in PHP*
- ▶ *Fetching data from PHP using jQuery* in *Chapter 2*

# 5
# Working with Forms

In this chapter, we will cover:

- ▶ Adding input fields dynamically in a form
- ▶ Searching for a user-inputted string in a page
- ▶ Checking for empty fields using jQuery
- ▶ Validating numbers using jQuery
- ▶ Validating e-mail and website addresses using regular expressions
- ▶ Displaying errors as user types: performing live validation
- ▶ Strengthening validation: validating again in PHP
- ▶ Creating a voting system
- ▶ Allowing HTML inside textareas and limiting HTML tags that can be used

## Introduction

Forms and pages are the only part of your web application that the end-user uses directly. It is, therefore, the responsibility of a web developer to make forms that are easy to use, easy to navigate, and interactive. Moreover, attackers can try to damage your application by trying to input malicious data through your forms.

This chapter deals with forms and form validations like searching for data in a form both on the browser and the server side. Though validation can be done on the browser with the help of jQuery, validating data on the server side is more important. If JavaScript is disabled on the browser, then the client-side validation will not work. Validation on the client side makes your application user-friendly and less error prone. You will learn how to validate forms for different types of data such as empty fields, numbers, e-mail or web addresses, and so on later in this chapter.

Validation on the server side is a must and the client-side
validation should not be seen as a replacement for it because
client-side validation can be disabled.

# Adding input fields dynamically in a form

We will create a form where you will be able to add more fields to a form without making a
trip to the server side. In our form, we will present the user with a single textbox and we will
provide buttons for adding and removing additional textboxes.

## Getting ready

Create a folder for this recipe named Recipe1 in the Chapter5 directory. Do not forget to
put the jquery.js file inside the Recipe1 folder.

## How to do it...

1.  Create a file and save it as index.html in the Recipe1 folder and write an HTML
    code that will create a list with only one list item. This list item will only have a single
    textbox. In the end, we'll see a button that will add more fields to our form.

```html
<html>
  <head>
    <title>Add rows dynamically</title>
    <style type="text/css">
      fieldset{width:450px;}
      ul{padding:2px;list-style:none;}
      label{float:left;width:100px;}
    </style>
  </head>
  <body>
    <form action="process.php" method="post">
      <fieldset>
        <legend>Websites you visit daily</legend>
        <ul id="sites">
          <li>
            <label>Name</label><input type="text" value=""/>
          </li>
        </ul>
        <input type="button" id="add" value="Add More"/>
      </fieldset>
```

```
    </form>
  </body>
</html>
```

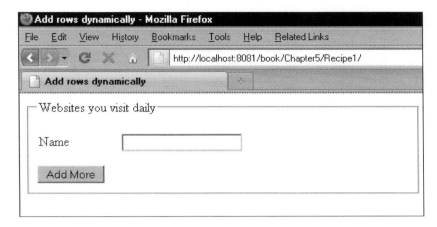

2. Now, include jQuery and write event handlers. The first event handler will be for the **Add More** button that will add more textboxes and also a button to remove them. We will write another event handler that will remove selected textboxes.

```
<script type="text/javascript" src="../jquery.js"></script>
<script type="text/javascript">
  $(document).ready(function ()
  {
    $('#add').click(function()
    {
      var str = '<li>';
      str+= '<label>Name</label><input type="text" value=""/> ';
      str+= '<input type="button" value="remove"
               class="remove"/>';
      str+= '</li>';
      $('#sites').append(str);
    });

    $('.remove').live('click', function()
    {
      $(this).parent('li').remove();
    });
  });
</script>
```

3. Run the file in your browser. Clicking on the **Add More** button will add more textboxes to the page. You can also remove specific textboxes by clicking on the **remove** button next to the textbox.

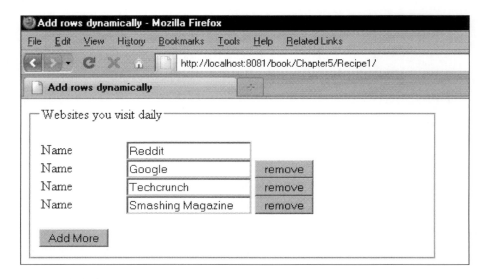

## How it works...

The event handler for the **Add More** button creates a new li with a textbox and a **remove** button inside it, and then uses jQuery's append method to append it to an existing list of sites.

Note that all **remove** buttons have a class called remove specified. We used the live method to attach the event handler for elements having this class. If you remember, the live method adds an event handler to those elements that are already present in the form as well as those that will be created in the future.

Therefore, clicking on the **remove** button on any row finds its parent li and removes it from the DOM.

## There's more...

### Getting values on server side

All these textboxes are generated on the client side that is using jQuery. To access these on the server side, all of these should have a name attribute. Since all of these belong to the same group (websites), we can provide a name attribute in array format that will allow us to get all filled values in the form of an array.

Simply add `name="sites[]"` to the existing textbox as well as when we create it from jQuery. Now if the form is submitted you can access all the filled values from the array `$_POST['sites']`. Given below is the `$_POST` array after submitting the form with some values:

```
Array
(
    [sites] => Array
        (
            [0] => Purple
            [1] => Violet
            [2] => Red
            [3] => Green
            [4] => Yellow
        )

)
```

# Searching for user-inputted string in a page

We will use jQuery to highlight a word entered by the user. The data on the browser can be made available from the server side (or database) as well. For this example, we will use some text in an HTML page. The user will enter a search query in a textbox and after pressing a button all matching words in the content will be highlighted.

## Getting ready

Create a folder for this recipe in the `Chapter5` directory and name it as `Recipe2`.

## How to do it...

1.  Open a new file, name it as `index.html` and save it in the `Recipe2` folder. Let us begin by writing the markup now. Create some paragraphs and put some text inside them. In the end, place a textbox and two buttons. We have also defined a CSS class `highlight` that will create the highlight effect.

    ```
    <html>
      <head>
        <title>Search</title>
        <style type="text/css">
          p { border:1px solid black;width:500px;padding:5px; }
          .highlight { background-color:yellow; }
    ```

```
      </style>
    </head>
    <body>
      <form>
        <p>
          I consider that a man's brain originally is like a little
          empty attic, and you have to stock it with such furniture
          as you choose. A fool takes in all the lumber of every
          sort that he comes across, so that the knowledge which
          might be useful to him gets crowded out, or at best is
          jumbled up with a lot of other things, so that he has a
          difficulty in laying his hands upon it.
        </p>
        <p>
          I consider that a man's brain originally is like a little
          empty attic, and you have to stock it with such furniture
          as you choose. A fool takes in all the lumber of every
          sort that he comes across, so that the knowledge which
          might be useful to him gets crowded out, or at best is
          jumbled up with a lot of other things, so that he has a
          difficulty in laying his hands upon it.
        </p>
        <p>
          I consider that a man's brain originally is like a little
          empty attic, and you have to stock it with such furniture
          as you choose. A fool takes in all the lumber of every
          sort that he comes across, so that the knowledge which
          might be useful to him gets crowded out, or at best is
          jumbled up with a lot of other things, so that he has a
          difficulty in laying his hands upon it.
        </p>
        <input type="text" id="text"/>
        <input type="button" id="search" value="Search"/>
        <input type="button" id="clear" value="Clear"/>
      </form>
    </body>
  </html>
```

2. Before the `body` tag closes, include jQuery. Now in the form we have two buttons. The first button is for searching the entered text and the second one is for clearing the highlighted parts. For searching, we'll call a `highlight` function by clicking on the **Search** button. This function searches the text on the page and on finding it, wraps it into HTML tags and applies the highlight class to it. The second button calls the `clearSelection` function that restores the page to normal.

```
<script type="text/javascript" src="../jquery.js"></script>
<script type="text/javascript">
  $(document).ready(function ()
  {
    $('#search').click(highlight);
    $('#clear').click(clearSelection);

    function highlight()
    {
      var searchText = $('#text').val();
      var regExp = new RegExp(searchText, 'g');
      clearSelection();
      $('p').each(function()
      {
        var html = $(this).html();
        var newHtml = html.replace(regExp,
                '<span class="highlight">'+searchText+'</span>');

        $(this).html(newHtml);
      });
    }

    function clearSelection()
    {
      $('p').each(function()
      {
        $(this).find('.highlight').each(function()
        {
          $(this).replaceWith($(this).html());
        });
      });
    }
  });
</script>
```

3.  Run the file in your browser and enter a search term in the textbox. Click on the **Search** button and all matching words will be highlighted on the page. Click on the **Clear** button to reset.

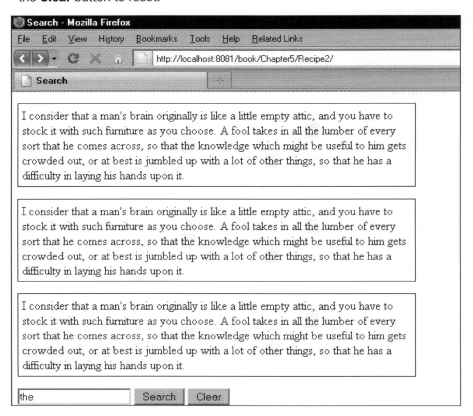

## How it works...

After entering a search term and clicking on the **Search** button, the `highlight` function is called. This function first clears any highlights on the page by calling the `clearSelection` function. We will see what `clearSelection` does in a moment. Next, we get the entered search term in variable `searchText`. After that, we create an object using the `RegExp` method of JavaScript. This regular expression will perform an actual search for the entered text.

Then we iterate through each paragraph on the form. We get the HTML of each paragraph and we get to use JavaScript's `replace` function on that HTML. The `replace` function takes two parameters. The first parameter is the regular expression object and the second one is the text with which we have to replace the matched text. We have just wrapped the search text in a span and assigned CSS class `highlight` to it. The `replace` function will return the whole text with the replaced words. We then replace the original HTML of the current paragraph with this new one.

There's more...

## Search and replace

You can extend this idea and could create a simple utility for "search and replace". Rather than highlighting the selected text, you can ask for a string to replace it with.

# Checking for empty fields using jQuery

Validation is an important technique in client-side scripting. Validation on the client side can significantly reduce round trips to the server by providing instant feedback in the form of messages. Even so, it is NOT recommended to rely on the client-side validation alone. JavaScript on the users' browsers might be turned off; therefore, validation should ALWAYS be done again on the server side as well.

## How to do it...

1.  Create a file for this recipe and name it `index.html`. Create a form with some text fields and an `input` button. Note that all textboxes except `city` has a class name `required` assigned to them. This will be used while validating the fields.

    ```html
    <html>
      <head>
        <title>Validate empty fields</title>
        <style type="text/css">
          body{font-family:"Trebuchet MS",verdana;width:450px;}
          .error{ color:red; }
          #info{color:#008000;font-weight:bold; }
        </style>
      </head>
      <body>
        <form>
          <fieldset>
            <legend><strong>Personal</strong></legend>
            <table>
              <tbody>
                <tr>
                <td>Name:* </td>
                <td><input type="text" class="required" /></td>
                </tr>
    ```

```
              <tr>
              <td>Address:* </td>
              <td><input type="text" class="required"/></td>
              </tr>
              <tr>
                <td>City: </td>
                <td><input type="text"/></td>
              </tr>
              <tr>
                <td>Country:* </td>
                <td><input type="text" class="required"/></td>
              </tr>
            </tbody>
          </table>
        </fieldset>
        <br/>
        <span id="info"></span>
        <br/>
        <input type="button" value="Check" id="check" />
      </form>
    </body>
</html>
```

2.  Now, include the jQuery before the `<body>` tag closes. Write the validation code that attaches a `click` event handler to the `input` button. The `validate` function will be called on clicking this button that will check the text fields for empty values.

```
<script type="text/javascript" src="../jquery.js"></script>
<script type="text/javascript">
  $(document).ready(function ()
  {
    $('#check').click(validate);
    function validate()
    {
      var dataValid = true;
      $('#info').html('');
      $('.required').each(function()
      {
```

```
        var cur = $(this);
        cur.next('span').remove();
        if ($.trim(cur.val()) == '')
        {
          cur.after('<span class="error"> Mandatory field
                    </span>');
          dataValid = false;
        }
      });
      if(dataValid)
      {
        $('#info').html('Validation OK');
      }
    }
  });
</script>
```

3.   Launch your browser and run the index.html file. Try clicking on the **Check** button without filling in values for the textboxes. You will see an error message next to each textbox that needs to be filled:

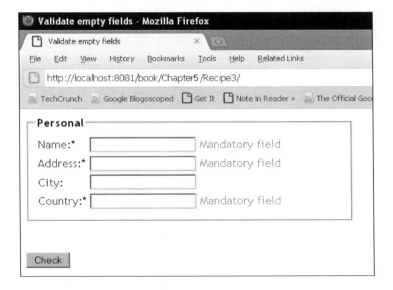

After filling the required values in each of the textboxes, click on the button again and this time you will see the **Validation OK** message appearing above the **Check** button as shown in the following screenshot:

## How it works...

We start by assigning a class name required to each textbox that we wish to make mandatory. This way we will be able to use jQuery's class selector to select all such textboxes.

First of all, in the jQuery code, we have attached an event handler to the **Check** button that calls the validate function. This function starts by declaring a variable dataValid to true and then it selects all the textboxes that have CSS class required. It then iterates in this collection and removes any span elements next to the textbox. These span elements maybe previous error messages. If we do not remove them, we will have multiple similar looking error messages next to a single textbox.

After this, the if condition checks the value of the current textbox. Note the use of jQuery utility function trim here. Since blank spaces are not considered valid values, we trim these from the text value. If a blank value is found, we append a span with an error message next to the current textbox and variable dataValid is set to false.

After all the iterations are done using jQuery's each method, we check the value of dataValid. If it's still true, that means no field is blank and we display a **Validation OK** message on the screen.

### Validating fields one by one

If you do not want to show all errors at once but instead want to make sure that the user has filled the first field and then proceeded to the next, you can do so by modifying the previous code.

To do that, change the `if` condition as follows:

```
if ($.trim(cur.val()) == '')
{
  cur.after('<span class="error"> Mandatory field</span>');
  dataValid = false;
}
```

And remove this code:

```
if(dataValid)
{
  $('#info').html('Validation OK');
}
```

## See also

▶  *Validating numbers using jQuery*

▶  *Validating e-mail and website addresses using regular expressions*

▶  *Displaying errors as user types: performing live validation*

# Validating numbers using jQuery

In the last recipe, we validated empty fields. In this recipe, we will extend that behavior and will check for numbers along with empty fields.

## Getting ready

Create a new folder `Recipe4` inside the `Chapter5` directory.

## How to do it...

1. Create a new file and save it as `index.html` in the `Recipe4` folder. We will take the same code form as used in the previous recipe and will add another section to it. So, copy the code from the previous recipe to the `index.html` file. Now, we will add another section to it through which a user will be able to enter some numbers. Create another section named **Other Details** after the **Personal** section. It is important to note that these fields have another CSS class named `number` along with `required` assigned to them. This way we will be able to validate for empty fields as well as for numbers.

```
<fieldset>
  <legend><strong>Other Details</strong></legend>
  <table>
    <tbody>
      <tr>
      <tr>
        <td>Age:* </td>
        <td><input type="text" class="required number"/></td>
      </tr>
      <tr>
        <td>Monthly Expenses:* </td>
        <td><input type="text" class="required number"/></td>
      </tr>
      </tr>
    </tbody>
  </table>
</fieldset>
```

2. Now, let's look at the jQuery code. Once again, include the jQuery library and write the code for validating empty fields as well as numbers. Clicking on the button this time will first check for blank fields. If any of the fields are empty, the user will be notified and we will jump out of the function. Once all the fields have passed the blank field validation, jQuery will check for those textboxes that should have numbers only. Here is the complete jQuery code:

```html
<script type="text/javascript" src="../jquery.js"></script>
<script type="text/javascript">
  $(document).ready(function ()
  {
    $('#check').click(validate);

    function validate()
    {
      var dataValid = true;
      $('.required').each(function()
      {
        var cur = $(this);
        cur.next().remove();
        if ($.trim(cur.val()) == '')
        {
          cur.after('<span class="error"> Mandatory field
                    </span>');
          dataValid = false;
        }
      });
      if(!dataValid) return false;

      $('.number').each(function()
      {
        var cur = $(this);
        cur.next().remove();
        if (isNaN(cur.val()))
        {
          cur.after('<span class="error"> Must be a number
                    </span>');
          dataValid = false;
        }
      });
      if(dataValid)
      {
        $('#info').html('Validation OK');
      }
    }
  });
</script>
```

## How it works...

In the previous code, we first check for empty fields by iterating on elements with class name `required`. After the iterations are complete we check the value of the `dataValid` field. If it is `false`, we'll return immediately from the function. Once all the fields are non-empty, we proceed to check for numbers.

We select all the elements with class name or number and use the each method to check each element. JavaScript function `isNaN` (is Not a Number) can be used to determine if a value is a number or not. If a value is found that is not a number, we append the appropriate error message after that element.

If all elements pass this validation, the message **Validation OK** gets displayed near the **Check** button.

## See also

▶ *Checking for empty fields using jQuery*

▶ *Validating e-mail and website addresses using regular expressions*

▶ *Displaying errors as user types: performing live validation*

# Validating e-mail and website addresses using regular expressions

While filling out web forms it is common to ask a user for an e-mail ID and a website name. These values are a little bit different from the normal strings as they have a fixed pattern. E-mail addresses require @ symbol whereas website addresses generally start with http or https. These and many other conditions are required by such addresses.

This is where regular expressions come to the rescue. This recipe will show you the use of regular expressions to validate patterns like e-mail addresses and URLs.

## Getting ready

Create a new folder named `Recipe5` inside the `Chapter5` directory.

## How to do it...

1.  Create a file named `index.html` inside the `Recipe5` folder. Similar to the previous recipe, create two textboxes—one for entering the e-mail address and another for the website address. Also, assign a CSS class `mail` to the first textbox and `site` to the second one.

```html
<html>
  <head>
    <title>Search</title>
    <style type="text/css">
      body{font-family:"Trebuchet MS",verdana;width:450px;}
      .error{ color:red; }
      #info{color:#008000;font-weight:bold; }
    </style>
  </head>
  <body>
    <form action="process.php" method="post">
      <fieldset>
      <legend><strong>Contact Details</strong>- both fields are
              mandatory</legend>
        <table>
          <tbody>
            <tr>
            <tr>
              <td>Email: </td>
              <td><input type="text" class="required mail"/></td>
            </tr>
            <tr>
              <td>Website:<br/>(start with http://) </td>
              <td><input type="text" class="required site"/></td>
            </tr>
            </tr>
          </tbody>
        </table>
      </fieldset>
      <br/>
      <span id="info"></span>
      <br/>
```

```
        <input type="button" value="Check" id="check" />
    </form>
  </body>
</html>
```

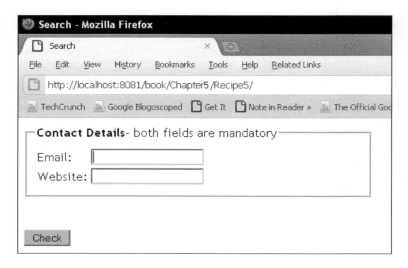

2. To make our validations actually work, first include the jQuery library. Then add an event handler for the **Check** button. It will first search for all elements with class name `mail` and will validate the entered e-mail address against a regular expression. After that, it will validate the website address entered by the user, again against a regular expression. If no match is found, an error will be displayed next to that textbox.

```
<script type="text/javascript" src="../jquery.js"></script>
<script type="text/javascript">
  $(document).ready(function ()
  {
    $('#check').click(validate);

    function validate()
    {
      var dataValid = true;

      $('.mail').each(function() {
        var cur = $(this);
        cur.next('span').remove();
        var emailPattern = /^([a-z0-9_\.-]+)@([\da-z\.-]+)\.([a-
                          z\.]{2,6})$/;
        if (!emailPattern.test(cur.val()))
```

```
            {
              cur.after('<span class="error"> Invalid Email Id
                        </span>');
              dataValid = false;
            }
          });
          if(!dataValid)          return;

          $('.site').each(function() {
            var cur = $(this);
            cur.next('span').remove();
            var urlPattern = /^(http(s?))\:\/\/www.([0-9a-zA-Z\-
                            ]+\.)+[a-zA-Z]{2,6}(\:[0-9]+)?(\/\S*)?$/;
            if (!urlPattern.test(cur.val()))
            {
              cur.after('<span class="error"> Invalid URL</span>');
              dataValid = false;
            }
          });
          if(dataValid)
          {
            $('#info').html('Validation OK');
          }
        }
      });
    </script>
```

## How it works...

On clicking the **Check** button, the `validate` function is called. This function first defines the variable `dataValid` to `true`. Then it gets all textboxes with class name `mail` and iterates in the selection. We declare a variable `emailPattern`, which defines a regular expression. Then, inside the `if` condition, we use JavaScript `test` function to check the value of textbox against the regular expression. If the pattern does not match, we append an error message next to the textbox and set the `dataValid` variable to `false`.

We then repeat the same procedure for elements with class name `site`. For URL validation, another regular expression has been used.

If all validations pass, we show the message **Validation OK** to the user.

**There's more...**

### References for regular expressions

You can refer to the below mentioned links for further study of regular expressions:

- ► `http://www.regular-expressions.info/`
- ► `http://en.wikipedia.org/wiki/Regular_expression`

**See also**

- ► *Checking for empty fields using jQuery*
- ► *Validating numbers using jQuery*

# Displaying errors as user types: Performing live validation

Wouldn't it be better if we could validate the data as soon as the user starts typing? We will not have to wait until the button is clicked and this will be quite informative for the user too.

This recipe is a major enhancement on previous recipes and will show you how you can use live validation in your forms. Users will be notified of errors as they are inputting data in a field.

**Getting ready**

Create a folder named `Recipe6` inside the `Chapter5` directory.

**How to do it...**

1. Create a new file inside `Recipe6` folder and name it as `index.html`. Write the HTML that will create two panels, one for **Personal details** and the other for **Other details**. Textboxes of the first panel will have class name `required` assigned to them. Similarly, the second panel textboxes will have class names `required` and `number` assigned to them.

```html
<html>
  <head>
    <title>Live validation</title>
    <style type="text/css">
      body{font-family:"Trebuchet MS",verdana;width:450px;}
      .error{ color:red; }
```

```
            #info{color:#008000;font-weight:bold; }
        </style>
</head>
<body>
    <form action="process.php" method="post">
        <fieldset>
            <legend><strong>Personal</strong></legend>
            <table>
                <tbody>
                    <tr>
                        <td>Name:* </td>
                        <td><input type="text" class="required" /></td>
                    </tr>
                    <tr>
                        <td>Address:* </td>
                        <td><input type="text" class="required"/></td>
                    </tr>
                    <tr>
                        <td>Country:* </td>
                        <td><input type="text" class="required"/></td>
                    </tr>
                </tbody>
            </table>
        </fieldset>
        <fieldset>
            <legend><strong>Other Details</strong></legend>
            <table>
                <tbody>
                    <tr>
                    <tr>
                        <td>Age:* </td>
                        <td><input type="text" class="required number"/>
                        </td>
                    </tr>
                    <tr>
                        <td>Monthly Expenses:* </td>
                        <td><input type="text" class="required number"/>
                        </td>
                    </tr>
                    </tr>
                </tbody>
            </table>
        </fieldset>
```

```
                <span id="info"></span>
                <br/>
                <input type="button" value="Save" id="save" />
            </form>
        </body>
    </html>
```

2. To bring our form to life, include the jQuery library first. Then write an event handler for textboxes that will execute when any of the textboxes gets focus or a key is released in any of the textboxes. This code will execute as the user is typing and will show an error message on a failed validation condition. Finally, add an event handler for the **Check** button also because the user might click on the **Check** button without entering any data in the form.

```javascript
<script type="text/javascript" src="../jquery.js"></script>
<script type="text/javascript">
  $(document).ready(function ()
  {
    $('input:text').bind('focus keyup',validate);

    function validate()
    {
      var cur = $(this);
      cur.next().remove();
      if(cur.hasClass('required'))
      {
        if ($.trim(cur.val()) == '')
        {
          cur.after('<span class="error"> Mandatory field
                    </span>');
          cur.data('valid', false);
        }
        else
        {
          cur.data('valid', true);
        }
      }

      if(cur.hasClass('number'))
      {
        if (isNaN(cur.val()))
        {
          cur.after('<span class="error"> Must be a number
                    </span>');
          cur.data('valid', false);
```

```
        }
        else
        {
          dataValid = true;
          cur.data('valid', true);
        }
      }
    }


    $('#save').click(function()
    {
      var dataValid = true;
      $('.required').each(function()
      {
        var current = $(this);
        if(current.data('valid') != true)
        {
          dataValid = false;
        }
      });

      $('.number').each(function()
      {
        var current = $(this);
        if(current.data('valid') != true)
        {
          dataValid = false;
        }
      });

      if(dataValid)
        $('#info').html('Validation OK');
      else
        $('#info').html('Please fill correct values in fields.');
    });
  });
</script>
```

The output should look similar to the following screenshot on a failed validation:

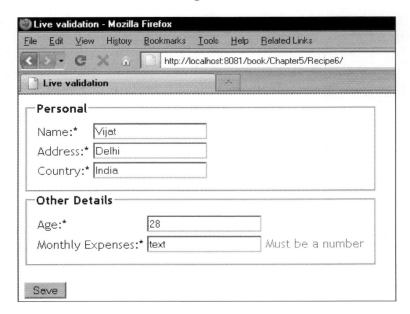

## How it works...

Since we are going to validate all the fields instantly as user types we attach two event handlers to the textboxes—focus and keyup. keyup will execute when the user releases a key on the keyboard and focus will execute when the user places the cursor in a textbox either by clicking it through a mouse or by using the *Tab* key. Both event handlers will call the same validate function. This way we will be able to validate the value as soon as it is entered in a textbox.

The validate function will now perform the same functions as we have seen in the last few recipes. It will get the value of textbox and check it for blank values and numeric values, as specified by the class name of the target textbox.

However, there is one problem here. If the user does not fill any values and just clicks on the **Save** button, we will not be able to detect if any values are filled or not. To resolve this, we will take two steps.

First, while validating in the validate function, we will save a value true or false for each textbox. This will be done by using the data() method of jQuery that stores data with DOM elements. If a field validates we save the value with key valid to it. The value against the key will be either true or false.

There is also an event handler attached to the **Save** button. Now suppose the user clicks the **Save** button without doing anything with the textboxes. We then select the textboxes and check if there is data associated with the textboxes or not. The key name should be `valid` and its value should be `true`. If we do not get a value `true`, it means the fields have not been validated yet and we set the variable `dataValid` to `false`. We then repeat the same process with textboxes and with the CSS class `number`. Finally, we show a message to the user depending on the value of the `dataValid` variable.

## See also

▶ *Checking for empty fields using jQuery*

▶ *Validating numbers using jQuery*

▶ *Validating e-mail and website addresses using regular expressions*

▶ *Strengthening validation: validating again in PHP*

# Strengthening validation: validating again in PHP

As mentioned previously, client-side validation should always be accompanied by server-side validation. If users turn off JavaScript on their browser and there is no server-side validation, then they can enter whatever they want. This could lead to disastrous results like your database being compromised and so on.

This recipe will go through the validation methods and functions available in PHP, which we can use to validate the data.

## Getting ready

Create a new folder named `Recipe7` inside the `Chapter5` directory .

 Make sure your version of PHP is >5.2. We will be using filter functions that are available only after PHP >=5.2

## How to do it...

1. Create a file named `index.php` inside the newly-created `Recipe7` folder. Create a form with different type of fields for entering strings, numbers, e-mail addresses, and website addresses.

```html
<html>
  <head>
    <title>Server Side validation</title>
    <style type="text/css">
      body{font-family:"Trebuchet MS",verdana;width:450px;}
      .error{ color:red; }
      .info{color:#008000;font-weight:bold; }
    </style>
  </head>
  <body>
    <form method="post">
      <fieldset>
        <legend><strong>Information form</strong>
            (All fields are mandatory)</legend>
        <table>
          <tbody>
            <tr>
              <td>Name: </td>
              <td><input type="text" name="userName"/></td>
            </tr>
            <tr>
              <td>Address: </td>
              <td><input type="text" name="address"/></td>
            </tr>
            <tr>
            <tr>
              <td>Age: </td>
              <td><input type="text" name="age"/></td>
            </tr>
            <tr>
              <td>Mail: </td>
              <td><input type="text" name="email"/></td>
            </tr>
            <tr>
              <td>Website: </td>
              <td><input type="text" name="website"/></td>
            </tr>
            </tr>
```

```
        </tbody>
      </table>
    </fieldset>
    <br/>
    <input type="submit" name="save" value="Submit"/>
  </form>
 </body>
</html>
```

The form should look similar to the following screenshot:

2.  When the form is submitted, it will go to the index.php file. Hence, we will place our validations at the beginning of this file. Shown below is the PHP code that needs to be placed at the beginning of the index.php file. This code checks all the fields and upon finding any error it pushes an error message into an array.

```php
<?php
  if(isset($_POST['save']))
  {
    $name = trim($_POST['userName']);
    $address = trim($_POST['address']);
    $age = trim($_POST['age']);
    $email = trim($_POST['email']);
    $website = trim($_POST['website']);
```

```php
$errorArray = array();
if($name == '' || $address == '' || $age == '' || $email == ''
                || $website == '')
{
  array_push($errorArray, 'Please fill all fields.');
}
if(filter_var($age, FILTER_VALIDATE_INT) == FALSE)
{
  array_push($errorArray, 'Please enter a number for age.');

}
if(filter_var($email, FILTER_VALIDATE_EMAIL) == FALSE)
{
  array_push($errorArray, 'Email address is incorrect.');
}
if(filter_var($website, FILTER_VALIDATE_URL) == FALSE)
{
  array_push($errorArray, 'Website address is incorrect.');
}
    }
?>
```

3.  As you can see in the previous code, we are creating an array of error messages (if any). The following code will print these error messages on the browser. Place this code just after the `<form>` tag opens:

```php
<?php
        if(count($errorArray) > 0)
        {
?>
        <p class="error">
<?php
          foreach($errorArray as $error)
          {
            echo $error.'<br/>';
          }
?>
        </p>
<?php
        }
?>
```

4.  Open your browser and point it to the `index.php` file. Enter some incorrect values in the form and click on the **Submit** button. You will see error messages in the form of a list in your browser.

## How it works...

First, we confirm the form submission using the `isset` function for `$_POST['save']`. Then, we collect the values of all form variables in separate variables. Next, we declare an array `$errorArray` that will collect all the error messages. After that, we check if the fields are blank or not. If any of the field is found blank, we push an error message in the `$errorArray` array.

Next comes the use of PHP's `filter_var()` function. This function takes three parameters out of which the last two are optional. The first parameter is the value that is to be filtered. The second parameter is the ID of the Validate filter that defines the type of validation to be done. For example, `FILTER_VALIDATE_INT` validates the value as integer. In the previous example, we have used three of them, `FILTER_VALIDATE_INT`, `FILTER_VALIDATE_EMAIL`, and `FILTER_VALIDATE_URL`.

`filter_var()` returns the filtered value on success, and `false` on failure. In the previous code if we encounter a `false` value, we push a related error message to the `$errorArray` array.

Then in the form we check the count for $errorArray. If the number of elements in this array is not equal to zero, then there is some error. So, we iterate in this array and print all the error messages.

## There's more...

### List of Validate filters

- ▶  FILTER_VALIDATE_INT
- ▶  FILTER_VALIDATE_FLOAT
- ▶  FILTER_VALIDATE_EMAIL
- ▶  FILTER_VALIDATE_URL
- ▶  FILTER_VALIDATE_BOOLEAN
- ▶  FILTER_VALIDATE_REGEXP
- ▶  FILTER_VALIDATE_IP

To see the list of all Validate filters available in PHP, you can refer to this URL from the PHP site: http://www.php.net/manual/en/filter.filters.validate.php.

### Sanitizing data

Apart from validation filter_var() can also be used to sanitize the data. Data sanitizing refers to removing any malicious or undesired data from the user's input. The syntax remains the same, the only difference is that instead of passing Validate filters as the second parameter, Sanitize filters are passed. Here are some commonly-used Sanitize filters:

- ▶  FILTER_SANITIZE_EMAIL
- ▶  FILTER_SANITIZE_NUMBER_FLOAT
- ▶  FILTER_SANITIZE_NUMBER_INT
- ▶  FILTER_SANITIZE_SPECIAL_CHARS
- ▶  FILTER_SANITIZE_STRING
- ▶  FILTER_SANITIZE_URL
- ▶  FILTER_SANITIZE_ENCODED

A list of all Sanitize filters can be found on the PHP website at this URL : http://www.php.net/manual/en/filter.filters.sanitize.php

## See also

- ▶  *Validating numbers using jQuery*
- ▶  *Validating e-mail and website addresses using regular expressions*
- ▶  *Displaying errors as user types: performing live validation*

# Creating a voting system

We will create an example where users will be able to vote for their favorite browsers. Once voted, they will not be able to vote for another day, that is 24 hours. Votes will be stored in an XML file. We will also display the votes in a nice graphical format.

[  XML file has been used just for the example. In real world applications, data will be loaded from databases or web services (which can return anything like XML, JSON, or any other format). ]

## Getting ready

Create a folder named Recipe8 inside the Chapter5 directory.

## How to do it...

1.  OK. This recipe is going to be a bit long, so grab a mug of coffee and start. First of all, create an XML file in the Recipe8 folder and name it as browsers.xml. This file will have information about the browsers that we will display to the user.

    ```
    <?xml version="1.0"?>
    <browsers>
      <browser name="Firefox" value="FF" votes="200"/>
      <browser name="Google Chrome" value="GC" votes="130"/>
      <browser name="IE" value="IE" votes="30"/>
    </browsers>
    ```

2.  Now create a PHP file named index.php. We will read the XML file and present the user a list of browsers to select from. This file also contains the code that will handle form submission. Also, the user will not be able to vote more than once in a day.

    ```
    <?php
    if(isset($_POST['vote']))
    {
      if(isset($_COOKIE["voted"]))
      {
        $message = 'You have already voted. You cannot vote more than
                    once per day.';
      }
      else
      {
        $message = 'Your vote has been saved';
        $dom = new DOMDocument();
        $dom->load('browsers.xml');
    ```

```php
    $xpath = new DomXPath($dom);
    $units = $xpath->query('//browser');

    foreach ($units as $unit)
    {
      $value = $unit->getAttribute('value');
      if($value == $_POST['browser'])
      {
        $votes = $unit->getAttribute('votes');
        $unit->setAttribute('votes', ++$votes);

        setcookie("voted", true, time()+ (24*60*60));  /* expire
            in 24 hours */
        break;
      }


    }
    $dom->save('browsers.xml');
  }
}
?>
<html>
  <head>
    <title></title>
    <style type="text/css">
    body{font-family:"Trebuchet MS",verdana;width:350px;}
    ul{list-style:none;}
    </style>
  </head>
  <body>
    <form method="post">
      <fieldset>
        <legend>Which is your favorite browser?</legend>
        <ul>
    <?php
        $dom = new DOMDocument();
        $dom->load('browsers.xml');
        $xpath = new DomXPath($dom);
        $browsers = $xpath->query('//browser');

        foreach ($browsers as $browser)
        {
          $checked = $_POST['browser'] ==
                  $browser->getAttribute('value')? 'checked': '';
```

```
        echo '<li><input type="radio" '.$checked.'
name="browser" value="'.$browser->getAttribute('value').'">'.$brow
ser->getAttribute('name').'</li>';
        }
    ?>
        <li style="color:red;"><?php echo $message; ?></li>
        <li><input type="submit" name="vote" value="vote" /> OR
<a href="results.php" id="results">View Results</a></li>
        </ul>
      </fieldset>
    </form>
  </body>
</html>
```

3. Run the file in the browser and you will see some radio buttons and a **vote** button as shown in the following screenshot:

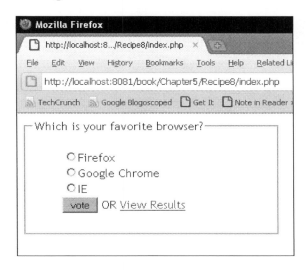

4. The above page also contains a link to view the results. To create that page, open a new file and save it as `results.php`. The code in this file will read the XML file and will display votes for each browser.

```
<html>
  <head>
    <title>Vote Results</title>
    <style type="text/css">
    body{font-family:"Trebuchet MS",verdana;width:350px;}
    ul{list-style:none;}
    li{height:25px;}
span{background-color:red;color:#fff;float:left;}
```

```
        </style>
      </head>
      <body>
        <fieldset>
          <legend>Poll Results</legend>
<?php
  $dom = new DOMDocument();
  $dom->load('browsers.xml');
  $xpath = new DomXPath($dom);
  $browsers = $xpath->query('//browser');

  echo '<ul  >';

  foreach ($browsers as $browser)
  {
    $name = $browser->getAttribute('name');
    $votes = $browser->getAttribute('votes');
    echo '<li>'.$name.' - '.$votes. ' votes</li>';
    echo '<li><span style="width:'.$votes.'px;"> </span></li
';style="width:'.$style="width:'.$
  }
  echo '</ul>';

?>
      </fieldset>
    </body>
</html>
```

5. All done and we are ready to run our example now. Run the index.php file in your browser and you will see the form. Select the last radio button and click on the **vote** button. You will see a message that says **Your vote has been saved**. Now select a browser and click the **vote** button again. This time you will see an error message that says **You have already voted. You cannot vote more than once per day**.

6. Now click on the **View Results** link. This will open a new page and you will see the number of votes for each browser. Your vote will increase the vote count for IE from 30 to 31.

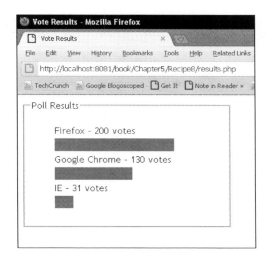

## How it works...

Let us start by examining the structure of the `browsers.xml` file. This XML contains three browser nodes, each defining one browser. Each node has three attributes: name, value, and nodes. Name will be displayed to the user, value will be used in internal processing, and votes are the number of votes for each browser.

Coming to the `index.php` file now, we will start from the HTML. Using the DOM Document functions we load the XML file and create an unordered list from it. A radio button is created for each browser. In the end, a button is created for **vote** and another link for **View Results**.

Now here's a summary of what happens after a form is submitted.

- To find out if a user has previously voted or not, we check the Superglobal `$_COOKIE`. If this cookie contains an entry for voted, this means the user has voted previously and we show an error message.
- If the user has not voted already, we increase one vote in the XML file.
- To add a vote for the selected browser, we load the XML using `DOMDocument`.
- Then we search through all browser nodes and check the attribute value against the value selected by the user. This value is available in `$_POST['browser']`.
- Once a match is found we increase the number of votes by one against that browser.
- Then we set a cookie named `voted`, which will sit on the user's browser. PHP's `setcookie` function is used to set the cookie and it is set to expire after 24 hours. This will prevent the user from voting more than once in a single day.
- Finally, save the XML using the `save` method of DOM.

To generate the page `results.php`, load the XML file using DOM Document again and iterate through all browser nodes. We create an unordered list again. For each browser, two list items are created. In the first `li`, we write the name of browser and number of votes cast against it. The second `li` creates a span element with its width set to the number of votes in pixels. This will create the effect of a bar chart.

## There's more...

### Cookie expiration time

In the previous example, we have set the cookie to expire after a day. You can change this as per your requirements. Just note that it is passed as a UNIX timestamp and hence you will have to pass it in seconds.

## See also

- ▶ *Reading an XML using DOM extension in Chapter 3*
- ▶ *Modifying an XML using DOM extension in Chapter 3*

# Allowing HTML inside text areas and limiting HTML tags that can be used

While a user is filling out some form, you may want to restrict the HTML tags that are allowed through user input. Some unwanted tags like `<script>` tags can cause potential harm to your site and its data.

This recipe will teach you how to filter the tags from data entered in a web form and accept only specific tags.

## Getting ready

Create a folder named `Recipe9` inside the `Chapter5` directory.

## How to do it...

1. Create a new file and save it as `index.html`. Now, create two textarea elements and a button. The first textarea is where the user will enter the text in HTML format. The second textarea will show the HTML after disallowed tags are stripped from it.

```html
<html>
  <head>
    <title>Strip tags</title>
```

```html
<style type="text/css">
  body{font-family:"Trebuchet MS",verdana;width:700px;}
</style>
</head>
<body>
  <form>
    <table>
      <tr>
        <td valign="top">Write some HTML in the box<br/>
        (Only allowed HTML tags are<br/>&lt;b&gt;,&lt;u&gt;,&lt;
        i&gt; and &lt;strong&gt;.<br/>Other tags will
        be removed):</td><td>
          <textarea id="comment" cols="50" rows="10"></textarea>
        </td>
      </tr>
      <tr>
        <td valign="top">This is how your HTML will look:</td>
        <td>
          <textarea id="stripped" cols="50" rows="10">
          </textarea>
        </td>
      </tr>
    </table>
    <input type="button" value="Check" id="check" />
  </form>
</body>
</html>
```

2.  Include the `jquery.js` file and then add an event handler for the **Check** button. Clicking on this button will send the data of the first textarea to a PHP file, `validate.php`. On receiving a response, it will be set inside the second textarea.

```html
<script type="text/javascript" src="../jquery.js"></script>
<script type="text/javascript">
  $(document).ready(function ()
  {
    $('#check').click(function()
    {
      $.post(
        "validate.php",
        { comment: $('#comment').val() },
        function(data)
        {
          $('#stripped').val(data);
        });
    });
  });
</script>
```

3. Create another file for the PHP code and name it `validate.php`. The code in this file will strip the disallowed HTML tags from the input data and will echo them back to the browser.

```php
<?php
$text = $_POST['comment'];
echo trim(strip_tags($text, '<b><u><i><strong>'));
?>
```

4. Now, open your browser and run the `index.html` file. Write some HTML in it and click on the **Check** button. The second textarea will show the HTML after disallowed tags are stripped from it.

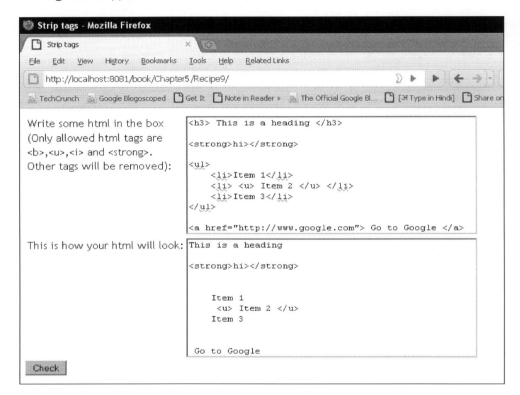

## How it works...

On clicking the **Check** button, an AJAX request is sent to the PHP file `validate.php`. Here comes the main part. We get the data received from the POST request. Then we use the PHP function `strip_tags()`. This function removes the HTML tags from the input string. The first parameter to this function is the input string that we need to strip tags from. The second parameter is optional. If not passed, this function will strip all HTML tags from the input string. In our example, we want to allow four tags: `<b>`,`<u>`,`<i>`, and `<strong>`, therefore we passed these as second parameters. The function will now remove all HTML tags from the input string except these four. It returns the resulting string that you can now safely save to a database or perform other operations on. In this example, we echo it to the browser to see how it will look. On the browser, jQuery inserts it into the second textarea.

## There's more...

### PHP tags are stripped too

Any HTML comments in input string and PHP tags are automatically stripped.

# 6

# Adding Visual Effects to Forms

In this chapter, we will cover:

- ▶ Creating a Tic-Tac-Toe game with effects
- ▶ Informing a user while an AJAX request is in progress
- ▶ Creating expandable and collapsible boxes (accordion)
- ▶ Fading an element after updating it
- ▶ Floating a box on demand
- ▶ Updating items in a shopping cart

## Introduction

Adding jQuery to web pages can result in amazing effects and user interaction if used wisely. There are many plugins in jQuery that already provide most of the utilities and widgets presented in this chapter. But most of the time these plugins try to be so complete that unnecessary features creep in.

In this chapter we will be creating widgets, such as accordion, floating DIVs, and yellow fade techniques that are common in modern AJAX applications. We will create these in the simplest manner with minimum code.

# Creating a Tic-Tac-Toe game with effects

Web forms should be as user-friendly as possible to ease the life of users. Users should be clear as to which part they are interacting with.

In this recipe we will create a game of Tic-Tac-Toe. You may have already played this game as a kid. This will present a good example of how different sections of a page can be highlighted for a user to let him or her know where he or she is interacting on the page.

Ours will be a two-player game where we will present the user with a grid of 3*3 or 5*5 depending on his selection. Hovering over a box in the grid will highlight that box and clicking on a box will put either a cross or a circle depending on the player's turn. With every mark made on the grid, we will switch user turns and check if a user has won or not.

## Getting ready

Create a folder named `Recipe1` inside the `Chapter6` directory. For this recipe we will need two more images: one for a cross and one for a circle as the game demands. Using paint or any other simple image editing programs we can create these two images. I have used the following images in this recipe:

## How to do it...

1. First create a CSS file `main.css` in the `Recipe1` folder. This file will contain the following CSS styles for our game:

```
body{color:#FA6766;font-family:Trebuchet MS,arial,verdana;margin:2
0px;padding:0pt;}
h3{margin:0pt:padding:0pt;}
div{float:left;}
#table{ width:100%; }
.row {width:100%;}
.col {width:75px;float:left;height:75px;cursor:pointer;}
```

```css
.hr{ border-right:2px solid #FA6766;}
.vr{ border-bottom:2px solid #FA6766;}
.cross{background-image:url(cross.png);}
.round{background-image:url(round.png);}
#log{clear:both;margin:0pt;padding:0pt;}
.reset{cursor:pointer;display:none;text-decoration:underline;}
```

2.  After defining styles, create another file in the same folder and name it as `index.html`. This file includes the `main.css` file. Then create a combo box from where the user will select a grid size (3*3 or 5*5). Then create two `h2` elements. The first element will be used to display the player's turns and the second element will be used to reset the game when it ends. Lastly, create a DIV with ID `container` that will hold the grid for a game. It will be created using jQuery.

3.  In the end add the reference to the jQuery library. Since the jQuery code will be a bit lengthy, we will keep it in a separate file that we will call `tictactoe.js`. Add a reference to this file also.

```html
<html>
  <head>
    <title>Tic-Tac-Toe</title>
    <link rel="stylesheet" href="main.css" />
  </head>
  <body>
    <div>
      <strong>Grid Size:</strong><select id="size">
        <option value="3">3 * 3</option>
        <option value="5">5 * 5</option>
      </select>
    </div>
    <p> </p>
    <h2 id="log">Waiting for Player 1</h2>
    <h2 class="reset">Reset</h2>
    <p> </p>
    <div id="container"></div>
    <script type="text/javascript" src="../jquery.js"></script>
    <script type="text/javascript" src="tictactoe.js"></script>
  </body>
</html>
```

4. Now create the `tictactoe.js` file in the `Recipe1` directory. This code will define a separate namespace `game` in which we will keep all our variables and functions. The code in this file has a function `createGrid()`, which will create a grid according to selected size and other functions. Then it will add event handlers for clicking on the grid.

```javascript
$(document).ready(function()
{
  function game() {};

  game.init = function(size)
  {
    if(parseInt(size,10) <=0)  return;
    this.gridSize = size;
    this.player = 0;  // 0 - player 1; 1- player 2
    this.marker;
    //create grid
    this.createGrid();

    $('.col').hover(function(){$(this).css('background-color',
    '#FBF9EA');},function(){$(this).css('background-color',
    '#FFF');});
    $('.col').click(function()
    {
      //check if already clicked
      if($(this).hasClass('cross') || $(this).hasClass('round'))
        { return; }// cant
      var who = (game.player ==0 ) ? "Player 1" : "Player 2";
      game.marker = (game.player == 0 ) ? 'cross' : 'round';
      $(this).addClass(game.marker);
      var won = game.checkForWin(this);
      if(!won)
      {
        //change players turn
        game.player = (game.player == 0) ? 1 : 0;
        var player = (game.player ==0 ) ? "Player 1" : "Player 2";
        $('#log').html('Waiting for '+ player);
      }
      else
      {
        $('.col').unbind('click');
        $('#log').html(who + ' Wins!!!');
        $('h2:last').show('slow');
      }
    });
  }
```

5. Another function `checkForWin()` is defined that will check if a player has won a game after clicking on a box in the grid. Finally, there are event handlers for both `h2` elements. In the last line of code we start the game by calling the `init` function.

```
game.checkForWin = function(current)
{
  var size = this.gridSize;
  var row = $(current).attr('i');
  var col = $(current).attr('j');
  //check horizontal and vertical rows
  var hDone = true, vDone = true;
  for(var i=0; i< size; i++)
  {
    if($('#'+(row + i)).hasClass(this.marker) != true)
        hDone = false;
    if($('#'+(i + col)).hasClass(this.marker) != true)
        vDone = false;
  }
  if(hDone == true || vDone == true) return true;

  //check diagonals
  if(row == col || ((parseInt(row) + parseInt(col)) ==
      (this.gridSize)-1))
  {
    var ldDone = true, rdDone = true;
    for(var i = 0, j = size-1; i< size; i++, j--)
    {
      if($('#'+i+i).hasClass(this.marker) != true)
        ldDone = false;
      if($('#'+i+j).hasClass(this.marker) != true)
        rdDone = false;
    }
    if(ldDone == true || rdDone == true) return true;
  }
  return false;
}

game.createGrid = function()
{
  var size = this.gridSize;
  var str = '<div id="table">';
  for(var i=0; i<size; i++)
  {
    str+= '<div class="row">';
    for(var j=0; j<size; j++)
    {
      var cssClass='col';
      if(j< size-1)  cssClass+= " hr";
      if(i< size-1)  cssClass+= " vr";
```

```
            str+= '<div id="'+i+j+'" class="' + cssClass +'" i="'+i+'"
                    j="'+j+'"></div>';
        }
        str+= '</div>';
    }
    $('#container').html(str);
}

$('#size').change(function()
{
    game.init($(this).val());
    $('#log').html('Waiting for Player 1');
});

$('h2:last').click(function()
{
    game.init($('#size').val());
    $('#log').html('Waiting for Player 1');
    $(this).hide('slow');
});

game.init(3);
});
```

6. Our game is complete and is ready to be played now. Run the file `index.html` in your browser and you will see a nice 3*3 tic-tac-toe grid.

7. Start playing the game now. Taking the mouse pointer over a box will make it yellow. Clicking in any box will place cross and circle symbols alternatively. After a player wins the game, the screen will look similar to the following screenshot:

## How it works...

First, define a global object `game`. This will be our namespace under which we will keep all variables and functions for our game.

We start with the `init` function where we pass a number. This number is the size of the grid that we will create. There is another variable, `player`, whose value will be 0 if it's Player 1's turn and 1 if it's Player 2's turn. The variable `marker` will decide which icon to place (cross or circle) depending on the player's turn. In the case of Player 1 it will be a cross and a circle if it is Player 2's turn.

Next comes `createGrid()` that creates the actual game grid. This function creates a DIV with rows and columns and assigns CSS classes to them that define the look and feel of the grid. If the grid size is 3, it will create a 3*3 grid. After creating the HTML for the grid, it inserts it into the `container` DIV. Each column in the grid has also been assigned two custom attributes `i` and `j` whose value is the index value of the matrix. The following figure will explain this:

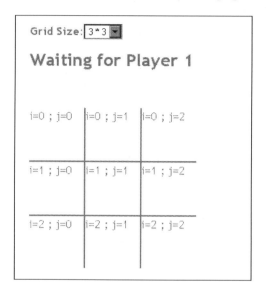

Before proceeding, make note of two important CSS classes: `cross` and `round`. `cross` will add a background image of a cross to a column and `round` will add the background image of a circle.

Our UI is ready and now we need to add event listeners. There are two important event handlers. First is when a user hovers the mouse pointer over a box in the grid. For this we use the jQuery `.hover` listener that changes the color to yellow while the mouse pointer is over a box and back to white if the mouse pointer goes out of the boundaries of a box.

The most important event is the `click` event on a box on the grid. On clicking a box or column, we first check if it has the `cross` or `round` class. If it has, we simply return from the function as we can place icons or markers on already empty columns.

As mentioned above, the variable `who` defines which player is playing and `marker` defines the CSS class to be applied. We then apply the suitable class after checking which player is playing.

After placing the CSS class we check if a player has won or not. We check this in function `checkForWin()`. If we get `true`, it means that the current player has won the game and we unbind the `click` event from the columns. With this we also display an information message and the game ends.

If, however, `checkForWin()` returns `false`, we switch the player's turn by changing the value of variable `player` and displaying it on the UI too.

The function `checkForWin()` actually checks for three same CSS classes in a row, column, or diagonal, which indicates a win situation. Horizontal and vertical rows are checked first with the help of a `for` loop.

Next, we check for diagonals using two `for` loops. The logic is simple. If all elements in a row, column, or diagonal have the same CSS class then a player has won. Accordingly, we return either a `true` or `false` value from this function.

Two other event handlers are present: one for the select box, which calls the `init` function when a user changes the grid size from the combo box and the other is for the **Reset** button, which becomes visible after a player wins.

 Note that this code of ours is generic. You can create a grid of any size by passing the value in the `init` function.

## There's more...

### Exercise—checking for a draw

If you observe closely, you will find that our example only shows the **Reset** link if a player wins. In case of a draw, the user is stuck and cannot reset the game again. I will leave this as an exercise for you.

To check for a draw you just need to count the clicks according to the size of the draw. For example, if grid size is 3*3, after nine clicks the game is a draw unless function `checkForWin` has returned `true`.

# Informing a user while an AJAX request is in progress

As AJAX applications do not have full page reloads, if an AJAX request is pending to the server, and the user can't see any notification, they may get confused.

It is, therefore, necessary that a user must be provided some kind of information while an AJAX request is in process. This is an important point worth noting while creating AJAX applications that should not be ignored.

In this recipe, you will learn how users can be notified that an AJAX request is taking place and how to provide the feedback of the progress to the user.

## Getting ready

Create a folder named `Recipe2` inside the `Chapter6` directory. The other thing that you need to do is visit either of these websites `http://ajaxload.info/` or `http://preloaders.net/`. Here you will find animated images of loading icons. Choose an image and download it. You will need this image for this recipe. For this recipe I have used the following image from `http://ajaxload.info/`.

## How to do it...

1.  Create a new file in the `Recipe2` folder and name it as `index.html`.

2.  We will create a form where the user will fill some information and it will then be sent to the server. Create this form and also create an image tag with its path set to the previously mentioned image. For the moment, hide this image using CSS style. Also create a paragraph element where response from the server will be displayed.

```html
<html>
  <head>
    <title>User feedback</title>
    <style type="text/css">
      body{font-family:"Trebuchet MS",verdana;width:450px;}
      #info{color:#008000;font-weight:bold; }
    </style>
  </head>
  <body>
    <form>
      <fieldset>
        <legend>
          <strong>Please fill the information</strong>
        </legend>
        <table>
          <tbody>
            <tr>
              <td>Name:</td>
              <td><input type="text" id="name" /></td>
            </tr>
            <tr>
              <td>Address:</td>
```

```
            <td><input type="text" id="address"/></td>
          </tr>
          <tr>
            <td>City:</td>
            <td><input type="text" id="city"/></td>
          </tr>
          <tr>
            <td>Country:</td>
            <td><input type="text" id="country"/></td>
          </tr>
          <tr>
            <td colspan="2"><img src="ajax-loader.gif"
              style="display:none;" id="loading"/></td>

          </tr>
          <tr>
            <td colspan="2"><input type="button" value="Save"
              id="save" /></td>
          </tr>
        </tbody>
      </table>
    </fieldset>
  </form>
  <p id="info"></p>
  </body>
</html>
```

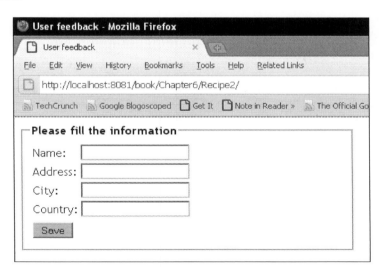

3. Now let's create the jQuery code that will collect the form values and will send them to a PHP script `process.php` on the server side. On receiving a response it will hide the form and will display the received data. This code will also be responsible for displaying the progress indicator while the PHP script processes the data.

```javascript
<script type="text/javascript" src="../jquery.js"></script>
<script type="text/javascript">
  $(document).ready(function ()
  {
    $('#save').click(function()
    {
      $('#loading').show();
      $(this).val('Please wait...');
      $.post(
        "process.php",
        {
          name : $('#name').val(),
          address : $('#address').val(),
          city : $('#city').val(),
          country : $('#country').val()
        },
        function(data)
        {
          $('#loading').hide();
          $('form').hide();
          $('#info').html(data);
        });
    });
  });
</script>
```

4. Create another file in the `Recipe2` folder and name it as `process.php`. This file will echo back the information received from the HTML form in a formatted string. To simulate the delay on the server side so that the browser has enough time to display the progress indicator we use the `sleep` function to halt the execution for five seconds.

```php
<?php
  sleep(5);
  $str = 'Your following information has been submitted:';
  $str.= '<br>';
  $str.= 'Name - '. $_POST['name'];
  $str.= '<br>';
  $str.= 'Address - '. $_POST['address'];
  $str.= '<br>';
  $str.= 'City - '. $_POST['city'];
  $str.= '<br>';
  $str.= 'Country - '. $_POST['country'];
  echo $str;
?>
```

5. We are good to go with this. Run the `index.html` file in your browser. Fill the form with values and click on the **Save** button. A progress bar will appear, which will stay for five seconds until the response is received from the PHP script. After the response is received you will see the values you earlier filled on the screen.

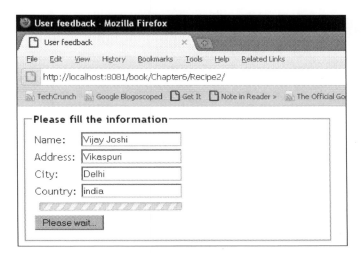

6. The following screenshot shows the screen after the response is received from the PHP script:

## How it works...

We have an event handler for the **Save** button that executes when the button is clicked. When the button is clicked, the image which has ID `loading` is displayed using the jQuery `show()` function and the button's display text is changed to **Please wait...**. Then an AJAX request is sent to `process.php` with the form values. On receiving these values, the PHP script waits for five seconds and then echoes the values to the browser.

On receiving a response from PHP, jQuery hides the progress bar, and the form and values received from the server are displayed on the page.

In this way, the user can be made aware that some processing is taking place and he or she should wait until the request finishes.

## There's more...

### Using text instead of images

If you do not want to use images as a progress indicator, you can use some text instead of it.

### Using overlays to stop a user from interacting with the form

In the previous example, while the request is in progress, a user can click on the **Save** button again, which will send a new request to the server. To avoid this, you can disable the **Save** button or, alternatively, you can use an overlay that covers the form till the request completes. This will convey the message clearly to the user that since a request is in progress, he or she must not interact with the form until it finishes.

## See also

▶   *Sending data to PHP in Chapter 2*

# Creating expandable and collapsible boxes (accordion)

Accordions are good examples of widgets where more information can be displayed in less space in an interactive and attractive manner. This recipe will teach you to create a simple accordion using jQuery.

## Getting ready

Create a folder named `Recipe3` inside the `Chapter6` directory.

## How to do it...

1. Create a new file inside the `Recipe3` folder and name it as `index.html`.

2. Now define the HTML markup for the accordion. The accordion will be a collection of `div` elements each having an `h1` tag for the section title and a DIV for that section's content. Put some title for each section and also some content for it. Also define some CSS styles in the `head` section that will give the accordion a nice look and feel.

```html
<html>
  <head>
    <title>Accordion</title>
    <style type="text/css">
      body{ margin:50px auto;font-family:"trebuchet MS",
            Arial;font-size:14px;width:500px;}

      div{ border:1px solid #FA6766;width:500px;}

      h1{cursor:pointer;font-size:20px;font-weight:bold;
            text-align:center;}

      .active{color:red;}

      .container{background-color:#F0F8FF;padding:5px;
                  text-align:justify;width:488px;}
    </style>
  </head>
  <body>
    <div>
      <div>
        <h1 href="#">PHP: PHP Hypertext Preprocessor</h1>
        <div class="container">PHP is a widely used, server side
          scripting language that is used to create dynamic web
          applications. PHP is very much popular among web
          developers and many top websites use PHP for their
          sites.</div>
      </div>

      <div>
        <h1 href="#">jQuery - The write less, do more
          javascript</h1>
```

```
        <div class="container">From the jQuery site: jQuery is
        a fast and concise JavaScript Library that simplifies
        HTML document traversing, event handling, animating, and
        Ajax interactions for rapid web development. jQuery is
        designed to change the way that you write
        JavaScript.</div>
    </div>

    <div>
      <h1 href="#">AJAX - Asynchronous JavaScript and XML</h1>
      <div class="container">Ajax is a group of web development
        techniques used on the client-side (browser) to create
        interactive web applications. AJAX can be used to
        retrieve data from the server  asynchronously in the
        background. XMLHttpRequest objects is generally used to
        contact the server side.</div>
    </div>

    <div>
      <h1 href="#">JSON - JavaScript Object Notation</h1>
      <div class="container">
        <p>JSON which stands for JavaScript Object Notation can
          be defined as a lightweight data interchange format. It
          is also said a fat-free lightweight alternative to xml.
          It is a text format which is programming language
          independent and is native data form of JavaScript. It
          is lighter and faster than xml. The credit to make json
          popular goes to Douglas Crockford.
        </p>
        <p>
        Since JSON is the native data form of JavaScript,
        it can be used on the client side in an Ajax application
        more easily then XML.
        </p>
      </div>
    </div>
  </div>
  </body>
</html>
```

The result will be similar to the following screenshot:

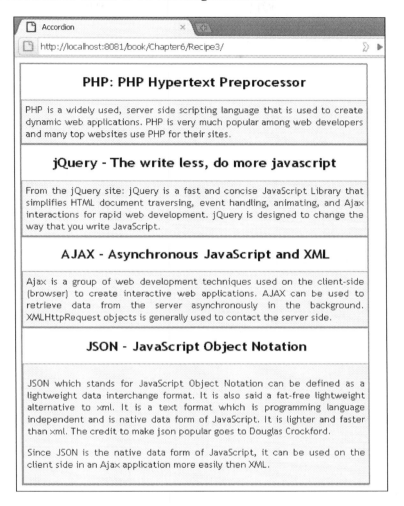

3. Before the `body` tag closes, include the jQuery library. Now write the jQuery code that will convert our HTML markup into a working accordion.

```
<script type="text/javascript" src="../jquery.js"></script>
<script type="text/javascript">
  $(document).ready(function ()
  {
    $('.container').hide();

    $('h1').click(function()
    {
```

```
        var h1 = $(this);
        $('h1.active').removeClass('active');
        h1.addClass('active');
        $(".container:visible").slideUp('fast');
        h1.next('div').slideToggle('fast');
    });
  });
</script>
```

4. With this the accordion is ready now. Launch your browser and run the `index.html` file. You will see four sections in the accordion. Clicking on a section will reveal its content and will hide any other open sections.

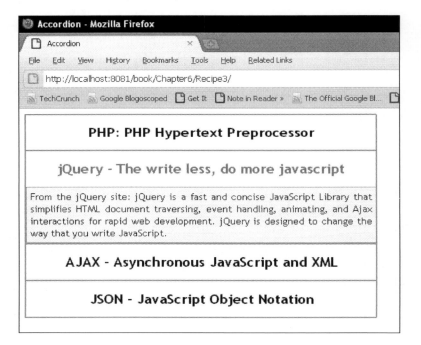

## How it works...

The HTML in the above code has a main DIV that has four DIV elements inside it. These four DIVs are four sections of the accordion. Each section has two parts: an `h1` tag and another DIV with class set to `container`. The `h1` tag will serve as the header for that section and the DIV will hold the HTML for that section. The CSS in the `head` section gives the look that you saw in the previous screenshot. This creates our basic structure that we will convert to an accordion using jQuery.

Now comes the jQuery part that does all the work.

First, we hide all the DIV elements with `container` class so that only header sections of the accordion are visible at first. Then we add an event handler for the `h1` tag. Note that we have defined a CSS class named `active` that will be applied to the clicked `h1`.

On clicking an `h1`, we first remove the `active` class from any `head` section that might have it. Then we add an `active` class to the current `h1`, which makes its text red in color. The selector expression `.container:visible` selects any content DIV elements that might be visible and hides them using jQuery's `slideUp()` method. Finally, we get the DIV next to the current `h1` and apply the `toggleSlide()` effect to it that shows or hides it. This gives us the feel of an accordion.

In summary, what we did is as follows:

- Get the `h1` that was clicked
- Remove the `active` class if any `h1` has it
- Add the `active` class to the clicked `h1`
- Hide any visible content containers
- Make the `container` DIV next to the clicked `h1` visible

## There's more...

### Using different markup for accordion

You are not restricted to the markup that can be used for the accordion. In the previous example we used `h1` and DIV elements for the header and content sections respectively. You can also use unordered lists, anchors, and virtually any kind of markup to achieve the same effect. Just remember that the jQuery code will change accordingly. Also do not forget to change the CSS styles depending on which elements you are using, as different elements are rendered differently on a browser.

You can try implementing the accordion using `ul` and `li` elements as an exercise.

# Fading an element after updating it

In modern web applications where parts of a page are updated without loading the entire page, it is necessary to inform the user about the change that has happened. Without it, a user may not know that a certain part of a page has been changed.

One of the commonly used techniques for this is known as the **Yellow Fade Technique** or the **YFT**. The basic idea behind it is simple: when a part of a page is changed or is required to be highlighted, that part is highlighted with a yellow color which gradually fades to its original colour. This attracts the user's attention to that part and the user notices the change. Although simple, this technique should be used while creating rich AJAX applications.

jQuery core does not provide this effect in itself but jQuery UI has this effect. However, to use this effect with jQuery you need to include two separate files `effects.core.js` and `effects.highlight.js` of the jQuery UI (which is an overload in itself) or you can use the jQuery easing plugin that is available from `http://gsgd.co.uk/sandbox/jquery/easing/`.

This recipe will teach you how to create a similar effect in a few lines of code and that too without having to use any other files.

## Getting ready

Create a folder named `Recipe4` inside the `Chapter6` directory.

## How to do it...

1. Create a new file and save it as `index.html` in the `Recipe4` folder.

2. In this file create a textbox and a button. Also create a `p` element, which will display the highlight effect.

```
<html>
  <head>
    <title>Fade</title>
    <style type="text/css">
      body{ margin:50px auto;font-family:"trebuchet MS",
            Arial;font-size:14px;width:500px;}
      p{ border:1px solid #FA6766;width:315px;height:50px;}
    </style>
  </head>
  <body>
<label for="textVal">Whats your name?</label>
    <input type="text" id="textVal"/>
    <input type="button" value="Show"/>
    <p id="result"></p>
  </body>
</html>
```

3. Now include jQuery and write the code that will take the value of the textbox and insert it into the `p` element on clicking the button. The `p` element will then be highlighted using the `fade()` function.

```
<script type="text/javascript" src="../jquery.js"></script>
<script type="text/javascript">
  $(document).ready(function ()
  {
    var base,interval;
```

```
$('input:button').click(YFT);
function YFT()
{
  $('#result').html('Hello ' + $('#textVal').val());
  base = 100;
  interval = setInterval(fade,100);
}
function fade()
{
  if(base > 255)
    clearInterval(interval);
  else
    $('p').css({'background-color':'rgb(255,255,'+ (base+=10)
+')'});
  }
});
</script>
```

4.  We are done and ready to see our highlight effect now. Run the index.html file in your browser and enter a name in the textbox. Now click on the **Show** button. You will see that the value of textbox is inserted into the p element and the paragraph will fade from yellow to its original colour.

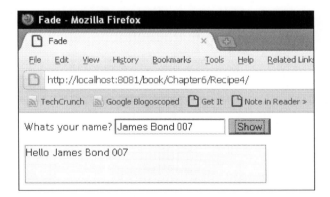

## How it works...

Here is the concept: to fade an element from yellow to white, we will have to start with the yellow colour and will have to change its RGB value until it turns white. That's what we will do here. We will start with a shade of yellow whose RGB value is 255,255,100 and we will step up the last value by 10 until we reach a RGB value of 255,255,255, that is, white colour. To repeatedly increment the value, we will use JavaScript's setInterval function to step up the value every 100 milliseconds.

Start by declaring two variables `base` and `interval`. Then an event handler is attached to an input button that calls the `YFT` function. Inside the `YFT` function we take the value from the textbox and insert it inside the `p` element. Then we define the value of the `base` as 100. Next, we use the `setInterval` JavaScript function to call the `fade` function every 100 milliseconds.

Inside the `fade` function we check the value of the variable `base`. If the value of `base` exceeds 255, we clear the interval and the `fade` function is not called anymore. This means the background color of the paragraph has now become white. If the value of `base` is still under 255, we set the background color of paragraph by changing its RGB value. R and G remain 255, and we increment the value of B by 10. As mentioned, `setInterval` keeps on executing the `fade` function until the value of base becomes 255.

# Floating box on demand

Imagine a page having a long list of products where you can select multiple products and the list gets updated in a separate container. On reaching the bottom of such a page, you may forget what you have selected previously as the box holding your selections is sitting at the top of the page.

Would it not be great if such a container box also scrolled as you scroll on the page? In other words, how about a floating box that scrolls on the page as you go up or down the page.

This recipe will show you how to create a floating box that will scroll on the page automatically as you scroll up or down on a page.

## Getting ready

Create a folder named `Recipe5` inside the `Chapter6` directory.

## How to do it...

1. Create a file named `index.html` inside the newly created `Recipe5` folder.

2. In order to demonstrate a floating DIV we must create a really long page. We do this by creating multiple paragraph elements with dummy text on the page, each with height set to `200px` in CSS. After that create a DIV which we will float using jQuery and assign CSS class and ID `float` to it. While defining CSS properties for this DIV, do not forget to assign `position` as `absolute`. It is necessary to be able to make this DIV floating.

```html
<html>
  <head>
    <title>Float</title>
    <style type="text/css">
```

```
      body{ font-family:"trebuchet MS",Arial;
            font-size:14px;width:500px;}
    p
    {
      border:1px solid black;
      height:200px;
      width:300px;
    }
    .float
    {
      border:1px solid black;
      position:absolute;
      right:50px;
      height:100px;
      width:100px;
      padding:10px;
    }
  </style>
</head>
<body>
  <p>
    This is some text
  </p>
  <p>
    This is some text
  </p>
  <p>
    This is some text
  </p>
  <p>
    This is some text
  </p>
  <p>
    This is some text
  </p>
  <p>
    This is some text
  </p>
  <p>
    This is some text
  </p>
  <p>
    This is some text
  </p>

  <div id="float" class="float">Floating box</div>
</body>
</html>
```

3. Now when our markup is done, let us proceed to make this DIV floating. First, include the awesome jQuery library. Then, write the `floatDiv` function that will make the DIV floating. After defining this function add an event handler for window scroll, which will be called each time you scroll up or down on the page. Finally, call the `floatDiv` function to float the DIV as the page loads.

```
<script type="text/javascript" src="../jquery.js"></script>
<script type="text/javascript">
  $(document).ready(function ()
  {
    var defaultOffset = 50;
    function floatDiv()
    {
      var offsetTop = $(document).scrollTop() + defaultOffset;
      $('#float').animate({top: offsetTop +
          "px"},{duration:500,queue:false});
    }

    $(window).scroll(floatDiv);
    floatDiv();
  });
</script>
```

4. Run the `index.html` file in your browser and scroll the page up or down using either the mouse or keyboard. You will see that the floating DIV sits on the top right-hand side of the page no matter where you are on the long page.

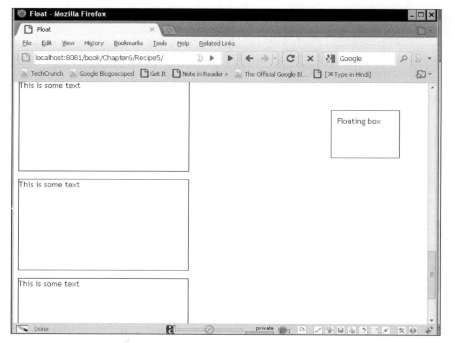

## How it works...

Two functions are responsible for the floating behavior of the DIV. The first function is the `$(document).scrollTop()` that gives us an integer value which is the number of pixels from the top of the browser window to current scroll bar start position. Second is the `animate` method that is used to create custom animations with jQuery.

We have attached a scroll event to the window object that calls the `floatDiv` function. This function is called each time the user scrolls on the web page using either the mouse or keyboard. Inside the `floatDiv` function we get the `scrollTop()` value of document and add it to variable `defaultOffset` to get another variable `offsetTop`. We have defined variable `defaultOffset` to 50 so that the DIV on floating is always 50 pixels below the top of the browser.

Then the `animate` function is used to set the top value for the DIV. Note the options where we have set the `duration` to 500. This means that the animation will take 500 milliseconds to complete. As another option `queue` is set to `false`, jQuery will not wait for any previous animation to finish before starting a new one.

Finally, we have called the `floatDiv()` function independently on DOM load. We have done this to float the DIV automatically on page load. Try this by scrolling to the bottom of the page and then pressing *F5*. The DIV will float according to the positions of the page (whether the user is at top or bottom).

## There's more...

### Important note about animate

Other properties that have numeric values can also be animated using the animate function. Properties having non-numeric values like `color` and `background-color` cannot be animated. For example, see the following code:

```
$('#float').animate({backgroundColor: "#ffffcc"},{duration:500,queue:
false});
```

The above code is an invalid use of `animate`. However, the following code is perfectly valid.

```
$('#float').animate({width: 500},{duration:500,queue:false});
```

# Updating items in a shopping cart

We will try to create a simple page with a list of items with their price and quantity. The user will be able to select any number of a particular item and that information will be sent to the server side. The server-side script will calculate the prices of selections and will show the net price to the user.

This is similar to a shopping cart as you might have seen in many sites. The difference is that a page reload will not occur and the user will have to wait less. This recipe is a basic example and you can enhance it in many ways to suit your requirements.

## Getting ready

Create a folder named `Recipe6` inside the `Chapter6` directory. Next, under the same directory, create an XML file that will have a list of some books. Each book will have an ID, name, and a price. We will use this XML to display the list of books and select some books. Name this file as `books.xml`.

```xml
<?xml version="1.0"?>
<books>
  <book id="1">
    <name>PHP Book</name>
    <price>35</price>
  </book>
  <book id="2">
    <name>jQuery Book</name>
    <price>35</price>
  </book>
  <book id="3">
    <name>The Twitter API Book</name>
    <price>35</price>
  </book>
  <book id="4">
    <name>Fundamentals of Facebook</name>
    <price>35</price>
  </book>
</books>
```

## How to do it...

1. Create a file named `index.php` in the `Recipe6` folder. This file will save an empty array in session which we will use as a cart to hold selected books. Next, define a DIV for the cart. After that create a list of books and their prices by reading data from the XML file using `simplexml` functions of PHP. Each book will have its name, price, a select box for selecting quantity, and a button to save selections. A hidden field will also be created for each book to hold its ID.

```php
<?php
  session_start();
  $booksInfo  = array();
  $_SESSION['cart'] = $booksInfo;
?>
<html>
  <head>
        <title>Cart</title>
    <style type="text/css">
      body{ font-family:"trebuchet MS",Arial;
            font-size:14px;width:500px; }
      div
      {
        border:1px solid black;
        padding:20px;
        width:250px;
        margin-top:10px;
      }
      .cart
      {
        border:1px solid black;
        float:right;
        right:50px;
        position:absolute;
        width:300px;
        padding:10px;
      }
    </style>
  </head>
  <body>
    <div class="cart">
      <strong>Your Cart</strong>
      <p id="cart">Cart is empty</p>

    </div>
    <?php
```

```php
$objXML = simplexml_load_file('books.xml');
foreach($objXML->book as $book)
{
  echo '<div>';
  echo 'Name - '. $book->name,'<br/>';
  echo 'Price - $'. $book->price,'<br/>';
?>
  Quantity -
  <select>
    <option value="1">1</option>
    <option value="2">2</option>
    <option value="3">3</option>
  </select>
  -
  <input type="hidden" value="<?php echo $book['id']; ?>"/>
  <input type="button" value="select this book"/>
<?php
  echo '</div>';
}
?>
</body>
</html>
```

The following screenshot shows the output:

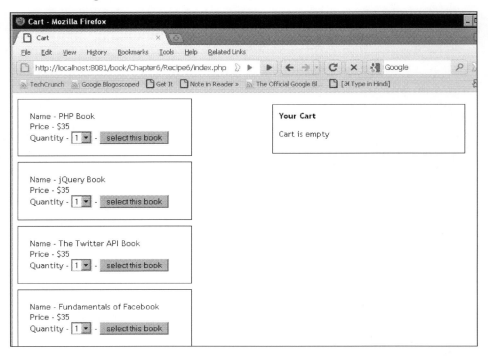

2. Now include the jQuery and write an event handler for the **select this book** button. On clicking this button an AJAX request will be sent to a PHP file called `calculate.php`. This request will contain the selected book ID and the quantity of that book. On receiving a response from the PHP file it will be inserted inside the element with the ID `cart`.

```
<script type="text/javascript" src="../jquery.js"></script>
<script type="text/javascript">
$(document).ready(function()
{
  $('input:button').click(function()
  {
    $.post('calculate.php',
      {
        bookId : $(this).prev('input:hidden').val(),
        quantity: $(this).prev().prev('select').val()
      },
      function(data)
      {
        $('#cart').html(data);
      }
    )
  });
});
</script>
```

3. Switching to server side now, create another file in same directory named `calculate.php`. This file will process the AJAX request. It will check if the selected book already exists in session or not. If not then book ID and its quantity will be saved in session otherwise its existing quantity will be updated. At last, the HTML for the cart will be created, which will list all the selected books, their quantity, price, and the net price for all the books.

```
<?php
  session_start();

  $booksInfo = $_SESSION['cart'];
  if(count($booksInfo) > 0)
  {
    $bookFound = false;
    for($i=0; $i< count($booksInfo); $i++)
    {
      if($booksInfo[$i]['bookId'] == $_POST['bookId'])
      {
        $booksInfo[$i]['quantity'] = $_POST['quantity'];
        $bookFound = true;
```

```php
            break;
        }
    }
}
if(!$bookFound)
{
    $book = array('bookId' => $_POST['bookId'],
                  'quantity' => $_POST['quantity']);
    array_push($booksInfo, $book);
}
$_SESSION['cart'] = $booksInfo;

$grossTotal = 0;
for($i=0; $i< count($booksInfo); $i++)
{
    $aBook = $booksInfo[$i];
    $bookName = getBookName($booksInfo[$i]['bookId']);
    $bookPrice = getPriceForBook($booksInfo[$i]['bookId']);
    $totalPrice = $bookPrice * $booksInfo[$i]['quantity'];
    $grossTotal+= $totalPrice;
    $str.= '<strong>Name - </strong>'.$bookName;
    $str.= '<br/>';
    $str.= ' <strong>Copies - </strong>'.$booksInfo[$i]['quantity'];
    $str.= '<br/>';
    $str.= '<strong>Price - </strong>$'.$bookPrice. ' * '
            .$booksInfo[$i]['quantity'].' = $'.$totalPrice;
    $str.= '<br/><br/>';
}
$str.= '<strong>Net Amount - </strong>$'.$grossTotal;
echo $str;


function getBookName($id)
{
    $objXML = simplexml_load_file('books.xml');
    foreach($objXML->book as $book)
    {
        if($book['id'] == $id)
        {
            return $book->name;
        }
    }
    return false;
```

```
    }
    function getPriceForBook($id)
    {
      $objXML = simplexml_load_file('books.xml');
      foreach($objXML->book as $book)
      {
        if($book['id'] == $id)
        {
          return $book->price;
        }
      }
      return false;
    }
?>
```

4.  All done now. We are ready to play with our example. Run the `index.php` file in your browser. You will see the list of books and an empty cart on the right-hand side. Select a quantity for a book and click on the **select this book** button. The cart will be updated on the right-hand side. Try selecting multiple books and changing quantities. The cart will reflect the corresponding values as per selection.

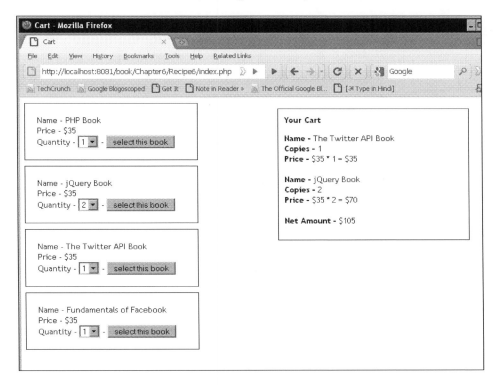

## How it works...

The PHP part in `index.php` file is simple. We created an empty array `$booksInfo` and put it in session. This array will hold the user selections. Next, we used the `simplexml_load_file` function to load the `books.xml` file. We created some HTML from it by iterating in each of the books so that we have a list of books ready on the page. Along with each book we also created a hidden variable that holds the book ID. We will need the book ID to send it to the server.

Let us analyze the jQuery code now. On clicking the **select this book** button we get the value of the selected book and the hidden variable (`bookId`) using jQuery selectors and send them to a PHP file called `calculate.php` using a Post AJAX request. The successful callback of this request simply inserts a server response into the element with the ID `cart`.

The real magic happens on the server side in the `calculate.php` file. First of all let us see the structure of the `$booksInfo` array. This array will hold selected books with the quantity and book ID of each book. It will have the following structure:

```
Array
(
    [0] => Array
        (
            [bookId] => 1
            [quantity] => 1
        )

    [1] => Array
        (
            [bookId] => 3
            [quantity] => 2
        )

)
```

The `calculate.php` file starts with line `session_start()` that initiates the current session in PHP. Then we pull out the `$booksInfo` array from the session. We now check if the selected book, the ID of which is in variable `$_POST['bookId']`, is already present in `$booksInfo` array or not. If book ID is already in the array we just update the existing book quantity with the new quantity we have received from the AJAX request (`$_POST['quantity']`). If the book was not present in the `$booksInfo` array, we create a new array and push it in the `$booksInfo` array.

Next we push back the updated `$booksInfo` array into the session.

We then proceed to calculate the price of all the selected books. For this, we iterate in the $booksInfo array and get the name and price of each book. To get the name of a book we have created function getBookName(). This function accepts a book ID and searches the books.xml for that particular ID. On finding a match it returns the book name. Similarly, function getPriceForBook() returns the unit price of a book. After getting these two values we create some HTML for each book and its price. At last we also display the **Net Amount** in it. When all selected books have been processed, we echo the result back to the browser.

jQuery on receiving the data inserts it into the DIV with ID cart.

This recipe makes an important point. We could have done the calculations on the client side itself with jQuery, then why a trip to the server side for each selection? The answer is that calculation on the client side can be manipulated by making changes using tools such as Firebug. We did the calculations on the server side and then displayed the results on the browser. In such a case the user cannot manipulate the calculations and we can trust the server side for correct calculations.

## There's more...

### Removing items from the cart

Similar to adding items to your cart you can modify this recipe to remove items from the cart too. For this simply place a link against each item in the cart. Clicking that link will initiate an AJAX request that will take the book ID to the server side. PHP on the server side can then check the book ID and can remove the corresponding book from the $booksInfo array and session.

## See also

▶  _Loading XML from files and strings using SimpleXML in Chapter 3_

▶  _Accessing elements and attributes using SimpleXML in Chapter 3_

# 7
# Creating Cool Navigation Menus

In this chapter, we will cover:

- ► Creating a basic drop-down menu
- ► Creating a menu that changes background on mouse-over
- ► Creating an accordion style menu
- ► Creating a floating menu
- ► Creating an interface for tabbed navigation
- ► Adding more tabs
- ► Creating a wizard using tabs

## Introduction

Menus are the lifeline of a website. Imagine a website without menus. It will be impossible to navigate it. A site having good navigation links proves to be very helpful to users. Good navigation menus are key to a good user experience.

This chapter will introduce to you a variety of techniques using which you will be able to create different types of menus.

We will start with basic drop-down menus and will gradually proceed to accordion and floating menus.

Finally, we will create tabs for navigation and will look at several ways in which tabs can be implemented.

# Creating a basic drop-down menu

In this recipe we will create a basic drop-down menu that will have three menu items. Hovering the mouse pointer over a menu item will display a submenu and taking the pointer away from it will hide it.

## Getting ready

Create a folder in the `Chapter7` directory and name it as `Recipe1`. Now create a file named `index.html` inside it.

## How to do it...

Start by creating the structure of menus and the CSS styles for them. Our menu will be an unordered list where each list item will be a menu header. Inside the list item will be an anchor which will contain the text for a menu. Next to it will be another unordered list whose list items will serve as menu items. Each of these menu items will contain a link which can be used to navigate to a page on a website.

1. While writing markup, we will also take care of the fact that a menu should be available on the page even if JavaScript is turned off in the user's browser. The following code defines the markup that we require:

```
<html>
  <head>
    <title>jQuery Menu</title>
<link rel="stylesheet" type="text/css" href="style.css">
  </head>
  <body>
    <div>
      <ul>
        <li class="menuHeader about">
          <a href="#">About us</a>
          <ul class="menuItem">
            <li><a href="http://google.com">Company</a></li>
            <li><a href="#">Culture</a></li>
            <li><a href="#">Motto</a></li>
          </ul>
        </li>
        <li class="menuHeader products">
          <a href="#">Products</a>
          <ul class="menuItem">
            <li><a href="#">Shopping Cart</a></li>
```

```
              <li><a href="#">CMS</a></li>
              <li><a href="#">Blog Software</a></li>
            </ul>
          </li>
          <li class="menuHeader tech">
            <a href="#">Technology</a>
            <ul class="menuItem">
              <li><a href="#">PHP</a></li>
              <li><a href="#">JavaScript</a></li>
              <li><a href="#">MySql</a></li>
            </ul>
          </li>
        </ul>
      </div>
    </body>
</html>
```

2. Now create a new file named `style.css`, which we have referenced in `index.html` and add the following CSS styles in it:

```css
body
{
  font-family:"Trebuchet MS",verdana;
}
ul
{
  list-style:none;
  margin:0;
  padding:0;
}
li.menuHeader
{
  border:1px solid #fff;
  float:left;
  padding:5px 10px;
  text-align:center;
  width:120px;
}
ul.menuItem
{
  margin-top:5px;
}
.menuItem > li
{
  padding:5px 10px;
```

```
}
a
{
  color:#fff;
}
.about{ background-color:#6D9931;}
.products{ background-color:#D63333;}
.tech{ background-color:#D49248;}
```

The screenshot shows how the page will look with styles applied to the markup:

3.  Now include the `jquery.js` file before `body` tag closes. Now hide the submenus and write the event handler that will show and hide the submenu on mouse-over.

```
<script type="text/javascript" src="../jquery.js"></script>
<script type="text/javascript">
$(document).ready(function(){
  $('ul.menuItem').hide();
  $("li.menuHeader").hover(
  function(){
      $('ul', this).slideDown();
  },
  function(){
      $('ul', this).slideUp();
  });

});
</script>
```

4.  Save the file, open your browser and open the file in your browser. You will see three menus. Hover the mouse pointer over any of them and the submenu will appear. Taking the mouse pointer out will again hide the menu.

## How it works...

We begin by creating the HTML structure for menus. We created an unordered list that will hold all menus and submenus. Each list item has a `menuHeader` class. Inside each list item is an anchor that will hold menu text. In real world uses you will assign an `href` value to it for navigating to the other pages. After the anchor is another unordered list, which is a placeholder for menu items for that particular menu. This list may contain multiple menu items each with an anchor for navigation.

When the DOM has loaded jQuery hides all elements with class `menuItem`. As explained previously, these elements refer to items for a menu that should be hidden when a page loads. So, only menus will be visible at page load. Next, we make use of the `hover` function to animate the menus. As you know from previous recipes, the `hover` method accepts two functions as parameters the first of which is executed when the mouse pointer enters an element and the second one is executed when the mouse pointer leaves that element.

In the first function, we select the `ul` inside the current list item and apply the `slideDown` function to it, which shows the submenu. Similarly, the second function uses the `slideUp` function to hide the menu when the mouse leaves it.

## There's more...

### Opening menus on click

You can also code the menu to open on click. The following code will open a submenu and will hide any other submenus that are already open:

```
$(".menuHeader > a").click(function(){
  $('.menuItem:visible').slideToggle();
  $('ul', $(this).parent()).slideToggle();
});
```

## See also

▸ *Creating a menu that changes background on mouse-over*

▸ *Creating an accordion style menu* later in this chapter

# Creating a menu that changes background on mouse-over

This recipe will teach you to create a menu that will allow you to highlight a menu item when the mouse pointer hovers over it. Other menus will be faded and only the menu having mouse focus will be highlighted.

## Getting ready

Create a folder named `Recipe2` inside the `Chapter7` directory. Also create a file named `index.html` inside the `Recipe2` folder. Create three images that will serve as backgrounds for our menu items. I have used the following three images. Each image has dimensions of 120px * 41px:

## How to do it...

1. First of all create the HTML structure for menus. Create an unordered list with three list items. Each list item has a class name `menuHeader` that will be used by jQuery. Another class name will add a background image to it. Put an `anchor` tag inside each `li` element and set its `href` to the page that you wish to navigate to.

```
<html>
<head>
    <title>jQuery Fading Menu</title>
<link rel="stylesheet" type="text/css" href="style.css">
</head>
  <body>
    <div>
      <ul>
        <li class="menuHeader about">
          <a href="http://google.com">google
          </a>
```

```
      </li>
      <li class="menuHeader products">
        <a href="http://yahoo.com">yahoo</a>
      </li>
      <li class="menuHeader tech">
        <a href="http://bing.com">bing</a>
      </li>
    </ul>
  </div>
 </body>
</html>
```

2. Now create a stylesheet file named `style.css` and add the following styles in it:

```css
body{ font-family:"Trebuchet MS",verdana; }
ul
{
  list-style:none;
  margin:0;
  padding:0;
}
li.menuHeader
{
  border:1px solid #fff;
  cursor:pointer;
  float:left;
  padding:5px 10px;
  text-align:center;
  width:120px;
}
a{ color:#fff;}
.about{ background-image:url(1_1.png);}
.products{ background-image:url(1_2.png);}
.tech{ background-image:url(1_3.png);}
```

3. Now include the jQuery library. After including the library, set the opacity of all menu items to 0.5 so that they look faded when the page loads. Attach a `hover` event handler to each list item that will highlight the menu item on which users will place their mouse pointer. As soon as the mouse pointer leaves a menu item, it will be restored to its previous condition.

```html
<script type="text/javascript" src="../jquery.js"></script>
<script type="text/javascript">
$(document).ready(function(){
  $("li.menuHeader").css("opacity","0.5");

  $("li.menuHeader").hover(function ()
  {
    $(this).stop().animate({ opacity: 1}, 'slow');
  },
```

```
function ()
{
  $(this).stop().animate({ opacity: 0.5 }, 'slow');
});

});
</script>
```

4.  Run the `index.html` file in your browser and you will see three menu items that are faded. Move your mouse pointer over a menu and it will be highlighted slowly. After highlighting, its text will be changed to a larger size and to uppercase. The following screenshot shows the capture when the mouse is over the last menu item:

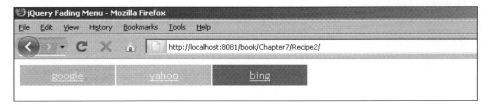

## How it works...

First of all we set the opacity of all menu items using `$("li.menuHeader").css("opacity","0.5")` to 0.5 that makes them look faded. Once again the `hover` function comes to the rescue. This function is called on hovering over list items. The first function (that is, when the mouse enters a list item) uses the `animate` function to set hovered list items' opacity back to 1. We have passed `slow` as the second parameter to `animate` and the third parameter is a callback function that executes when an animation is complete. This function finds the first child of the current list item (which is an anchor) and sets its `font-weight` and `text-transform` CSS properties that make the anchor text bold and uppercase.

## See also

▶  *Creating a basic drop-down menu* in this chapter

▶  *Creating an accordion style menu*

# Creating an accordion style menu

Accordions can also be used as a menu. The content part of an accordion can be used in many ways. In this recipe, we will create a simple accordion and will use it as a menu. Headers of the accordion reveal the content section. This content section will have some text and a Read More link. Clicking on this link will request the related content from a PHP script and will display it on the page.

It can be very handy in cases when you want to show the user only a summary of something (say a product) instead of lengthy details. If the user finds the summary interesting, he can click the link and can read the full details on the page. It can save a lot of space, which means more data can be displayed in the saved space.

## Getting ready

Create a new folder under the Chapter7 directory and name it Recipe3.

## How to do it...

1.  Create a file named index.html inside the Recipe3 folder. Now we have to create a page with three sections. On the top will be a header that will have the page name. Below it the page will be divided into two sections: we will call them left panel and right panel respectively. The left panel will have the markup for an accordion. h1 tags will be used as headers for the accordion. Below each h1 there will be a DIV with class container, which will have the content for it. There will also be an anchor tag in the end of each DIV that will be used to fetch content from the server related to that section. Right panel can have some text or HTML in it. In the head section of this page are some CSS styles for the elements on the page.

```html
<html>
  <head>
    <title>Accordion Menu</title>
    <style type="text/css">
      body{ margin:0px auto;font-family:"trebuchet MS",Arial;
            font-size:14px;width:900px; }
      .header{ background-color:#FA6766;color:#fff;height:100px;
               text-align:center; }
      .accordion{ border:1px solid #FA6766;width:300px;}
      .accordion > h1{cursor:pointer;font-size:14px;
                      font-weight:bold;text-align:center;}
      .active{color:#ff0000;}
      .container{background-color:#F0F8FF;padding:5px;
                 text-align:left;width:288px;}
      p,div{ padding:0pt;margin:0pt; }
      #leftPanel{ float: left; width: 300px; }
      #rightPanel{ float: left; margin: 0pt 0pt 0pt 10px;
                   padding: 0pt;text-align:justify;width: 590px; }
    </style>
  </head>
  <body>
    <div id="main">
      <div class="header">
        <h1>My Awesome Page</h1>
      </div>
```

```
            <div class="content">
              <div id="leftPanel">
                <div class="accordion">
                  <h1>PHP</h1>
                  <div class="container">PHP is a widely used,
                    server side scripting language that is used to ...
                    <a href="data.php?page=php">Read More</a></div>
                </div>
                <div class="accordion">
                  <h1>jQuery</h1>
                  <div class="container">From the jQuery site: jQuery
                      is a fast and concise JavaScript Library that...
                    <a href="data.php?page=jQuery">Read More</a></div>
                </div>
                <div class="accordion">
                  <h1>AJAX</h1>
                  <div class="container">Ajax is a group of web
                    development techniques used on the browser...
                    <a href="data.php?page=ajax">Read More</a></div>
                </div>

                <div class="accordion">
                  <h1>JSON</h1>
                  <div class="container">JSON which stands for
                      JavaScript Object Notation can be defined as...
                    <a href="data.php?page=json">Read More</a></div>
                </div>

              </div>

              <div id="rightPanel">
                <h2>Select a term from the left menu to know more
                      about it.</h2>
              </div>
            </div>
          </div>
        </body>
      </html>
```

The following screenshot shows how the page will look:

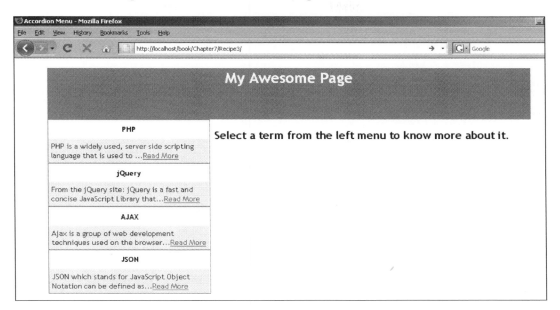

2. The page in the previous screenshot has no JavaScript or jQuery yet. Switching to jQuery now, include the jQuery library using the correct path first. We have to do two things now: first, write code for left panel so that it changes into an accordion and second, on click of the **Read More** link, fetch the corresponding data from the server. In order to do this two event handlers will be written. The first one will be called on clicking accordion headers and the second one will be called on click of **Read More** link which will call a function `getData`. The `getData` function will request data from a PHP script called `data.php`. jQuery will send information regarding which link was clicked.

```
<script type="text/javascript" src="../jquery.js"></script>
<script type="text/javascript">
  $(document).ready(function ()
  {
    $('.container').hide();
    $('.accordion >h1').click(function()
    {
      $('h1.active').removeClass('active');
      $(".container:visible").slideUp('fast');
      $(this).addClass('active').next('div').slideToggle('fast');
    });

    $('.container > a').click(getData);
```

```
function getData()
{
  var url = ($(this).attr('href'));
  $.get(url, {}, function(data)
  {
    $('#rightPanel').html(data);
  });
  return false;
};
});
</script>
```

3. To handle the AJAX request create another file named data.php in the same directory. In this file write the code that will echo response based on parameters received in the get request.

```
<?php
$page = $_GET['page'];
switch($page)
{
  case 'php':
  echo 'PHP is a widely used, server side scripting language
        that is used to create dynamic web applications. PHP is
        very much popular among web developers and many top
        websites use PHP for their sites.';
  break;
  case 'jQuery':
  echo 'From the jQuery site: jQuery is a fast and concise
        JavaScript Library that simplifies HTML document
        traversing, event handling, animating, and Ajax
        interactions for rapid web development. jQuery is
        designed to change the way that you write JavaScript.';
  break;
  case 'ajax':
  echo 'Ajax is a group of web development techniques used on
        the browser (client-side) to create interactive web
        applications. AJAX can be used to retrieve data from the
        server asynchronously in the background. XMLHttpRequest
        objects is generally used to contact the server side.';
  break;
  case 'json':
  echo 'JSON which stands for JavaScript Object Notation can be
        defined as a lightweight data interchange format. It is
        also said a fat-free lightweight alternative to xml. It
        is a text format which is programming language
        independent and is native data form of JavaScript. It is
        lighter and faster than xml. The credit to make json
```

```
                popular goes to Douglas Crockford.';
        break;
    }

?>
```

4.  Once this is done, run the `index.html` file in your browser and click on any header
    of the accordion. It will expand while hiding any open sections and you will see a
    summary and a link. Click on this link now and jQuery will load data from the
    `data.php` file related to that link. If you clicked **Read More** on the **AJAX** tab,
    you will see detailed information related to AJAX on the right panel.

## How it works...

DIV elements with the class name set to `container` represent sections of the
accordion which hold data. In jQuery, after a document loads, we hide all of these using
`$('.container').hide()` so that only accordion headers are visible. After that we register
a `click` event handler for all `h1` elements of the accordion. Clicking on an `h1` first removes
its `active` class. Then any visible content sections are hidden. Finally, we add class `active`
to the clicked `h1`, and toggle its next DIV, which makes the summary related to that section
visible. This completes our first task of creating an accordion.

Secondly, we have to activate the **Read More** link. For this, we add an event listener to an
element of the `container` DIV. Note that the `href` attribute of each anchor has a variable
`page` as part of the query string whose value is different for each section of the accordion.
Clicking on the link calls the `getData` function. This function gets the `href` attribute from the
clicked link and then uses jQuery's `$.get` method to send an AJAX request to that address.

This request is received by a PHP page `data.php` that analyzes the value of variable page in `$_GET` array and then uses a switch case to send back an appropriate response to the client. On receiving a response jQuery inserts it inside the right panel which has ID `rightPanel`.

 Do not forget to return false from the `getData` function otherwise the page will navigate to the URL specified for the **Read More** link.

## There's more...

### jQueryUI Accordion

For more features and functionality you can use the jQueryUI Accordion. It is available from the jQuery UI website at `http://jqueryui.com/demos/accordion/`.

## See also

▶ *Creating expandable and collapsible boxes in Chapter 6*
▶ *Fetching data from PHP using jQuery in Chapter 2*

# Creating a floating menu

In the previous chapter *Adding Visual Effects to Forms*, we learnt to create a floating box that shifts its position as the user scrolls up or down on a page so that it is always visible. We can use this effect to create menus, which will be helpful for users if the pages are too long. In a normal case, if the user has scrolled too much down on a page, they will have to go all the way up to access any menus or submenus.

We can design a menu inside the floating box itself so that it is available to users all the time while they are on the page. This recipe will explain how you can design such menus.

Clicking on a menu item will reveal submenus inside it. Menus can be multiple levels deep also.

## Getting ready

Create a folder named `Recipe4` inside the `Chapter7` directory.

## How to do it...

1. Create a new file inside the `Recipe4` folder and name it as `index.html`.

2. We will create menus in such a way that we can have as many submenus as possible without having to change our jQuery code. For this reason HTML needs to be structured in such a way that jQuery code could be applied to it as many levels deep as possible.

3. First of all create a long paragraph on the page so that we can see the floating effect. Now create a DIV for a floating box. Inside it will be the markup for our menu. The menu will be an unordered list with each list item working as a menu item. Each list item will have a `span` element immediately followed by another unordered list that will act as a submenu for that `span`. All `span` elements will have a CSS class `menu` and all unordered lists that are submenus will have class `menuItem`. Finally, the innermost list can have anchor tags that can be used to navigate to other pages. This structure can be nested as deep as you want. For this recipe we will write a three-level deep menu. The CSS styles required for all elements have been specified in the `head` section of the page.

```
<html>
  <head>
    <title>Floating Menu</title>
    <style type="text/css">
      body{ font-family:"trebuchet MS",Arial;
            font-size:14px;width:500px;}
      .longP,ul
      {
        margin:0; padding:0;
      }
      ul
      {
        list-style:none;
      }
      .longP
      {
        border:1px solid black;
        height:1000px;
        width:300px;
      }
      #floatingBox
      {
        border:1px solid black;
        padding:10px;
        position:absolute;
        right:50px;
```

```
        width:200px;
      }
      .menu
      {
        font-weight:bold;
        margin-top:10px;
      }
      .menuItem
      {
        margin:0;
        padding:10px;
      }
      span
      {
        color:#FA6766;
        cursor:pointer;
        text-decoration:underline;
      }
    </style>
  </head>
  <body>
    <div id="floatingBox">
      <ul>
        <li>
          <span class="menu">Menu Item 1</span>
          <ul class="menuItem">
            <li><a href="http://google.com">Sub Link 1</a></li>
            <li><a href="http://google.com">Sub Link 2</a></li>
            <li><a href="http://google.com">Sub Link 3</a></li>
          </ul>
        </li>
        <li>
          <span class="menu">Menu Item 2</span>
          <ul class="menuItem">
            <li>
             <span class="menu">Sub Menu</span>
             <ul class="menuItem">
               <li>
                 <span class="menu">3rd Level Menu</span>
                 <ul class="menuItem">
                  <li>
                   <a href="http://google.com">Sub Link 1</a>
                  </li>
                  <li>
                   <a href="http://google.com">Sub Link 1</a>
                  </li>
```

```
                <li>
                <a href="http://google.com">Sub Link 1</a>
                </li>
                </ul>
              </li>
            </ul>
          </li>
          <li><a href="http://google.com">Sub Link 1</a></li>
          <li><a href="http://google.com">Sub Link 1</a></li>
        </ul>
      </li>
    </ul>
  </div>
  <p class="longP">
    This is paragraph with height set to 1000 to create
    a long page
  </p>
  </body>
</html>
```

This will result in the menu being shown as seen in the following screenshot:

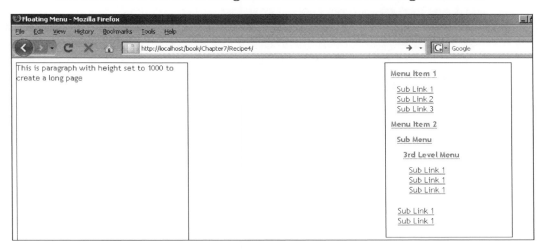

4. Since we have not hidden any submenus, this menu will work fine even if JavaScript is disabled on the user's browser. Let us now add some jQuery magic to make it live. Include the `jquery.js` file before the `body` tag closes. First add a listener for the window scroll event. It will position the floating box on the page depending on the user's position on page. After that hide all submenus and add a `click` event listener for elements with class `menuItems`.

```
<script type="text/javascript" src="../jquery.js"></script>
<script type="text/javascript">
```

```
$(document).ready(function ()
{
  $('.menuItem').hide();
  $(window).scroll(floatDiv);
  floatDiv();
});
function floatDiv()
{
  $('#floatingBox').animate({top: $(document).scrollTop() +
      "px"},{duration:250,queue:false});
}
$('span.menu').click(function()
{
  $(this).next('ul').slideToggle('fast');
});
</script>
```

5. All done now. Save your code and switch to the browser. Point it to the `index.html` file and there it is. You will see a long page with a scrollbar. On the right-hand side will be a box with two menu items. Scroll down the page a bit using the keyboard or mouse and the box will scroll with you. Now click any of the menu items. They will slide down to show you submenus. Try opening the second menu: **Menu Item 2**. It has a three-level deep nesting of menus. The following screenshot shows the page after all the submenus of **Menu Item 2** are opened:

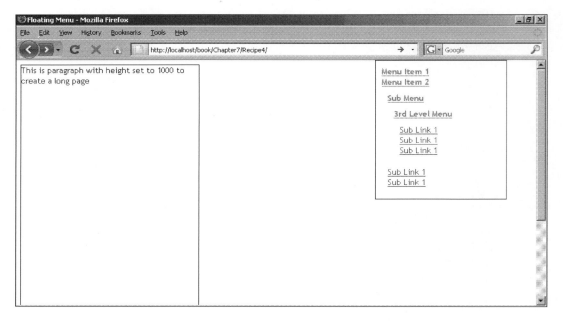

## How it works...

We will start with the floating box. The `floatDiv` function is called after page loads or the user scrolls on the page. This function gets the scrollbar position from the top of the page using jQuery's `$(document).scrollTop()` method. Then we use the `animate` method to set the `top` property of `floating box` over a period of 250 milliseconds. `floatDiv` is also called on page load so that it positions the floating box, by default, when the page opens.

After `floatDiv`, we get all elements with the class name `menuItem` and hide them. We did not do this from CSS because if JavaScript is off on the user's browser, the user will not be able to see submenus, which will make navigation a nightmare.

To toggle the submenus on click of a menu, we have attached another listener to the `span` elements with class `menu`. When a `span`, which has a class `menu`, is clicked we get its next unordered list element (which is a submenu) using the next method and use the `slideToggle` function to toggle its visibility. The `slideToggle` function toggles an element's visibility. Different from `show` and `hide` functions, it manipulates the element's height to achieve the sliding effect. This function accepts parameters similar to `show` and `hide` functions. You can pass either strings `slow`, `normal`, or `fast` to it or you can pass the number of milliseconds for which the effect will run.

## See also

▶ *Floating box on demand in Chapter 6*

# Creating an interface for tabbed navigation

Tabs are a very powerful tool for displaying more information in less space. We will go thorough some techniques in this recipe and the next few recipes that will allow us to create tabs for displaying data.

## Getting ready

Create a folder for this recipe in the `Chapter7` directory and name it as `Recipe5`.

## How to do it...

1.  Create a file named `index.html` in the `Recipe5` folder. In the same folder create another file named `tabs.css`. This file will be used to write the CSS rules for elements.

2. Open the `index.html` file in the text editor of choice. First of all, reference the `tabs.css` file in the `head` section. Now create the structure of the tabs. Tab headers will be an unordered list with each list item representing one tab header. Next to it will be a DIV that will have contents for each tab in a separate DIV. The first list item (tab) will have its contents in the first DIV, the second list them contents will be in the second DIV, and so on. Wrap the unordered list and the DIV containing the tab contents in a separate DIV.

```html
<html>
  <head>
    <title>Tabs</title>
    <link rel="stylesheet" type="text/css" href="tabs.css"
      media="screen" />
  </head>
  <body>
    <div class="tabContainer">
      <ul class="tabHeader">
        <li>Tab 1</li>
        <li>Tab 2</li>
        <li>Tab 3</li>
      </ul>
      <div class="contents">
        <div class="tabContent">
          <h3>Tab 1</h3>
          Content for tab1
        </div>
        <div class="tabContent">
          <h3>Tab 2</h3>
          Content for Tab 2
        </div>
        <div class="tabContent">
          <h3>Tab 3</h3>
          Content for Tab 3
        </div>
      </div>
    </div>
  </body>
</html>
```

3. Open the `tabs.css` file and define the CSS properties for elements. We have done only basic styling for this example but you can add images and make it more colorful and attractive.

```css
body
{
  font-family:"Trebuchet MS",verdana;
```

```
   margin: 50 auto;
   width:800px;
}
h3
{
   margin:0;padding:0;
}
ul
{
   float: left;
   list-style: none;
   margin: 0pt;
   padding: 0pt;
   width:600px;
}
li
{
   border-left:1px solid #000;
   border-right:1px solid #000;
   cursor:pointer;
   float:left;
   padding:5px;
   text-align:center;
   width:100px;
}
.tabContainer
{
   border:1px solid #000;
   float:left;
   width:600px;
}
.tabContent
{
   border-top:1px solid #000;
   float:left;
   height:100px;
   padding:5px;
   text-align:justify;
   width:590px;
}
.active
{
   background-color:#6AA63B;
   color:white;
}
```

The output will be similar to the following screenshot:

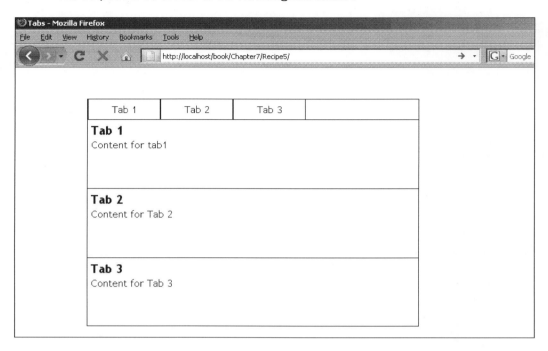

4. Include the jQuery library first using the correct path. Now let's see the jQuery code that will convert this structure to a tab format. This code will make the first tab look active and will have a function `showHideTabs` defined, which will be called on the click of a tab header. This function will make the clicked tab active and will display the content related to it.

```
<script type="text/javascript" src="../jquery.js"></script>
<script type="text/javascript">
  $(document).ready(function ()
  {
    $('.tabContent:gt(0)').hide();
    $('.tabHeader > li:eq(0)').addClass('active');
    $('.tabHeader > li').click(showHideTabs);
  });
  function showHideTabs()
  {
    var allLi = $('.tabHeader > li').removeClass('active')
    $(this).addClass('active');
```

```
        var index = allLi.index(this);
        $('.tabContent:visible').hide();
        $('.tabContent:eq('+index+')').show();
    }
</script>
```

5.  With this our tabs are ready. Run the `index.html` file in your browser. You will
    see three tabs with the first tab being shown as active and only its content being
    displayed. Clicking on another tab header will make it active and the related content
    will be displayed.

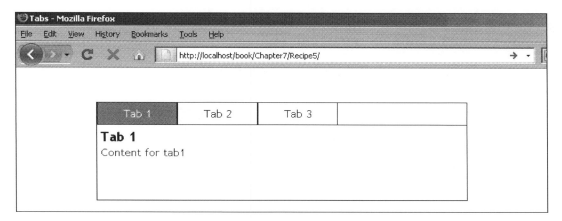

## How it works...

OK. Here is the logic. The contents of each tab are inside a tab that has class `tabContent`.
`$('.tabContent:gt(0)').hide()` hides all such containers that have an index greater
than 0. This means only the first DIV with class `tabContent` remains visible and all others
are hidden. The next line `$('.tabHeader > li:eq(0)').addClass('active')` adds
the active class to the first list item so that it is highlighted. In the next line we add an event
handler to the list items that call function `showHideTabs` whenever a tab header is clicked.
This function will take care of switching of the tabs.

Here is how `showHideTabs` works. First of all get all the list items and remove the `active`
class from all of them using the `removeClass` function. Then using the `addClass` function,
add the `active` class to the current item. This will take care of highlighting tab headers. To
display the content related to clicked tab, get the index of the clicked list item using jQuery's
`index` function. This function returns a 0 based index of an item from a collection. Now hide
the visible DIV elements that have class tab containers using the `:visible` selector. Finally,
display the DIV whose index is equal to the clicked list items index. If the second list item is
clicked, its index will be 1. The line `$('.tabContent:eq('+index+')').show()` will get
the DIV whose index is 1 and will show it.

# Adding more tabs

This recipe may be considered as an extension to the previous recipe. You learned to create tabs in the previous recipe. This recipe will explain how you can add new tabs to existing ones. You will be able to specify name and contents for a new tab.

## Getting ready

Create a folder for this recipe inside the `Chapter7` folder and name it `Recipe6`.

## How to do it...

1. Create a new file in the `Recipe6` folder and name it as `index.html`. Now create another file in the same folder for CSS rules and name it as `tabs.css`.

2. Open the `tabs.css` file and define the following CSS properties for elements. This file will have some more properties than the previous recipe because we will also create some elements for entering tab and content name.

```css
body{   font-family:"Trebuchet MS",verdana;}
ul
{
  float: left;
  margin: 0pt;
  padding: 0pt;
  list-style: none;
  width:600px;
}
li
{
  border-left:1px solid #000;
  border-right:1px solid #000;
  cursor:pointer;
  float:left;
  padding:5px;
  text-align:center;
  width:100px;
}
.tabContainer
{
  border:1px solid #000;
  float:left;
  width:600px;
}
.tabContent
{
```

```
    border-top:1px solid #000;
    float:left;
    height:200px;
    padding:5px;
    text-align:justify;
    width:590px;
}
.newTabHolder
{
    float:left;
    width:300px;
}
.active
{
    background-color:DarkBlue;
    color:white;
}
.hide
{
    display:none;
}
#error{ color:#ff0000;}
.remove{float: right;font-weight:bold;color:#ff0000;}
h4{  margin:0px;padding:0px;  }
label{float: left; width: 100px;}
input,textarea{ width:185px;}
```

3. Now let us write the markup for creating tabs. We will use the same structure as in the previous recipe. Before that we will create a textbox, a textarea, and an input button. We will enter the tab name in the textbox and the contents of the tab in textarea and the button will add the new tab to the existing structure. Open the index.html file in the text editor of choice. Now reference the tabs.css file in the head section and write the complete HTML markup as follows:

```
<html>
  <head>
    <title>Tabs</title>
    <link rel="stylesheet" type="text/css" href="tabs.css"
      media="screen" />
  </head>
  <body>
    <div class="newTabHolder">
      <h4>Add a New Tab</h4>
      <label for="tabName">Tab Name</label>
      <input type="text" id="tabName"/>
      <label for="tabHTML">Tab HTML</label>
      <textarea id="tabHTML" rows="10"></textarea>
```

```
          <input type="button" id="addTab" value="Add New Tab"/><br/>
          <span id="error"></span>
      </div>
      <div class="tabContainer">
        <ul id="tabHeader">
          <li>Tab 1</li>
          <li>Tab 2</li>
          <li>Tab 3</li>
        </ul>
        <div id="contents">
          <div class="tabContent">
            <h3>Tab 1</h3>
            Content for tab1
          </div>
          <div class="tabContent">
            <h3>Tab 2</h3>
            Content for Tab 2
          </div>
          <div class="tabContent">
            <h3>Tab 3</h3>
            Content for Tab 3
          </div>
        </div>
      </div>
    </div>
  </body>
</html>
```

The page will be similar to the following screenshot:

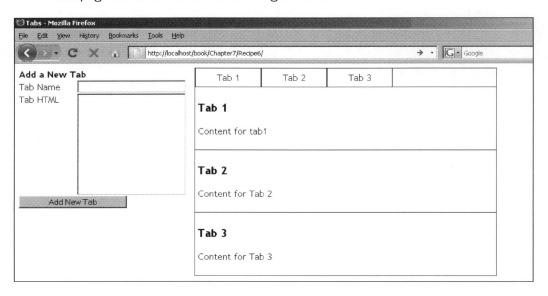

4. Include the jQuery library first using the correct path. Besides making the first tab active and hiding other content tabs, we will write a new function addTab, which will take the values for tab name and its contents and will create a new tab with it. From the previous recipe we already have the capability to switch tabs. For that purpose, we had created a function called showHideTabs, which made the clicked tab active and displayed the content related to it.

```
<script type="text/javascript" src="../jquery.js"></script>
<script type="text/javascript">
  $(document).ready(function ()
  {
    $('.tabContent:gt(0)').hide();
    $('#tabHeader > li:eq(0)').addClass('active');
    $('#tabHeader > li').live('click',showHideTabs);
    $('#addTab').click(addTab);

    function showHideTabs()
    {
      var allLi = $('#tabHeader > li').removeClass('active');
      $(this).addClass('active');
      var index = allLi.index(this);
      $('.tabContent:visible').hide();
      $('.tabContent:eq('+index+')').show();
    }

    function addTab()
    {
      if(jQuery.trim($('#tabName').val())!= '' &&
          jQuery.trim($('#tabHTML').val()) != '')
      {
        $('#error').empty();
        $('#tabHeader').append('<li>' + $('#tabName').val() +
          '</li>');
        $('#contents').append('<div class="tabContent hide">' +
            $('#tabHTML').val() + '</div>');
        //display the new tab by default
        $('#tabHeader > li').removeClass('active');
        $('#tabHeader > li:last').addClass('active');
        $('.tabContent:visible').hide();
        $('.tabContent:last').show();
      }
      else
      {
        $('#error').html('Please provide a Tab Name.');
      }
    }
  });
</script>
```

5. Save the `index.html` file and launch it in the browser. On the left-hand side you will see a textbox, a textarea, and a button. On the right-hand side will be three tabs with the first one already active. Fill some values in the elements on the left-hand side and click on the **Add New Tab** button. A new tab will be created and will be appended at the end of the existing ones.

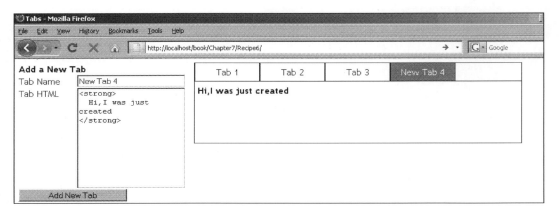

## How it works...

An important point to begin with, if you remember from the previous recipe, is that function `showHideTabs` was registered using the `click` event. In this recipe we are going to add new tabs, and we want the `click` event available to new tabs also. So, instead of adding the event with click, we will use `live` to add the event. `live()` adds events to elements that are created later.

Now back to adding a new tab. On clicking the **Add New Tab** button, function `addTab` is called. This function checks if the value of textbox or textarea is empty or not. If any of these values are empty, an error message is displayed. If there is no error, the tab can be added. First, the `span` element, which may have a previous error message, is emptied. In the very next line we create a list item with its HTML set to the tab name as in textbox and append it to the unordered list. Similarly, we create a DIV and set its HTML with the value in textarea and append it to the DIV with class name `contents`. We also assign this DIV another class called `hide`, which makes it hidden and currently the display is not affected. Clicking on this new tab header will now display its contents.

## There's more...

### Displaying new tab by default

In the previous code, a new tab is created but not displayed by default. You can set it to be active by default. Add these four lines of code in the end of the `if` block in the `addTab` function.

```
$('#tabHeader > li').removeClass('active');
$('#tabHeader > li:last').addClass('active');
$('.tabContent:visible').hide();
$('.tabContent:last').show();
```

Since the new tab is appended in the end, the first two lines remove the `active` class from all tab headers and add it to the last one. The last two lines hide all tab content DIV elements and then show the last one. Therefore, all other tabs are hidden and the new tab is now active.

## See also

▶ *Creating an interface for tabbed navigation* in this chapter

▶ *Adding events to elements that will be created later from Chapter 1*

# Creating a wizard using tabs

This recipe will explain how you can create a wizard in which you can guide a user step by step.

## Getting ready

Create a folder for this recipe and name it as `Recipe7`. Create an `index.html` file inside it.

## How to do it...

1. Similar to the previous recipe, create the structure for tabs using list items of an unordered list as tab headers and DIV elements with class `tabContent` as containers for respective tabs. Do not forget to define the CSS styles in the `head` section.

```
<html>
  <head>
    <title>Tabs</title>
    <style type="text/css">
```

```css
body
{
  font-family:"Trebuchet MS",verdana;
  margin: 50px auto;
  width:600px;
}
.tabContainer
{
  border:1px solid black;
  float:left;
  width:600px;
}
ul
{
  float: left;
  margin: 0pt;
  padding: 0pt;
  list-style: none;
  width:600px;
}
li
{
  border-left:1px solid black;
  border-right:1px solid black;
  cursor:pointer;
  float:left;
  padding:5px;
  text-align:center;
  width:100px;
}
.tabContent
{
  border-top:1px solid black;
  float:left;
  height:200px;
  padding:5px;
  text-align:justify;
  width:590px;
}
.active
{
  background-color:#6AA63B;
  color:white;
}
```

```
      .prev{ float:left;}
      .next{ float:right;}
      #order
      {
        border:0px solid #000;
      }
      </style>
</head>
<body>
   <form action="">
      <div class="tabContainer">
        <ul class="tabHeader">
          <li>Name</li>
          <li>Selections</li>
          <li>Confirmation</li>
        </ul>
        <div class="contents">
          <div class="tabContent">
            <p>
              <strong>Please enter your name</strong>
              <input type="text" id="userName"/>
            </p>
            <input type="button" value="Next >>" class="next"/>
          </div>
          <div class="tabContent">
            <p>
              <strong>Please select a product</strong>
              <select id="product">
                <option>Shirt</option>
                <option>Jeans</option>
                <option>Shoes</option>
              </select>
              <br/><br/>
              <strong>Select quantity</strong>
              <select id="quantity">
                <option value="1">1</option>
                <option value="2">2</option>
                <option value="3">3</option>
              </select>
            </p>
            <input type="button" value="<< Previous"
              class="prev"/>
            <input type="button" value="Next >>" class="next"/>
          </div>
```

```
            <div class="tabContent last">
              <p>
                <strong>Review</strong>
                <div id="order"></div>
              </p>
              <input type="button" value="<< Previous"
                class="prev"/>
            </div>
          </div>
        </div>
      </form>
    </body>
  </html>
```

There will be some more elements in these tabs. The first tab has a textbox and a **Next** button, which will be used to navigate to next tab. The second tab will have a few select boxes and **Previous** and **Next** buttons that will take a user to the previous and next tabs respectively. The third and final tab has an extra class name `last` and it has a DIV with ID `order`. It also has a **Previous** button. The page is similar to the following screenshot:

2. Now include the jQuery file and add event handlers for the previous and next buttons. To keep it simple, we will not add event handlers for tab headers this time so that the user cannot jump directly to any tab. Event handlers for buttons will first get the index of the current tab, and will then call the function showHideTabs. The showHideTabs function will switch tabs according to the passed value. It will also check if the tab is last. If it is, jQuery will collect the information from the previous tabs and will display it in the last tab.

```javascript
<script type="text/javascript" src="../jquery.js"></script>
<script type="text/javascript">
  $(document).ready(function ()
  {
    $('.tabContent:gt(0)').hide();
    $('.tabHeader > li:eq(0)').addClass('active');

    $('input:button').click(function()
    {
      var currentTabIndex = getCurrentTabIndex(this);
      if($(this).hasClass('prev'))
      {
        showHideTabs(--currentTabIndex);
      }
      else if($(this).hasClass('next'))
      {
        showHideTabs(++currentTabIndex);
      }
    });

    function getCurrentTabIndex(el)
    {
      var parent = $(el).parent('.tabContent');
      return $('.tabContent').index(parent);
    }
    function showHideTabs(index)
    {
      $('.tabHeader > li.active').removeClass('active');
      $('.tabHeader > li:eq('+index+')').addClass('active');

      $('.tabContent:visible').hide();
      $('.tabContent:eq('+index+')').show();

      if($('.tabContent:eq('+index+')').hasClass('last'))
      {
        displaySelectedValues();
      }
```

```
        }
        function displaySelectedValues()
        {
          var name = $('#userName').val();
          var product = $('#product').val();
          var quantity = $('#quantity').val();
          var strHtml = 'Hello ' + name + ', ';
          strHtml+= 'Please confirm your selection:<br/>';
          strHtml+= '<strong>Item:</strong> ' + product;
          strHtml+= '<br/>';
          strHtml+= '<strong>Quantity:</strong> ' + quantity;
          strHtml+= '</ul>';
          $('#order').html(strHtml);
        }
      });
    </script>
```

3.  Save the file and open it in your browser. You will see three familiar tabs. Enter some value in the first tab and click on the **Next** button. Then select a product and its quantity from the second tab and click on the **Next** button. The final tab will show you a confirmation message with the values that you have selected.

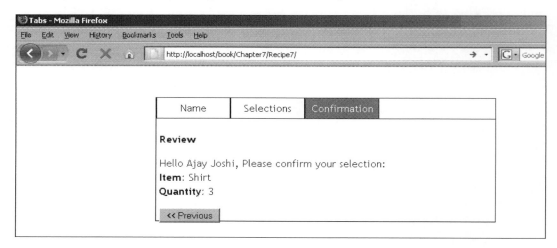

# How it works...

First we hide all tabs except the first one. Then add class `active` to the first tab. Then comes the event handler for the **Previous** and **Next** buttons. When a button is clicked, we get the index of its parent DIV in variable `currentTabIndex` using the `getCurrentTabIndex` function. Then the handler function checks the class of the clicked button. If it is `prev`, which means user wants to navigate to previous tab, we then decrease the value of `currentTabIndex` and pass it to the `showHideTabs` function. Similarly, if the button has class `next`, we pass the incremented value of `currentTabIndex` to the `showHideTabs` function.

Function `showHideTabs` first removes the class `active` from the list item. Then it finds the list item whose index is equal to the passed index and adds class `active` to it. Then the visible `tabContent` DIV is hidden and the DIV whose index matches the passed index is displayed.

In the end, the code checks if the tab is the last one or not by checking for class `last`. If it is the last tab then function `displaySelectedValues` is called.

Function `displaySelectedValues` takes the values of the `userName` textbox and the `product` and `quantity` select boxes and creates a nicely formatted information message in the form of HTML and inserts it into the DIV with ID `order`.

# See also

- ▶ *Creating an interface for tabbed navigation*
- ▶ *Adding more Tabs*

# 8
# Data Binding with PHP and jQuery

In this chapter, we will cover:

- ▶ Fetching data from a database and displaying it in a table format
- ▶ Collecting data from a form and saving it to a database (Registration form)
- ▶ Filling chained combo boxes that depend upon each other
- ▶ Checking username availability from a database
- ▶ Paginating data for large record sets
- ▶ Adding auto suggest functionality to a textbox
- ▶ Creating a tag cloud

## Introduction

This chapter will explain some recipes where we will use a database along with PHP on the server side. A database is an essential part of almost every dynamic web application. PHP provides a large number of functions to interact with the database. The most commonly used database along with PHP is MySQL. In this chapter, we will be using another version of MySQL called MySQLi or MySQL improved. It provides significant advantages over the MySQL extension; most important of them being the support for the object-oriented interface as well as the procedural interface. Other features include support for transactions, prepared statements, and so on.

You can read more about MySQLi on the PHP site at `http://www.php.net/manual/en/book.mysqli.php`.

MySQLi extension is available with PHP version 5.0 or higher. So, make sure you have the required PHP version. If you are running PHP 5 or a higher version, you will have to configure MySQL separately as a default PHP support, for MySQL was dropped starting from PHP versions 5.0 and higher.

**Cleaning data before use**

Throughout the recipes in this book, we have used user input directly by pulling these from $_GET or $_POST arrays. Although this is okay for examples, in practical websites and applications, user data must be properly cleaned and sanitized before performing any operations on it to make your application safe from malicious users. Below are some links where you can get more information on how to make your data safe, and security in general.

PHP Security Consortium: `http://phpsec.org/`

PHP Manual: `http://php.net/manual/en/security.php`

# Fetching data from a database and displaying it in a table format

This is a simple recipe where we will get some data from a table and we'll display it in a page. Users will be presented with a select box with options to choose a programming language. Selecting a language will get some functions and their details from the database.

## Getting ready

Create a new folder named `Recipe1` inside the `Chapter8` directory. Now, using phpMyAdmin create a table named `language` in the `exampleDB` database using the following query.

```
CREATE TABLE `language` (
  `id` int(3) NOT NULL auto_increment,
  `languageName` varchar(50) NOT NULL,
  PRIMARY KEY  (`id`)
);
```

Insert two records for `languageName` in this table, namely PHP and jQuery. Now, create another table `functions` that will have function names and details related to a language.

```
CREATE TABLE `functions` (
  `id` int(3) NOT NULL auto_increment,
  `languageId` int(11) NOT NULL,
```

```
`functionName` varchar(64) NOT NULL,
`summary` varchar(128) NOT NULL,
`example` text NOT NULL,
PRIMARY KEY (`id`)
);
```

languageId is the ID of the language that is in the language table. Now, insert some records in this table using phpMyadmin with some data for PHP and some for jQuery. Here is a snapshot of what the functions table will look like after filling it with data:

| id | languageId | functionName | summary | example |
|---|---|---|---|---|
| 1 | 1 | simplexml_load_file | Interprets an XML file into an object | $xml = simplexml_load_file('test.xml'); print_r($... |
| 2 | 1 | array_push | Push one or more elements onto the end of array | $arrPets = array('Dog', 'Cat', 'Fish' ); array_pu... |
| 3 | 1 | ucfirst | Make a string's first character uppercase | $message = 'have a nice day; $message = ucfirst($... |
| 4 | 1 | mail | used to send email | $message = "Example message for mail"; if(mail('t... |
| 5 | 2 | $.get | Load data from the server using a HTTP GET request... | $.ajax({ url: url, data: data, success: s... |
| 6 | 2 | hover | hover method accepts 2 functions as parameters whi.. | $(selector).hover( function() { //executes on m... |
| 7 | 2 | bind | Attach a handler to an event for the elements. | $(element).bind('click', function() { alert('... |
| 8 | 2 | jQuery.data | Store arbitrary data associated with the specified.. | jQuery.data(element, key, value); |

## How to do it...

1. Create a file named index.php in the Recipe1 folder. Using methods of MySQLi class, select data from the language table, and populate a select box with list of languages. Also, create a p element that will show the functions for the selected language.

```html
<html>
  <head>
    <style type="text/css">
    body{font-family: "Trebuchet MS", Verdana, Arial;width:600px;}
    div {  background-color: #F5F5DC;  }

    </style>
  </head>
  <body>
```

```php
<?php
$mysqli = new mysqli('localhost', 'root', '', 'exampleDB');
if (mysqli_connect_errno())
{
    die('Unable to connect!');
}
else
{
  $query = 'SELECT * FROM language';
  if ($result = $mysqli->query($query))
  {
    if ($result->num_rows > 0)
    {
?>
      <p>
        Select a language
        <select id="selectLanguage">
          <option value="">select</option>
<?php
      while($row = $result->fetch_assoc())
      {
?>
        <option value="<?php echo $row[0]; ?>"><?php echo $row[1];
?></option>
<?php
      }
?>
        </select>
    </p>
    <p id="result"></p>
<?php
    }
    else
    {
      echo 'No records found!';
    }
    $result->close();
  }
  else
  {
    echo 'Error in query: $query. '.$mysqli->error;
  }
}
$mysqli->close();
?>
  </body>
</html>
```

2. Now, add a reference to the jQuery file. After this, write the event handler for a select box that will be fired on selecting a value from the combo box. It will send an AJAX request to a PHP file `results.php`, which will get the data for the selected language and will insert it into the `p` element.

```
<script type="text/javascript" src="../jquery.js"></script>
<script type="text/javascript">
  $(document).ready(function()
  {
    $('#selectLanguage').change(function()
    {
      if($(this).val() == '')  return;
      $.get(
        'results.php',
        { id : $(this).val() },
        function(data)
        {
          $('#result').html(data);
        }
      );
    });
  });
</script>
```

3. Create another `results.php` file that will connect to the database `exampleDB` and will get data specific to a language from the database. It will then create the formatted HTML from the results and will send it back to the browser where jQuery inserts it into the `p` element.

```
<?php
$mysqli = new mysqli('localhost', 'root', '', 'exampleDB');
$resultStr = '';
$query = 'SELECT functionName, summary, example FROM functions
where languageId='.$_GET['id'];
if ($result = $mysqli->query($query))
{
  if ($result->num_rows > 0)
  {
    $resultStr.='<ul>';
    while($row = $result->fetch_assoc())
    {
      $resultStr.= '<li><strong>'.$row['functionName'].'</strong>
      - '.$row['summary'];
      $resultStr.= '<div><pre>'.$row['example'].'</pre></div>';
      '</li>';
    }
```

```
      $resultStr.= '</ul>';
    }
    else
    {
      $resultStr = 'Nothing found';
    }
  }
  echo $resultStr;
  ?>
```

4. Now, run the `index.php` file in the browser and you will see a combo box with two options: PHP and jQuery. Select any option and you will see the results in the form of a bulleted list.

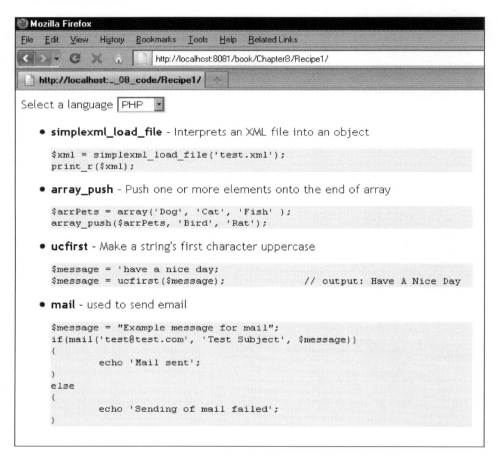

## How it works...

First, we create a new object of MySQLi class using its constructor. We pass the host, database user name, password, and database name to it. Then, we check for errors, if any, while connecting to the database. In case of an error, we display an error message and terminate the script.

Then, we use the `query` method of the `mysqli` class to select all data from the language table. If the query is successful we get the result object in the `$result` variable. The `$result` variable that we have is an object of the `MySQLi_Result` class. The `MySQLi_Result` class provides several methods to extract data from the object. We have used one such method called `fetch_assoc()` that fetches a row as an associative array. Using a `while` loop, we can iterate in the `$result` object one row at a time. Here, we create a select box with ID `selectLanguage` and fill the language names as its options and `languageId` as values for the options.

In jQuery code, we have an event handler for the `change` event of the combo box. It takes the value of the select box and sends it to the `results.php` file, using a GET AJAX request.

The `results.php` file connects to the `exampleDB` database and then writes a query for selecting data for a particular language. jQuery sends an `id` parameter with an AJAX request that will be used in the query. Like the `index.php` page, we get the results in the `$result` variable. Now, we iterate over this result and create an unordered list and assign it to the `$resultStr` variable. Each list item contains a function name, a brief description about it, and an example. In case of any error, the variable `$resultStr` is assigned an error message.

Finally, we echo the `$resultStr` variable received by jQuery. jQuery then inserts the received HTML in the `p` element with ID `result`.

## There's more...

### What is a constructor?

In object-oriented programming, a constructor is a method that is invoked whenever a new object of that class is created. A constructor has the same name as the class name.

```
$mysqli = new mysqli('localhost', 'root', '', 'exampleDB');
```

The above line creates a new object of `mysqli` class, which has a constructor that takes four arguments.

One thing to keep in mind is: in PHP5 and above versions, a constructor is defined as `__construct()` whereas in prior versions the constructor has the same name as the class name. To read more about constructors in PHP refer to the PHP site: `http://www.php.net/manual/en/language.oop5.decon.php`

# Collecting data from a form and saving to a database

Using the same two tables of the previous recipe, we will create a form that will allow the user to select a language, add a function name, its summary, and related examples. We will then save this information to the `functions` table with the selected language.

## Getting ready

Create `Recipe2` folder inside the `Chapter8` directory.

## How to do it...

1. Create a file named `index.php` inside the `Recipe2` folder. Now, create a form with four fields. First, create a select box and query the `language` table to fill languages in it. Next, create two textboxes for **Function name** and **Summary**. Finally, create a textarea in which users will enter the example for that function. Assign a CSS class named `required` to each of these elements.

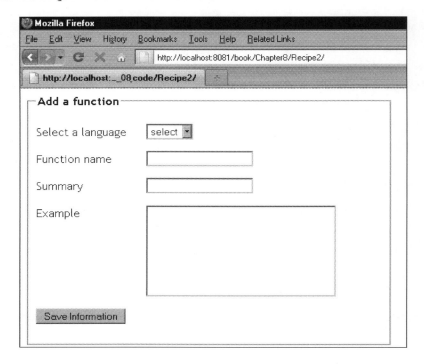

2. Before the closing of `body` tag, include the `jquery.js` file and after that, write the event handler function for the form's `submit` event. This function will perform a basic validation by checking each element's value. If any of the fields is blank, it will display an error message. If there are no errors, the form will be submitted.

```
<script type="text/javascript" src="../jquery.js"></script>
<script type="text/javascript">
  $(document).ready(function()
  {
    $('#frmMain').submit(function()
    {
      var flag = true;
      $('#error').empty();
      $('.required').each(function()
      {
        if(jQuery.trim($(this).val()) == '' )
        {
          flag = false;
        }
      });
      if(!flag)
      {
        $('#error').html('Please fill all the fields');
        return false;
      }
      else
      {
        return true;
      }
    });
  });
</script>
```

3. Now, when the form is submitted, PHP will take the values for each element from the global `$_POST` array and will assign them to different variables, after escaping them. Then an `INSERT` query will execute and will insert these values into the database. An appropriate message will be displayed, depending on whether the query has succeeded or failed. Below is the full code for the `index.php` file.

```
<html>
  <head>
    <style type="text/css">
    body{ font-family: "Trebuchet MS", Verdana, Arial;
          width:500px; }
    input,textarea { vertical-align:top; }
    label{ float:left; width:150px;}
```

```php
    </style>
  </head>
  <body>
<?php
$mysqli = new mysqli('localhost', 'root', '', 'exampleDB');
if(isset($_POST['save']))
{
  $language = $mysqli->real_escape_string($_POST['language']);
  $functionName = $mysqli->real_escape_string($_
POST['functionName']);
  $summary = $mysqli->real_escape_string($_POST['summary']);
  $example = $mysqli->real_escape_string($_POST['example']);
  $query = 'INSERT INTO functions (
      languageId ,
      functionName ,
      summary ,
      example
      )
      VALUES ('.$language.', "'.$functionName.'", "'.$summary.'","
'.$example.'")';
        if ($mysqli->query($query))
  {
    echo 'Data Saved Successfully.';
  }
  else
  {
    echo 'Cannot save data.';
  }

}
$query = 'SELECT * FROM language';
if ($result = $mysqli->query($query))
{
  if ($result->num_rows > 0)
  {
?>
    <fieldset>
    <legend><strong>Add a function</strong></legend>
    <form action="" method="post" id="frmMain">
      <p>
        <label>Select a language</label>
          <select name="language" class="required">
            <option value="">select</option>
<?php
            while($row = $result->fetch_array())
            {
```

```php
?>
                <option value="<?php echo $row[0]; ?>">
                  <?php echo $row[1]; ?></option>
<?php
           }
?>
           </select>
       </p>
       <p>
         <label>Function name </label>
         <input type="text" name="functionName"  class="required"/>
       </p>
       <p>
         <label>Summary</label>
           <input type="text" name="summary" class="required"/>
       </p>
       <p>
         <label>Example</label> <textarea rows="10" cols="30"
             name="example" class="required"></textarea>
       </p>
       <p>
         <strong id="error"></strong>
       </p>
       <p>
         <input type="submit" name="save"
             value="Save  Information"/>
       </p>
     </form>
     </fieldset>
<?php
   }
   else
   {
     echo 'No records found!';
   }
   $result->close();
}
else
{
   echo 'Error in query: $query. '.$mysqli->error;
}

$mysqli->close();
?>
   </body>
</html>
```

4. Now, run the file in your browser and fill some values in the form. Click on the **Save Information** button and it will save the values to the `functions` table in the database. You will also see a message **Data Saved Successfully** on successful execution of the query. Leaving any fields blank and trying to submit the form will display an error message.

## How it works...

First, we connect to the database using the constructor of `mysqli` class. Next, the `if` statement checks whether the form has been submitted or not. Hence, this part will be executed after the form submission. We will look into this part in detail later in this chapter.

```
if(isset($_POST['save']))
{
}
```

Outside the above condition, we query the `language` table using a `SELECT` statement that gets us the languages from the database. We then fill these languages and their values inside the select box. Other fields include two textboxes and a textarea.

After the form is submitted with non-blank values, PHP fetches these values from the `$_POST` Superglobal and escapes it using `real_escape_string()` method of `mysqli` class. This function escapes the user data so that it is ready to be used in a query. Then, we insert the values for the language, function name, and example using an `INSERT` query. `query()` will return `true` on success and `false` on failure. We then display the final message to the user based on this return value.

## There's more...

### real_escape_string() function

The `real_escape_string()` function is used to escape special characters in a string. SQL queries may throw an error if the data present in them is not escaped properly. You should always use it in your database queries.

Also note that you need to be connected to a database to be able to use this function.

### Return values for mysqli->query()

For statements such as `SELECT`, `SHOW`, and so on, this method returns an object of class `MySQLi_Result`. For statements like `INSERT`, `UPDATE`, and `DELETE`, it returns either `TRUE` or `FALSE`.

## See also

▶  *Checking for empty fields using jQuery in Chapter 5*

# Filling chained combo boxes that depend upon each other

This recipe tries to solve a very common task that is seen in many web applications, that is, filtering contents of a combo box according to the selection made in its previous combo box.

We will create an example where the user will be presented with three select boxes—one each for country, state, and town. Selecting a country will get its states and selecting a state will get its towns. Finally, on selecting a town we will display some information related to it.

The most important point here is that there will not be any page reloads. Instead, we will use AJAX to filter the contents silently. This will create a better user experience compared to classic web application behavior where it would have required a full-page reload on each selection.

## Getting ready

Create a folder named `Recipe3` inside the `Chapter8` directory. Now, we will require four tables in our database. Once again, open phpMyadmin, create these four tables, and fill them with the desired values.

▶  Country

```
CREATE TABLE `country` (
  `id` int(11) NOT NULL auto_increment,
  `countryName` varchar(64) NOT NULL,
  PRIMARY KEY  (`id`)
);

INSERT INTO `country` (`id`, `countryName`) VALUES
(1, 'India');
```

▶  States

```
CREATE TABLE `states` (
  `id` int(11) NOT NULL auto_increment,
  `countryId` int(11) NOT NULL,
  `stateName` varchar(64) NOT NULL,
  PRIMARY KEY  (`id`)
);

INSERT INTO `states` (`id`, `countryId`, `stateName`) VALUES
(1, 1, 'U.P.'),
(2, 1, 'Uttarakhand');
```

▶ Towns

```
CREATE TABLE `towns` (
  `id` int(11) NOT NULL auto_increment,
  `stateId` int(11) NOT NULL,
  `townName` varchar(64) NOT NULL,
  PRIMARY KEY  (`id`)
);

INSERT INTO `towns` (`id`, `stateId`, `townName`) VALUES
(1, 1, 'Lucknow'),
(2, 1, 'Bareilly'),
(3, 2, 'Pithoragarh'),
(4, 2, 'Dehradun'),
(5, 2, 'Nainital');
```

▶ Towninfo

```
CREATE TABLE `towninfo` (
  `id` int(11) NOT NULL auto_increment,
  `townId` int(11) NOT NULL,
  `description` text NOT NULL,
  PRIMARY KEY  (`id`)
);

INSERT INTO `towninfo` (`id`, `townId`, `description`) VALUES
(1, 3, 'Pithoragarh is a beautiful town situated in Kumaon region
of Uttarakhand. It has an average elevation of 1,514 metres (4,967
feet) above sea level.'),
(2, 4, 'Dehradun also known as Doon is the capital city of
Uttarakhand. It is around 250 Kilometers from national capital
Delhi.\r\nRice and Lychee are major products of this city.'),
(3, 1, 'Lucknow is the capital city of U.P. or Uttar Pradesh.\
r\nLucknow has Asia''s first human DNA bank.\r\nIt is popularly
known as The City of Nawabs, Golden City of the East and The
Constantinople of India.');
```

## How to do it...

1. Create a file `index.html` inside the `Recipe3` folder. Create three combo boxes for country, state, town, and a `p` element that will display the information about the selected town. Also write some CSS styles in `head` section for styling these elements. All values in these combo boxes will be filled using AJAX requests.

```
<html>
  <head>
    <style type="text/css">
    body{font-family: "Trebuchet MS", Verdana, Arial;width:600px;}
```

```
ul { list-style:none;margin:0pt;padding:0pt;width:525px;
     float:left; }
li{ float:left;padding:10px;}
p{border:1px solid #000; float:left;height:100px;width:500px;}
select { width:100px; }
</style>
</head>
<body>
  <ul>
    <li>
      <strong>Country</strong>
      <select id="countryList">
        <option value="">select</option>
      </select>
    </li>
    <li>
      <strong>State</strong>
      <select id="stateList">
        <option value="">select</option>
      </select>
    </li>
    <li>
      <strong>Town</strong>
      <select id="townList">
        <option value="">select</option>
      </select>
    </li>
  </ul>
  <p id="information"></p>
</body>
</html>
```

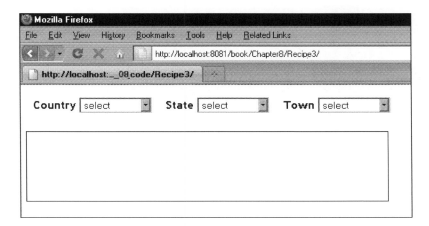

2. Before the `body` tag closes, add the jQuery library. Now, create a function `getList` that will be called whenever the value in the combo box changes. Depending on which combo box it is, a URL will be set with two parameters: `find` and `id`. Finally, an AJAX request will be sent to this URL which will fetch the corresponding results. Function `getList()` will be called once the document is ready so that we have values available in the **Country** combo box.

```
<script type="text/javascript" src="../jquery.js"></script>
<script type="text/javascript">
  $(document).ready(function()
  {
    $('select').change(getList);
    getList();
    function getList()
    {
     var url, target;
      var id = $(this).attr('id');
      var selectedValue = $(this).val();
      switch (id)
      {
        case 'countryList':
          if(selectedValue == '') return;
          url = 'results.php?find=states&id='+ selectedValue;
          target = 'stateList';
        break;

        case 'stateList':
          if($(this).val() == '') return;
          url = 'results.php?find=towns&id='+ selectedValue;
          target = 'townList';
        break;

        case 'townList':
          if($(this).val() == '') return;
          url = 'results.php?find=information&id='+ selectedValue;
          target = 'information';
        break;

        default:
          url = 'results.php?find=country';
          target = 'countryList';
      }
      $.get(
        url,
        { },
```

```
            function(data)
            {
              $('#'+target).html(data);
            }
          )
       }

     });
  </script>
```

3. The AJAX request will be sent to the `results.php` file. So, create a new file with this name. This file connects to the database and depending on the values of parameters `find` and `id`, it queries the appropriate table and fetches data from it. HTML is generated from this data and is sent back to the browser where jQuery displays it.

```php
<?php
$mysqli = new mysqli('localhost', 'root', '', 'exampleDB');
$find = $_GET['find'];
switch ($find)
{
  case 'country':
    $query = 'SELECT id, countryName FROM country';
  break;
  case 'states':
    $query = 'SELECT id, stateName FROM states WHERE
    countryId='.$_GET['id'];
  break;
  case 'towns':
    $query = 'SELECT id, townName FROM towns
     WHERE stateId='.$_GET['id'];
  break;
  case 'information':
    $query = 'SELECT id, description FROM towninfo
    WHERE townId='.$_GET['id'] .' LIMIT 1';
  break;
}
if ($mysqli->query($query))
{
  $result = $mysqli->query($query);
  if($find == 'information')
  {
    if($result->num_rows > 0)
    {
      $row = $result->fetch_array();
      echo $row[1];
    }
```

```php
    else
    {
      echo 'No Information found';
    }
  }
  else
  {
?>
    <option value="">select</option>
<?php
    while($row = $result->fetch_array())
    {
?>
      <option value="<?php echo $row[0]; ?>"><?php echo $row[1];
?></option>
<?php
    }
  }
}
?>
```

4. Run the index.html file in your browser and you will find the values in the **Country** combo box. Other boxes will be empty. Select a country and the **State** combo box will be filled with data. Selecting a state will fill the last combo box (**Town**). In the end, select a town and an AJAX request will get information related to it and will display it in the p element.

## How it works...

The HTML code of index.html is almost clear. We have created three combo boxes and a p element. Each element has been assigned an ID: countryList, stateList, townList, and information respectively.

In the jQuery code, we have added a `change` event listener for all select elements that call a function `getList()`. `getList()` defines two variables: URL and target. Then, it gets the ID and the value of the element whose value is changed. Next, is a `switch` case where the ID of the element is checked in four different cases. If the value from the combo box with ID `countryList` is selected, we set the `find` parameter in the URL to `states` and id parameter as its value. Similarly for `stateList` box, `find` is set to `towns` and for selectbox `townList`, we set the `find` parameter to `information` because on selecting a town we need to show information related to it. In the default case, `find` is set to `country` so that it gets all the countries from the database and fills them in first combo box. Along with setting the URL we also set the target element in which data will be inserted.

After the `switch` case, an AJAX `GET` request is sent from jQuery to the PHP file `results.php`. The response received from `results.php` will be inserted in the target element.

Let's go through the code of `results.php` now. This script first connects to our `exampleDB`. Then, we fetch the value of the `find` key from the `$_GET` Superglobal. A `switch` case checks the value of the `$find` variable and creates a query accordingly. If `find` is set to `states` it creates a query to retrieve data from the `states` table based on `countryId`. If case is `information`, it queries the `information` table for the `id` of a particular town.

Once the results are retrieved from the database, a `while` loop is used to iterate over them and a formatted HTML is sent back to the browser where jQuery inserts it into the appropriate target element.

# Checking username availability from database

We will write an example of a registration form that will match a user-entered name against all other names in the database and will notify the user whether that username is available or not.

## Getting ready

Create a folder for this recipe inside the `Chapter8` directory and name it as `Recipe4`. Open phpMyAdmin and create a new table named `users` with the following structure and data.

```
CREATE TABLE `users` (
  `id` int(11) NOT NULL AUTO_INCREMENT,
  `username` varchar(32) NOT NULL,
  `password` varchar(32) NOT NULL,
  PRIMARY KEY (`id`)
);
```

```
    INSERT INTO `users` (`id`, `username`, `password`) VALUES
(1, 'holmes', 'sherlockholmes'),
(2, 'watson', 'johnwatson'),
(3, 'sati', 'pranay'),
(4, 'mantu', 'ajayjoshi'),
(5, 'sahji', 'brijsah'),
(6, 'vijay', 'vijayjoshi'),
(7, 'brij', 'brijsah'),
(8, 'arjun', 'samant'),
(9, 'jyotsna', 'sonawane'),
(12, 'ravindra', 'pokharia'),
(13, 'prakash', 'joshi'),
(14, 'sahji2', 'aloklal'),
(15, 'basant', 'bhandari')
```

## How to do it...

1.  Create a file named `index.html` in the `Recipe4` folder. In this file, create two textboxes for login name and password. Next to the login name, create an anchor that will check the username on clicking it. Another element next to it will show whether that login name is available or not.

```html
<html>
  <head>
    <title>Check Username</title>
    <style type="text/css">
    body{ font-family: "Trebuchet MS", Verdana, Arial;
        width:555px; }
    input,textarea { vertical-align:top; }
label{ float:left; width:150px;}
    #error {font-weight:bold; color:#ff0000;}
    </style>
  </head>
  <body>
    <fieldset>
      <legend><strong>Add a function</strong></legend>
      <form action="" method="post" id="loginForm">
        <p>
          <label>Username </label>
          <input type="text" name="loginName" id="loginName"/>
          <a href="#" id="check"><strong>Check</strong></a>
          <span id="status" style="float:right;"></span>
        </p>
        <p>
```

```
            <label>Password</label>
            <input type="password" name="password"/>
          </p>
          <p>
            <span id="error"></span>
          </p>
          <p>
            <input type="submit" value="Save" name="dos"
               id="dosave"/>
          </p>
        </form>
      </fieldset>
    </body>
  </html>
```

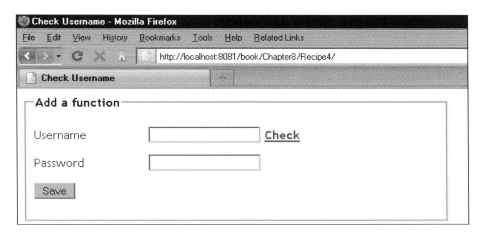

2. Now include the `jquery.js` file first. Next, write an event handler function that will be executed when the user clicks on the element with `check` ID. It will send an AJAX request to the PHP file, `check.php`, which will return either `true` or `false` depending on whether the username is available or not. Another event handler is for the `submit` event of the form that will allow the form to be submitted when the user has chosen an available username.

```
<script type="text/javascript" src="../jquery.js"></script>
<script type="text/javascript">
  $(document).ready(function()
  {
    var checked = false;
    $('#check').click(function()
    {
        $('#error').empty();
```

```
          var inputValue = $('#loginName').val();
          if(jQuery.trim(inputValue) == ''){return false; }
          $.post(
            'check.php',
            { username : inputValue },
            function(data)
            {
              if(data)
              {
                checked = true;
                $('#status').html('Username is available');
              }
              else
              {
                checked = false;
                $('#status').html('Username not available');
                return false;
              }
            }
          );
        });
        $('#loginForm').submit(function()
        {
          if(checked == false)
          {
            $('#error').html('Kindly check the username');
            return false;
          }
          else
          {
            return true;
          }
        });
        $('#loginName').focus(function()
        {
          checked == false;
        });
      });
    </script>
```

3. Create another file and name it as `check.php`. This file will check the values supplied by jQuery in the `users` table and will return `true` or `false`.

```php
<?php
$mysqli = new mysqli('localhost', 'root', '', 'exampleDB');
$selectQuery = 'SELECT username as user FROM users WHERE
username="'.$_POST['username'].'"';
$result = $mysqli->query($selectQuery);
if($result)
{
  if ($result->num_rows > 0)
  {
    echo false;
  }
  else
  {
    echo true;
  }
}
else
{
  echo false;
}
?>
```

4. Run the `index.html` file in the browser and enter a username that is already in the database and click on the **Check** link. You will see an error message **Username not available**. Entering an available username will show the message **Username is available**. Trying to submit the form without checking the username will display an error **Kindly check the username**.

## How it works...

On clicking the **Check** link an AJAX request is sent to `check.php` file. This file checks the `users` table for that username. If there are more than zero records in the table we can be sure that the username is already in use and we return false, otherwise we return true.

jQuery's `success` callback function checks the value provided by PHP and displays an error message accordingly.

Variable `checked` is used to prevent the form submission if it takes place without checking a username. Only if a username is available is the variable set to `true` and the form submission is allowed.

## There's more...

### Alternative methods for implementation

In this recipe, we are checking the username on the click of a button. The same check can be implemented on the `onkeydown` event of the textbox too. This has been left as an exercise for you.

# Paginating data for large record sets

It is best to break down a long list into separate pages and navigate them with buttons such as **Previous**, **Next**, and specific page numbers. In this recipe, we will take a long list of HTML elements and will paginate them into separate pages with a fixed number of items per page. We will also provide the user with options to jump to any page using a select box.

## Getting ready

Create a folder for this recipe inside the `Chapter8` directory and name it as `Recipe5`. Using phpMyAdmin, create a table named `movies` with the following structure:

```
CREATE TABLE IF NOT EXISTS `movies` (
  `id` int(11) NOT NULL AUTO_INCREMENT,
  `movieName` varchar(64) NOT NULL,
  PRIMARY KEY (`id`)
);
```

For pagination, we will require a long list so as to enter some movie names in this table, using phpMyAdmin. For this example, we have already inserted 100 names in the table. You can use the `movies.sql` file that will be supplied along with this book to populate the table. Names of movies in this list have been taken from: `http://www.thebest100lists.com/best100movies/`.

## How to do it...

1. Create a file named `index.php` inside the `Recipe5` folder. In this file, connect to the database and fetch all the movie names from the `movies` table and create an unordered list with movie names as the list items. Also, create a DIV with ID `navigation` where the pagination buttons will be placed. Some CSS properties are also defined in the `head` section for a proper look and feel.

```html
<html>
  <head>
<title>Top 100 movies</title>
    <style type="text/css">
    body{ font-family: "Trebuchet MS", Verdana,
        Arial;width:400px;}
    h3{ margin:0;padding:0;}
    ul{ list-style:none;margin:10px 0;padding:0;
        border:1px solid #000;}
    li{ padding:5px;}
    #prev{ float:left;width:100px;}
    #next{ float:right;width:100px;text-align:right;}
    #navigation {float: left; border: 1px solid; padding: 5px;
                width: 97%;}
    #navigation>div { float: left; text-align: center;
                    margin-left:40px; 200px;}
    select { width:100px; }
    strong { cursor:pointer; text-decoration:underline;}
    </style>
  </head>
  <body>
    <h3>Top 100 movies voted by people</h3>
    <a href="http://www.thebest100lists.com/best100movies/">
     http://www.thebest100lists.com/best100movies/</a>
    <ul id="list">
<?php
    $mysqli = new mysqli('localhost', 'root', '', 'exampleDB');
    if ($mysqli->connect_errno)
    {
      die('Connect Error: ' . $mysqli->connect_errno);
    }
    $query = 'SELECT movieName FROM movies';

    if ($mysqli->query($query))
    {
      $result = $mysqli->query($query);
      if($result->num_rows > 0)
      {
        while($row = $result->fetch_array())
```

```
        {
          echo '<li>'.$row[0].'</li>';
        }
      }
      else
      {
        echo 'No records';
      }
    }
    else
    {
      echo 'Query Unsuccessful';
    }
?>
    </ul>
    <div id="navigation"></div>
    <p> </p>
  </body>
</html>
```

2. The previous screenshot is a partial capture of what the page will look like. It will display all the 100 movies on the browser. Include the `jquery.js` file and write the jQuery code for paginating this list. First, define the number of items per page and total pages that will be displayed. In this example, we have defined the number of items per page as ten, which means that in total ten pages will be available. Then, define `createNavigation` function that will create links for the previous page, the next page, and a combo box with all page numbers. Then, write a function `setDataAndEvents` that will have event handler functions for these navigation links. Clicking on a navigation link or selecting a page number from the combo box will call another function `goToPage` that will display the movies for that page only.

```javascript
<script type="text/javascript" src="../jquery.js"></script>
<script type="text/javascript">
  $(document).ready(function()
  {
    var totalMovies =  $('#list>li').length;
    var moviesPerPage = 10;
    var totalPages = Math.ceil(totalMovies/moviesPerPage);

    createNavigation();
    setDataAndEvents();
    function createNavigation()
    {
      var navHTML = '<strong id="prev">Previous</strong>';
      navHTML+= '<div>';
      navHTML+= '<select id="goTo">';
      navHTML+= '<option value="">Go to page</option>';
      for(var i = 0; i< totalPages; i++)
      {
        navHTML+= '<option value="'+(i+1)+'">Page '+(i+1)+'
          </option>';
      }
      navHTML+= '</select>';
      navHTML+= '</div>';
      navHTML+= '<strong id="next">Next</strong>';

      $('#navigation').html(navHTML);
      $('#prev').hide();
      $('#goTo').val(1);
    }

    function setDataAndEvents()
    {
      $('#list').data('currentPage', 1);
      $('#list>li:gt(' + (moviesPerPage-1) + ')').hide();
```

```
$('#prev').click(function()
{
  var current = $('#list').data('currentPage');
  goToPage(--current);
});

$('#next').click(function(){
  var current = $('#list').data('currentPage');
  goToPage(++current);
});

$('#goTo').change(function()
{
  if($.trim($(this).val()) == '') return;
  goToPage($(this).val());
});
}

function goToPage(pageNumber)
{
  if(pageNumber == 1) $('#prev').hide();
        else $('#prev').show();
  if(pageNumber == totalPages) $('#next').hide(); else
$('#next').show();

  $('#list').data('currentPage', pageNumber);
  $('#goTo').val(pageNumber);
  var from = (pageNumber - 1) * moviesPerPage;
  var to = from + (moviesPerPage - 1);
  $('#list>li').show();
  $('#list>li:lt(' + (from) + ')').hide();
  $('#list>li:gt(' + (to) + ')').hide();

}
});
</script>
```

3.  Now run the file in your browser and you will see list of ten movies and navigation links available at the bottom. The page number will be set as 1 in the combo box. Because it will be the first page, only the **Next** button will be available. Clicking the **Next** button will change the list as well as page number at the bottom. Going to the last page will hide the **Next** button.

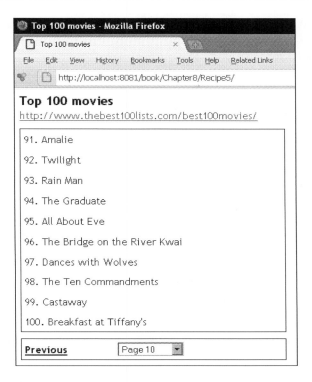

## How it works...

First of all, we retrieve the list of all movies from the database using `query` method of `mysqli` class. Then by iterating over results, we create an unordered list with ID `list`, using each movie name as a list item. After the list, there is a DIV with ID `navigation`, which will contain the navigation links. After the page is loaded, jQuery code executes. First, we get the length of all `li` element and assign it to the `totalMovies` variable. Then, we set the `moviesPerPage` variable to 10. After this, we calculate the total number of pages by dividing `totalMovies` with `moviesPerPage`.

Now, the `createNavigation` function is called. This function creates two elements inside the `navigation` DIV that act as **Previous** and **Next** buttons and assigns those `prev` and `next` IDs respectively. Another select element is created with ID `goTo`. It has page numbers as the options. Once these elements are created, they are inserted inside the DIV with ID `navigation`. After that, the **Previous** button is hidden and the value of select box `goTo` is set to 1.

Next is the `setDataAndEvents` function. To navigate between the previous and next pages, we need to know the current page number and then increase or decrease it for previous or next page respectively. This is achieved by jQuery's `data` function. We save data with the `ul` list having `currentPage` as its key with initial value set to 1. The next line uses the `:gt` selector that hides all `li` elements that have an index more than 10 (first page).

Event handlers for **Previous** and **Next** buttons come next. On clicking the **Previous** button, we get the saved value of `currentPage`; decrease it by 1 and pass it to the `goToPage` function. Similarly, value of `currentPage` is increased by 1 for **Next** button and passed to the function `goToPage`. The select box has a `change` event handler attached to it that takes the currently selected value and passes it to the `goToPage` function.

Function `goToPage` receives the passed value in the `pageNumber` variable. Value of this variable is the page where we have to navigate. Here we put two checks. If the user is on the first page, we hide the **Previous** button, and on last page, we hide the **Next** button. Then, we update the value of `currentPage` and then set the value of select box to `pageNumber`. To decide what list items are to be displayed for that page, we calculate two variables: `from` and `to`. The final three lines hide all other list items except the ones which do not fall in range between `from` and `to`.

# Adding auto-suggest functionality to a textbox

Perhaps the simplest example of explaining auto-suggest is the Google homepage. When you type a query in the search box, it displays a list of queries beneath it by matching your search terms.

We will create an example with the same functionality where text entered by the user will be matched against user names in a table and matching results will be displayed to the user in the form of a list just below the textbox in form of suggestions. The user will be able to use arrow keys to navigate up or down in a list and select a name from the list.

## Getting ready

Create a folder named `Recipe6` inside the `Chapter8` directory. To be able to match user input with the database, we will require a table. Open phpMyAdmin and create a new table named `users` with the following structure and data:

```
CREATE TABLE `users` (
  `id` int(11) NOT NULL AUTO_INCREMENT,
  `username` varchar(32) NOT NULL,
  `password` varchar(32) NOT NULL,
  PRIMARY KEY (`id`)
);
```

```
INSERT INTO `users` (`id`, `username`, `password`) VALUES
(1, 'holmes', 'sherlockholmes'),
(2, 'watson', 'johnwatson'),
(3, 'sati', 'pranay'),
(4, 'mantu', 'ajayjoshi'),
(5, 'sahji', 'brijsah'),
(6, 'vijay', 'vijayjoshi'),
(7, 'brij', 'brijsah'),
(8, 'arjun', 'samant'),
(9, 'jyotsna', 'sonawane'),
(12, 'ravindra', 'pokharia'),
(13, 'prakash', 'joshi'),
(14, 'sahji2', 'aloklal'),
(15, 'basant', 'bhandari'),
(16, 'ajay', 'gamer')
```

## How to do it...

1. Create a file named `index.html` inside the `Recipe6` folder. In this file, create a DIV with class `autosuggest`. Inside this DIV, create a textbox with ID `suggest`, and an unordered list with ID `suggestions`. This list will display the matched results. Now, create an image tag that will have a spinning loading indicator that will be displayed while script is busy getting data from the database. Finally, create a span element with ID `error` that will be displayed when there are no matched results.

```html
<html>
  <head>
    <title>Autocomplete</title>
    <link rel="stylesheet" type="text/css" href="style.css">
  </head>
  <body>
    <div class="autosuggest">
      <input type="text" id="suggest"/>
      <ul id="suggestions">
      </ul>
      <img src="ajax-loader.gif" alt="loading" title="loading"
          id="loader"/>
      <span id="error"></span>
    </div>
  </body>
</html>
```

2. Note that we have referred to a `style.css` file in the `head` section. CSS attributes are very important for this example as we have to position the `ul`, just under the textbox. Create a new file named `style.css` and place the following CSS properties in it:

```css
body{ font-family: "Trebuchet MS", verdana, arial;width:400px;margin:0 auto; }
.autosuggest
{
  width:200px;
  top:5px;
  position:relative;
}
input { width:200px;}
#suggestions
{
  position:absolute;
  list-style:none;
  margin:0;
  padding:0;
  width:200px;
  display:none;
  background-color:#ECECF6;
  top:20px;
  left:0px;
}
#suggestions li
{
  cursor:pointer;
  padding:5px;
  border-right:1px solid #000;
  border-bottom:1px solid #000;
  border-left:1px solid #000;

}
.active
{
  background-color:red;
  color:#fff;
}
#error
{
  top:25px;
  font-weight:bold;
  color:#ff0000;
```

```
}
#loader
{
  position:absolute;
  top:2px;
  right:0;
  display:none;
}
```

3. Focusing on jQuery now, add the `jquery.js` file before the closing of the `body` tag. Now define four event handlers that will get the suggestions from the database and display them in a list at a proper position. Call function `getSuggestions` on `keyup`. This is the core function that picks up keystrokes and gets matching results using an AJAX request. Value of textbox is sent through an AJAX request to a PHP file, `suggestions.php`. On receiving the `results` function, `showSuggestions` executes, which creates a list from received data and displays it.

4. Function `navigateList` will be executed on `keydown` event. It will take care of the navigation by adding functionality for up and down arrow keys and the *Enter* key for selecting a list item. Next are two functions for mouse movements. The first function `listHover` will execute whenever the mouse pointer enters or leaves a list item and will change the look and feel of list items. `listClick` function will be used to fill the textbox with the selected value when a mouse is clicked against a list item.

```
<script type="text/javascript" src="../jquery.js"></script>
<script type="text/javascript">
  $(document).ready(function()
  {
    var xhr;
    $('#suggest').keyup(getSuggestions);
    $('#suggest').keydown(navigateList);
    $('#suggestions>li').live(0'mouseover mouseout click',
      listHover);

    function getSuggestions(event)
    {
      var value = jQuery.trim($(this).val());
      if(value == '' || event.which == 27)
      {
        $('#suggestions').empty().hide();
        $('#loader').hide();
      }

      if((event.which >= 65 && event.which <= 90) ||
        event.which == 8 || event.which == 46)
      {
```

```
        $('#loader').show();
        if(xhr) xhr.abort();
        if(value.length >= 1)
        {
          xhr = $.getJSON
            (
             'suggestions.php',
             { input : value },
             showSuggestions
            );
        }
        else
        {
          $('#loader').hide();
        }
      }
    }


    function showSuggestions(data)
    {
      if(data == false)
      {
        $('#error').html('No results').show();
        $('#suggestions').empty().hide();
      }
      else
      {
        var str = '';
        $('#error').empty().hide();
        for(var i=0; i < data.length; i++)
        {
          str+= '<li>'+data[i]+'</li>';
        }
        $('#suggestions').html(str).show();
      }
      $('#loader').hide();
    }


    function navigateList(event)
    {
      switch(event.which)
      {
        case 38:  //up arrow
          if($('#suggestions>li.active').length > 0)
          {
```

```
              $('#suggestions>li.active').removeClass('active').
                prev().addClass('active');
          }
          else
          {
              $('#suggestions>li:last').addClass('active');
          }
       break;

       case 40:   //down arrow
          if($('#suggestions>li.active').length > 0)
          {
              $('#suggestions>li.active').removeClass('active').
                next().addClass('active');
          }
          else
          {
              $('#suggestions>li:first').addClass('active');
          }
       break;

       case 13:     //enter
              $('#suggest').val($('#suggestions>li.active').
                html());
            $('#suggestions').empty().hide();
          break;
      }
    }

    function listHover(event)
    {
       if (event.type == 'mouseover')
       {
          $('#suggestions>li.active').removeClass('active');
       }
       $(this).toggleClass('active');

       if(event.type == 'click')
       {
          $('#suggest').val($(this).html());
          $(this).parent().empty().hide();
          $('#suggest').focus();
       }
      }
    });
</script>
```

5. Create another file named `suggestions.php` in the same directory. Connect to the `exampleDB` database in this file, and using the value of textbox, write a query to fetch results from the database. Once results are retrieved, JSON is created and is sent back to the browser where it is displayed by jQuery.

6. Run the `index.html` file in the browser and press any key. The AJAX request will try to get the matching results and will show them in the list. Below is a sample response after pressing key **a**:

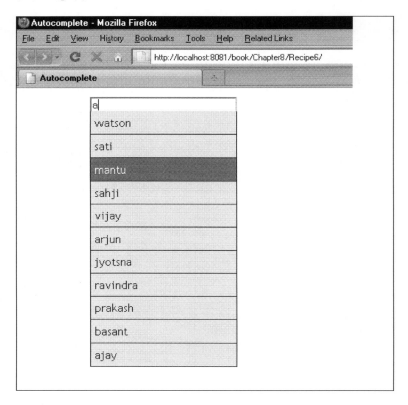

## How it works...

First, we will make sure that the `ul` always appears below the textbox. There is a clean and easy way to do it. First, make the CSS position of the outer DIV relative. This has been done in the CSS file. Now you can make the position of any element inside this DIV absolute, relative to the DIV. So, the following CSS properties of `ul` will place it just below the textbox.

```
position:absolute;
top:20px;
left:0px;
```

Rest of the properties define the look and feel for the `ul`. Similarly, we place the loaded image absolutely to the right.

Let us implement `autocomplete` now. First is the `keyup` event handler for the textbox. It executes a function `getSuggestions`. This function gets the value of the textbox and continues only if the value is not empty. Then, it checks which keys are pressed using `event.which` that is provided by jQuery. Pressing keys between *a-z*, *A-Z*, *Delete* key, or the *Backspace* key will change the value of textbox. So, we take this value from the textbox and send it with an AJAX request to the `suggestions.php` file. A callback function `showSuggestions` is provided for handling the response. `suggestions.php` returns a JSON that is used in `showSuggestions`. The response can be an array of matching names or `false` in case of any error or upon finding no records. If the response from `showSuggestions` is `false`, we show an error message. Otherwise we iterate over the response array and create a list item for each element in the array. After all list items are created, we insert them into the `ul` with ID `suggestions`. Just before the request is sent, we show the loading indicator image and after processing is done in `showSuggestions` we hide it.

We want to be able to use arrow keys to move up or down in the list and select a value by pressing *Enter*. Moving up and down in the list will highlight the item by adding a CSS class active to it. For this purpose, another event handler `navigateList` has been defined for the `keyDown` event. This function has a `switch` statement with three cases. First one is for Up arrow key whose key code is 38. It checks if any `li` element has already CSS class `active` or not. If not, it adds the `active` class to the last element that highlights the last item in the list. If a list item already has an `active` class attached to it, then on pressing the Up arrow key, an `if` condition is executed that removes the `active` class from the highlighted element and adds the same class to its previous element.

The code for the Down arrow key works in a similar way. If no element is highlighted and the Down arrow key is pressed, the first element of the list elements is selected If an item is already `active` and Down arrow key is pressed again, the `active` class is removed from it and is added to the next element.

The third and final case is for the *Enter* key, which has key code 13. On pressing *Enter*, the HTML of the currently-highlighted element is taken and is set as the value of the textbox. After that, the `ul` suggestions are emptied and hidden.

After keyboard navigation, we need to take care of mouse selections too. Hovering over a list item should add an `active` class to it and moving the mouse pointer out of it should remove this class. Also, clicking an item should select its value in the textbox. As no list item is present inside the `ul` tag at the beginning, we use the `live` method to add the `listHover` event handler. This function will execute whenever the mouse pointer enters a list item, leaves it, or it is clicked. In this function, if the event is `mouseover`, we first remove the `active` class from any previously active item. Then we use the `toggleClass` function to add or remove the `active` class from the current item. This will make a list item active when mouse pointer is over it and will remove the `active` class when the mouse pointer is taken away.

Finally, `listHover` also checks if a `li` was clicked, we take the active item's HTML and insert it into the textbox. Then the `ul` is emptied and hidden and focus is given to textbox.

On the server side, the PHP file `suggestions.php` receives the value of the textbox and queries the `users` table in the database to find all the matching records.

```
$query = 'SELECT username FROM users where username like "%'.
  $_GET['input']. '%"';
```

Use of `%` before and after the textbox value in our query indicates that any characters may precede or follow the value. This means if the input value was "ss", it will match both "pass" and "passed". After getting the results from the database, we iterate over them and create an array. This array is converted to JSON and echoed back to the browser.

Another important thing to note is variable `xhr`, which we have declared at the beginning of the file. If the user presses multiple keys, that number of requests will hit the server simultaneously. To avoid this, we assign `$.getJSON` to variable `xhr`. Now before sending a request to the server, we can abort any previous request using the `abort` method of `xmlHttpRequest` so that only the current request is processed.

## See also

▶ *Creating keyboard shortcuts in Chapter 1*

# Creating a tag cloud

A tag cloud is a visual representation of tags or keywords where each tag's size or color is determined by its weight. Consider a blog with many articles. Each article can be tagged to a category like PHP, jQuery, XML, JSON, and so on. Out of these, if PHP category has 50 articles, jQuery has 30, XML 10, and JSON has 22 articles, we can say that PHP has most weight and XML has the least weight. If we wanted to present these tags in a graphical manner so that a more weighted item is more emphasized, we can do so by setting their respective font size in proportion to their weights.

We will create a similar example where we have a list of cities in a database and each has a rating out of 100. We will present these tags in the form of a tag cloud such as with their sizes depending on their rating.

## Getting ready

Create a folder named `Recipe7` inside the `Chapter8` directory. For the list of cities and their ratings, use the following SQL query in phpMyAdmin to create a new table named `cities`:

```
CREATE TABLE `cities` (
  `id` int(3) NOT NULL AUTO_INCREMENT,
```

```
   `cityName` varchar(32) NOT NULL,
   `cityRating` int(3) NOT NULL,
   PRIMARY KEY (`id`)
);

INSERT INTO `cities` (`id`, `cityName`, `cityRating`) VALUES
(1, 'Udaipur', 71),
(2, 'Leh', 55),
(3, 'Mahabaleshwar', 28),
(4, 'Mount Abu', 31),
(5, 'Rishikesh', 15),
(6, 'Hampi', 81),
(7, 'Matheran', 29),
(8, 'Manali', 85),
(9, 'Mysore', 33),
(10, 'Jaipur', 55),
(11, 'Munnar', 89),
(12, 'Bangalore', 66),
(13, 'Wayanad', 42),
(14, 'Amritsar', 29),
(15, 'Gangtok', 69),
(16, 'Havelock Islands', 27),
(17, 'DharamShala', 57),
(18, 'Kashmir', 78),
(19, 'Tirupati', 22),
(20, 'Goa', 75)
```

## How to do it...

1. Create a file named `index.html` in the `Recipe7` folder. In this file, create a DIV with `cloud` ID and define some CSS styles for DIV and anchor elements that will be created in the page.

```html
<html>
  <head>
    <title>Create a tag cloud</title>
    <style type="text/css">
    body { font-family:"Trebuchet MS",Verdana,Arial; }
    div
    {
      width:600px;
      border:1px solid;
      float:left;
      position:relative;
    }
```

```
      a
      {
        float:left;
        text-decoration:none;
        padding:0px 5px;
        text-transform:lowercase;
      }
      span { font-size:12px; }
      </style>
    </head>
    <body>
      <h3>Popularity of Indian Tourist Destinations</h3>
      <div id="cloud"></div>
    </body>
  </html>
```

2.  Include the `jquery.js` file before closing the `body` tag. In jQuery code, send an AJAX request to the PHP file `tags.php`. Callback function is `createTagCloud` for this AJAX call. This function iterates over the response and creates tags on the page.

```
<script type="text/javascript" src="../jquery.js"></script>
<script type="text/javascript">
  $(document).ready(function()
  {
    $.getJSON(
      'tags.php',
      {},
      createTagCloud
    );
  });

  function createTagCloud(response)
  {
    var str = '', i=0;
    $.each(response.tags, function(index, tag)
    {
      var color = i%2 == 0 ? 'color:#A52A2A' : 'color:#6495ED';
      var fontSize = ((parseInt(tag.rating,10)/30));
      str+= '<a href="#" style="font-size:'+fontSize+'em;'+color+'
          " title="' + tag.city + '">' + tag.city + '</a>';
      i++;
    });
    $('#cloud').html(str);
  }
</script>
```

3. Create another file named `tags.php`. This file will connect to the database and will fetch the city information from the `cities` table. A JSON string will be created from the database results that will be sent to the browser where jQuery receives it and handles the tag creation.

```php
<?php
$mysqli = new mysqli('localhost', 'root', '', 'exampleDB');

if (mysqli_connect_errno())
{
    die('Unable to connect!');
}
$query = 'SELECT cityName, cityRating FROM cities';
$arr = array();
if ($result = $mysqli->query($query))
{
    if ($result->num_rows > 0)
  {
    while($row = $result->fetch_assoc())
    {
      array_push($arr, array('city' => $row['cityName'],
          'rating' => $row['cityRating']));
    }
  }
}
$result = array('tags' => $arr);
header('Content-Type:text/json');
echo json_encode($result);
?>
```

4. Run the `index.php` file in the browser and you will see a collection of city names in various sizes.

## How it works...

Once the document is ready, an AJAX request is sent to the PHP file `tags.php` using `$.getJSON` method. The callback function for this request is `createTagCloud`. In the `tags.php` file, a SELECT query is executed which fetches all city names and their ratings. Then we use the `fetch_assoc` method to retrieve results from each row and insert them into the `$arr` array.

Once all records are pushed in this array `$arr`, we assign it to an associative array `$result` having tags as the key.

Finally, we set the response type as `text/json` and convert the array `$result` to a JSON string using PHP's `json_encode` method. The JSON will look like the following:

```
{
    "tags":
    [
        {"city":"Udaipur","rating":"71"},
        {"city":"Leh","rating":"55"},
        {"city":"Mahabaleshwar","rating":"28"},
        {"city":"Mount Abu","rating":"31"},
        {"city":"Rishikesh","rating":"15"},
        {"city":"Hampi","rating":"81"},
        {"city":"Matheran","rating":"29"},
        {"city":"Manali","rating":"85"},
        {"city":"Mysore","rating":"33"},
        {"city":"Jaipur","rating":"55"},
        {"city":"Munnar","rating":"89"},
        {"city":"Bangalore","rating":"66"},
        {"city":"Wayanad","rating":"42"},
        {"city":"Amritsar","rating":"29"},
        {"city":"Gangtok","rating":"69"},
        {"city":"Havelock Islands","rating":"27"},
        {"city":"DharamShala","rating":"57"},
        {"city":"Kashmir","rating":"78"},
        {"city":"Tirupati","rating":"22"},
        {"city":"Goa","rating":"75"}
    ]
}
```

Now the response is available in the `createTagCloud` function inside a variable named `response`. We use jQuery's `each` method to iterate over the `tags` array in this JSON. For each element, we set different colors for alternate tags by checking the value of variable `i`. For deciding the font size, we divide the rating by 30. You can choose any number for division, depending on how large or small the font sizes need to be. Once the font size and colors are set, we create anchor tags, set these values, and keep on appending these anchors to a variable `str`. After the array has been traversed fully, we insert the value of variable `str` into DIV with ID `cloud`. The end result is a beautiful tag cloud.

## See also

- *Creating JSON in PHP in Chapter 4*
- *Accessing data from JSON in jQuery in Chapter 4*

# 9
# Enhancing your Site with PHP and jQuery

In this chapter, we will cover:

- ▸ Sending cross-domain requests using server proxy
- ▸ Making cross-domain requests with jQuery
- ▸ Creating an endless scrolling page
- ▸ Creating a jQuery plugin
- ▸ Displaying RSS feeds with jQuery and PHP

## Introduction

In this final chapter, we will look at some advanced techniques that can be used to enhance the functionality of web applications.

We will create a few examples where we will search for images the from Flickr and videos from YouTube using their respective APIs. We will parse a RSS feed XML using jQuery and learn to create an endless scrolling page like Google reader or the new interface of Twitter.

Besides this, you will also learn to create a jQuery plugin, which you can use independently in your applications.

# Sending cross-domain requests using server proxy

Browsers do not allow scripts to send cross-domain requests due to security reasons. This means a script at domain http://www.abc.com cannot send AJAX requests to http://www.xyz.com.

This recipe will show how you can overcome this limitation by using a PHP script on the server side. We will create an example that will search Flickr for images. Flickr will return a JSON, which will be parsed by jQuery and images will be displayed on the page. The following screenshot shows a JSON response from Flickr:

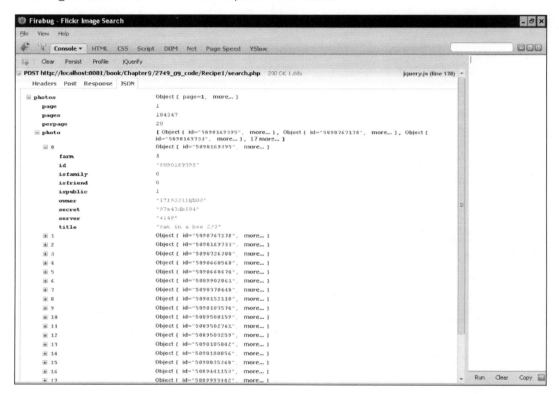

## Getting ready

Create a directory for this chapter and name it as Chapter9. In this directory, create a folder named Recipe1.

Also get an API key from Flickr by signing up at http://www.flickr.com/services/api/keys/.

## How to do it...

1. Create a file inside the `Recipe1` folder and name it as `index.html`. Write the HTML code to create a form with three fields: tag, number of images, and image size. Also create an `ul` element inside which the results will be displayed.

```html
<html>
  <head>
    <title>Flickr Image Search</title>
    <style type="text/css">
      body { font-family:"Trebuchet MS",verdana,arial;
             width:900px; }
      fieldset { width:333px; }
      ul{   margin:0;padding:0;list-style:none; }
      li{   padding:5px; }
      span{ display:block;float:left;width:150px; }
      #results li{ float:left; }
      .error{ font-weight:bold; color:#ff0000; }
    </style>
  </head>
  <body>
    <form id="searchForm">
      <fieldset>
        <legend>Search Criteria</legend>
        <ul>
          <li>
            <span>Tag</span>
            <input type="text" name="tag" id="tag"/>
          </li>
          <li>
            <span>Number of images</span>
            <select name="numImages" id="numImages">
              <option value="20">20</option>
              <option value="30">30</option>
              <option value="40">40</option>
              <option value="50">50</option>
            </select>
          </li>
          <li>
            <span>Select a size</span>
            <select id="size">
              <option value="s">Small</option>
              <option value="t">Thumbnail</option>
              <option value="-">Medium</option>
```

```
                <option value="b">Large</option>
                <option value="o">Original</option>
              </select>
            </li>
            <li>
              <input type="button" value="Search" id="search"/>
            </li>
          </ul>
        </fieldset>
      </form>
      <ul id="results">
      </ul>
    </body>
</html>
```

The following screenshot shows the form created:

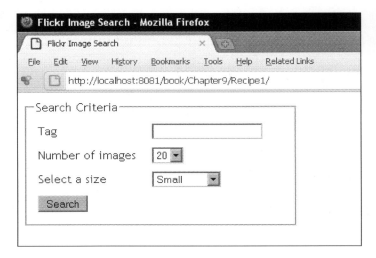

2. Include the `jquery.js` file. Then, enter the jQuery code that will send the AJAX request to a PHP file `search.php`. Values of form elements will be posted with an AJAX request. A callback function `showImages` is also defined that actually reads the JSON response and displays the images on the page.

```
<script type="text/javascript" src="../jquery.js"></script>
<script type="text/javascript">
  $(document).ready(function()
  {
    $('#search').click(function()
```

```
{
  if($.trim($('#tag').val()) == '')
  {
    $('#results').html('<li class="error">Please provide
       search criteria</li>');
    return;
  }
  $.post(
    'search.php',
    $('#searchForm').serialize(),
    showImages,
    'json'
  );
});

function showImages(response)
{
  if(response['stat'] == 'ok')
  {
    var photos = response.photos.photo;
    var str= '';
    $.each(photos, function(index,value)
    {
      var farmId = value.farm;
      var serverId = value.server;
      var id = value.id;
      var secret = value.secret;
      var size = $('#size').val();
      var title = value.title;

      var imageUrl = 'http://farm' + farmId +
        '.static.flickr.com/' + serverId + '/' + id + '_' +
         secret + '_' + size + '.jpg';
      str+= '<li>';
      str+= '<img src="' + imageUrl + '" alt="'
                 + title + '" />';
      str+= '</li>';
    });

    $('#results').html(str);
  }
  else
```

```
        {
          $('#results').html('<li class="error">an error
            occured</li>');
        }
      }
    });
  </script>
```

3. Create another file named `search.php`. The PHP code in this file will contact the Flickr API with specified search criteria. Flickr will return a **JSON** that will be sent back to the browser where jQuery will display it on the page.

```php
<?php

define('API_KEY', 'your-API-key-here');
  $url = 'http://api.flickr.com/services/rest/?method=flickr.
photos.search';
$url.= '&api_key='.API_KEY;
  $url.= '&tags='.$_POST['tag'];
  $url.= '&per_page='.$_POST['numImages'];
  $url.= '&format=json';
  $url.= '&nojsoncallback=1';

  header('Content-Type:text/json;');
  echo file_get_contents($url);
?>
```

4. Now, run the `index.html` file in your browser, enter a tag to search in the form, and select the number of images to be retrieved and the image size. Click on the **Search** button. A few seconds later you will see the images from Flickr displayed on the page:

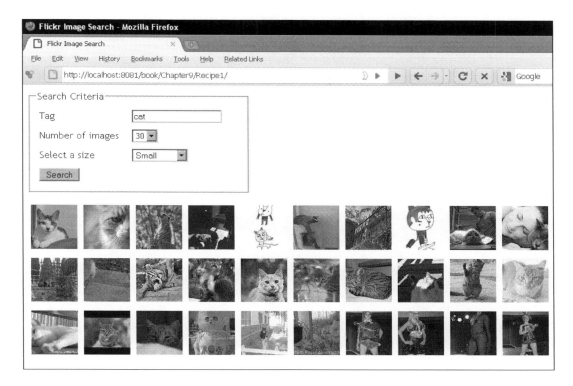

# How it works...

On clicking the **Search** button, form values are sent to the PHP file `search.php`. Now, we have to contact Flickr and search for images. Flickr API provides several methods for accessing images. We will use the method `flickr.photos.search` to search by tag name. Along with the method name we will have to send the following parameters in the URL:

- ▸ `api_key`: An API key is mandatory. You can get one from: `http://www.flickr.com/services/api/keys/`.

- ▸ `tags`: The tags to search for. These can be comma-separated. This value will be the value of textbox tag.

- ▸ `per_page`: Number of images in a page. This can be a maximum of 99. Its value will be the value of select box `numImages`.

- ▸ `format`: It can be JSON, XML, and so on. For this example, we will use JSON.

- ▸ `nojsoncallback`: Its value will be set to 1 if we don't want Flickr to wrap the JSON in a function wrapper.

Once the URL is complete we can contact Flickr to get the results. To get the results we will use the PHP function `file_get_contents`, which will get the results JSON from the specified URL. This JSON will be echoed to the browser.

jQuery will receive the JSON in callback function `showImages`. This function first checks the status of the response. If the response is OK, we get the photo elements from the response and we can iterate over them using jQuery's `$.each` method. To display an image, we will have to get its URL first, which will be created by combining different values of the photo object. According to Flickr API specification, an image URL can be constructed in the following manner:

```
http://farm{farm-id}.static.flickr.com/{server-id}/{id}_{secret}_
[size].jpg
```

So we get the `farmId`, `serverId`, `id`, and `secret` from the photo element. The size can be one of the following:

- s (small square)
- t (thumbnail)
- - (medium)
- b (large)
- o (original image)

We have already selected the image size from the select box in the form. By combining all these values, we now have the Flickr image URL. We wrap it in a `li` element and repeat the process for all images. Finally, we insert the constructed images into the results `li`.

## See also

- *Making cross-domain requests with jQuery*

# Making cross-domain requests with jQuery

The previous recipe demonstrated the use of a PHP file as a proxy for querying cross-domain URLs. This recipe will show the use of JSONP to query cross-domain URLs from jQuery itself.

We will create an example that will search for the videos from YouTube and will display them in a list. Clicking on a video thumbnail will open a new window that will take the user to the YouTube website to show that video.

The following screenshot shows a sample JSON response from YouTube:

```
{
  version: "1.0",
  encoding: "UTF-8",
  - feed: {
      xmlns$app: http://purl.org/atom/app#,
      xmlns: http://www.w3.org/2005/Atom,
      xmlns$media: http://search.yahoo.com/mrss/,
      xmlns$openSearch: http://a9.com/-/spec/opensearchrss/1.0/,
      xmlns$gd: http://schemas.google.com/g/2005,
      xmlns$yt: http://gdata.youtube.com/schemas/2007,
    + id: { _ },
    + updated: { _ },
    + category: [ _ ],
    + title: { _ },
    + logo: { _ },
    + link: [ _ ],
    + author: [ _ ],
    + generator: { _ },
    + openSearch$totalResults: { _ },
    + openSearch$startIndex: { _ },
    + openSearch$itemsPerPage: { _ },
    - entry: [
      - {
          - id: {
              $t: http://gdata.youtube.com/feeds/api/videos/Qit3ALTel0o
            },
          - published: {
              $t: "2007-09-05T14:33:15.000Z"
            },
          + updated: { _ },
          + category: [ _ ],
          - title: {
              $t: "The Mean Kitty Song",
              type: "text"
            },
          + content: { _ },
          - link: [
            - {
                rel: "alternate",
                type: "text/html",
                href: http://www.youtube.com/watch?v=Qit3ALTel0o&feature=youtube_gdata
              },
            - {
                rel: http://gdata.youtube.com/schemas/2007#video.responses,
                type: "application/atom+xml",
                href: http://gdata.youtube.com/feeds/api/videos/Qit3ALTel0o/responses
              },
            - {
                rel: http://gdata.youtube.com/schemas/2007#video.related,
                type: "application/atom+xml",
                href: http://gdata.youtube.com/feeds/api/videos/Qit3ALTel0o/related
              },
            - {
                rel: http://gdata.youtube.com/schemas/2007#mobile,
                type: "text/html",
                href: http://m.youtube.com/details?v=Qit3ALTel0o
              },
            - {
                rel: "self",
                type: "application/atom+xml",
                href: http://gdata.youtube.com/feeds/api/videos/Qit3ALTel0o
              }
            ],
          + author: [ _ ],
          - gd$comments: {
              - gd$feedLink: {
                  href: http://gdata.youtube.com/feeds/api/videos/Qit3ALTel0o/comments,
                  countHint: 177930
                }
            },
          + media$group: { _ },
          - gd$rating: {
              average: 4.7772064,
              max: 5,
              min: 1,
              numRaters: 248333,
              rel: http://schemas.google.com/g/2005#overall
            },
          + yt$statistics: { _ }
        },
      + { _ },
      + { _ },
      + { _ },
      + { _ },
      + { _ },
      + { _ },
      + { _ },
      + { _ },
      + { _ },
      + { _ },
      + { _ },
      + { _ },
      + { _ },
      + { _ },
      + { _ },
      + { _ },
      + { _ },
      + { _ },
      + { _ },
      + { _ },
      + { _ }
      ]
    }
}
```

## Getting ready

Create a folder named Recipe2 inside the Chapter9 directory.

## How to do it...

1. Create a file inside the Recipe2 folder and name it as index.html. Write the HTML code to create a form with a single field query and a DIV with results ID inside which the search results will be displayed.

```html
<html>
  <head>
    <title>Youtube Video Search</title>
    <style type="text/css">
      body {font-family:"Trebuchet MS",verdana,arial;width:900px;}
      fieldset { width:333px; }
      ul{  margin:0;padding:0;list-style:none; }
      li{  padding:5px; }
      span{ display:block;float:left;width:150px; }
      #results ul li{ float:left; background-color:#483D8B;
              color:#fff;margin:5px; width:120px; }
      .error{ font-weight:bold; color:#ff0000; }
      img{ border:0}
    </style>
  </head>
  <body>
    <form id="searchForm">
      <fieldset>
        <legend>Search Criteria</legend>
        <ul>
          <li>
            <span>Enter query</span>
            <input type="text" id="query"/>
          </li>
          <li>
            <input type="button" value="Search" id="search"/>
          </li>
        </ul>
      </fieldset>
    </form>
    <div id="results">
    </div>
  </body>
</html>
```

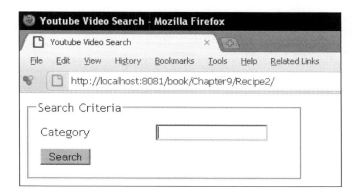

2. Include the `jquery.js` file before closing the `body` tag. Now, write the jQuery code that will take the search query from the textbox and will try to retrieve the results from YouTube. A callback function called `showVideoList` will get the response and will create a list of videos from the response.

```
<script type="text/javascript" src="../jquery.js"></script>
<script type="text/javascript">
  $(document).ready(function()
  {
    $('#search').click(function()
    {
      var query = $.trim($('#query').val());
      if(query == '')
      {
        $('#results').html('<li class="error">Please enter
          a query.</li>');
        return;
      }
      $.get(
        'http://gdata.youtube.com/feeds/api/videos?q=' + query +
          '&alt=json-in-script',
        {},
        showVideoList,
        'jsonp'
      );
    });
  });
  function showVideoList(response)
  {
    var totalResults =
      response['feed']['openSearch$totalResults']['$t'];
    if(parseInt(totalResults,10) > 0)
    {
```

```
                var entries = response.feed.entry;
                var str = '<ul>';
                for(var i=1; i< entries.length; i++)
                {
                  var value = entries[i];
                  var title = value['title']['$t'];
                  var mediaGroup = value['media$group'];
                  var videoURL = mediaGroup['media$player'][0]['url'];


                  var thumbnail = mediaGroup['media$thumbnail'][0]['url'];
                  var thumbnailWidth =
                      mediaGroup['media$thumbnail'][0]['width'];
                  var thumbnailHeight =
                      mediaGroup['media$thumbnail'][0]['height'];
                  var numComments =
                      value['gd$comments']['gd$feedLink']['countHint'];
                  var rating =
                      parseFloat(value['gd$rating']['average']).toFixed(2);
                  str+= '<li>';
                  str+= '<a href="' + videoURL + '" target="_blank">';
                  str+= '<img src="'+thumbNail+'" width="'+thumbNailWidth+'"
                      height="'+thumbNailWidth+'" title="' + title + '" />';
                  str+= '</a>';
                  str+= '<hr>';
                  str+= '<p style="width: 120px; font-size: 12px;">Comments:
                      ' + numComments + '';
                  str+= '<br/>';
                  str+= 'Rating: ' + rating;
                  str+= '</p>';

                  str+= '</li>';
                }
                str+= '</ul>';
                $('#results').html(str);
            }
            else
            {
              $('#results').html('<li class="error">No results.</li>');
            }
          }

    </script>
```

3. All done, and we are now ready to search YouTube. Run the `index.html` file in your browser and enter a search query. Click on the **Search** button and you will see a list of videos with a number of comments and a rating for each video.

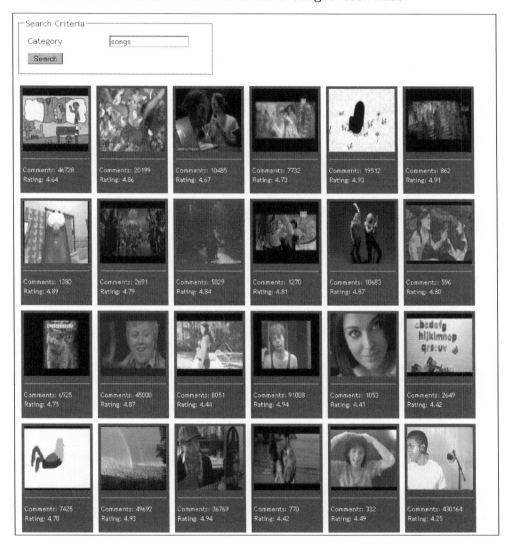

## How it works...

`script` tags are an exception to cross-browser origin policy. We can take advantage of this by requesting the URL from the `src` attribute of a `script` tag and by wrapping the raw response in a callback function. In this way the response becomes JavaScript code instead of data. This code can now be executed on the browser.

The URL for YouTube video search is as follows:

```
http://gdata.youtube.com/feeds/api/videos?q=' + query +
'&alt=json-in-script
```

Parameter `q` is the query that we entered in the textbox and `alt` is the type of response we want. Since we are using **JSONP** instead of **JSON**, the value for `alt` is defined as `json-in-script` as per YouTube API specification. On getting the response, the callback function `showVideoList` executes. It checks whether any results are available or not. If none are found, an error message is displayed. Otherwise, we get all the entry elements and iterate over them using a `for` loop. For each video entry, we get the `videoURL`, `thumbnail`, `thumbnailWidth`, `thumbnailHeight`, `numComments`, and `rating`. Then we create the HTML from these variables with a list item for each video. For each video an anchor is created with `href` set to `videoURL`. The video thumbnail is put inside the anchor and a `p` tag is created where we display the number of comments and rating for a particular video. After the HTML has been created, it is inserted in the DIV with ID `results`.

## There's more...

### About JSONP

You can read more about **JSONP** at the following websites:

- `http://remysharp.com/2007/10/08/what-is-jsonp/`
- `http://en.wikipedia.org/wiki/JSON#JSONP`

## See also

- *Sending cross-domain requests using server proxy*

# Creating an endless scrolling page

If you use Google reader or the new Twitter then you will understand what I am talking about. In both of these applications when you scroll and reach the bottom of the page they automatically load content that is appended to the bottom of the page. This behavior eliminates the need for pagination; the previous and the next buttons.

We will create an example that will have a similar functionality. On reaching the bottom of a page, an AJAX request will load data from a PHP script and will append it to the bottom of the page.

## Getting ready

Create a folder named `Recipe3` inside the `Chapter9` directory.

## How to do it...

1.  Create a new file named `index.html` inside the `Recipe3` folder. In this file, create a DIV with `container` ID along with some paragraphs so that the page becomes long enough for scrolling. Next to it create another paragraph that will show a loading text when data will be fetched from the server.

```html
<html>
  <head>
    <title>Endless Scroll</title>
    <style type="text/css">
      body{ font-family: "Trebuchet MS",verdana,arial;}
      #loading{ display:none; font-weight:bold;color:#FF0000;}
      p{padding:10px;}
    </style>

  </head>
  <body>
    <div id="container">
      <p>Test Paragraph 1</p>
      <p>Test Paragraph 2</p>
      <p>Test Paragraph 3</p>
      <p>Test Paragraph 4</p>
      <p>Test Paragraph 5</p>
      <p>Test Paragraph 6</p>
      <p>Test Paragraph 7</p>
      <p>Test Paragraph 8</p>
      <p>Test Paragraph 9</p>
      <p>Test Paragraph 10</p>
      <p>Test Paragraph 11</p>
      <p>Test Paragraph 12</p>
      <p>Test Paragraph 13</p>
      <p>Test Paragraph 14</p>
      <p>Test Paragraph 15</p>
      <p>Test Paragraph 16</p>
      <p>Test Paragraph 17</p>
      <p>Test Paragraph 18</p>
      <p>Test Paragraph 19</p>
      <p>Test Paragraph 20</p>
    </div>
    <p id="loading">loading data... </p>
    <p> </p>
  </body>
</html>
```

2. Include the `jquery.js` file before closing the `body` tag. Write the jQuery code that will add event handlers for window scroll. If the user reaches the window bottom while scrolling or using arrow keys, the code will send an AJAX request to a PHP file, `data.php`, to load the data. This data will be appended to the existing data.

```html
<script type="text/javascript" src="../jquery.js"></script>
<script type="text/javascript">
  $(document).ready(function()
  {
    $(window).scroll(loadData);
  });

    var counter = 0;
    function loadData()
    {
      if(counter < 5)
      {
        if   (isUserAtBottom())
        {
          getData();
        }
      }
    }
  function isUserAtBottom()
  {
     return (((($(document).height() - $(window).height()) -
$(window).scrollTop()) <= 50) ? true : false;
  }
  function getData()
  {
    $(window).unbind('scroll');
    $('#loading').show();

    $.get(
    'data.php',
    {},
    function(response)
    {
            counter++;
      $('#loading').hide();
      $('#container').append(response);
      $(window).scroll(loadData);
    });
  }
</script>
```

3. On the server side, create a new PHP file `data.php`. In this file, simply echo a line that will be sent to the browser.

```
<?php
  sleep(2);
  echo '<p>This data has been <br/>loaded from server...</p>';
?>
```

4. Run the `index.html` file in your browser. You will see a long list of paragraphs. Now scroll down the page using the mouse wheel or arrow keys. When you reach the bottom a loading indicator will appear.

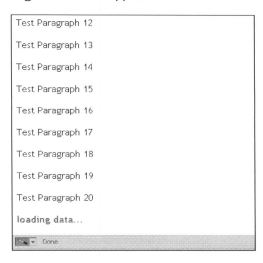

5. After the data has been loaded, this indicator will disappear and data received from the PHP script will be appended to the existing one.

## How it works...

First of all, we attached a scroll event handler to the window element. On scrolling the page through a mouse or arrow keys, the handler function `loadData` is called. Now before we load any data we will have to make sure that the user is indeed at the bottom of the page. For this purpose, a function `isUserAtBottom` is defined. To determine this we use following code:

```
return ((($(document).height() - $(window).height()) - $(window).
scrollTop()) <= 50) ? true : false;
```

`$(document).height()` is the height of the complete HTML page. `$(window).height()` is the height of the visible area of the browser or the viewport. `$(window).scrollTop()` indicates the vertical position of the scroll bar from the top. We have calculated the resulting value by subtracting the window height and scrollbar position from the document's total height. If this value is less than 50, that is, the user is 50 pixels above from the bottom of the browser, we return `true`, otherwise `false`.

Once we know that the user is at the bottom we call the `getData()` function. This function first unbinds the scroll event from the window so that no more requests could be processed until the current one completes. Then the loading indicator is displayed and an AJAX request is sent to the `data.php` file. In this example, this file echoes a single line. When the response is received in callback function, the loading indicator is hidden and the received data is appended to the DIV container. The scroll event is then again attached to the window that will allow the user to load more data. This process will continue until the value of variable counter is less than five. It means data will be fetched from the server a maximum of five times.

## There's more...

### Loading data from other sources

In this example, we have echoed a single line from PHP file. In real world applications, data will be fetched from databases or APIs. You should also allow a condition when there is no more data to load and show an appropriate response to the user.

# Creating a jQuery plugin

This recipe will explain how you can create a simple jQuery plugin. The user will be able to enter two numbers and the plugin will count from the first number to the second number while animating just like how a stopwatch changes. We will call it **Cash Counter**. You will also be able to specify how fast or slow the animation runs.

## Getting ready

Create a folder `Recipe4` inside the `Chapter9` directory.

## How to do it...

1. Create a file named `index.html` inside `Recipe4` folder. In this file, create two text boxes to enter starting and end numbers, an `h1` element to display the number as it changes, and a button to initiate the process.

```
<html>
  <head>
    <title>Cash Counter</title>
    <style type="text/css">
      body{ font-family:"Trebuchet MS",verdana,arial;
            width:900px;margin:0 auto; }
      ul{ list-style:none;padding:10px; }
      label{ display:block;float:left;width:75px; }
    </style>
  </head>
  <body>
    <ul>
      <li>
        <label>Start :</label><input type="text" id="start"/>
      </li>
      <li>
        <label>End :</label><input type="text" id="end"/>
      </li>
      <li>
        <h1 id="container"></h1>
      </li>
      <li>
        <input type="button" id="change" value="Change" />
      </li>
```

```
      </ul>
    </body>
  </html>
```

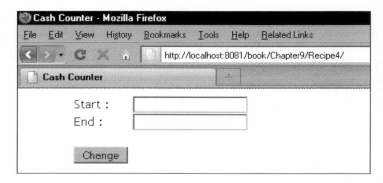

2.  Next, create a new JavaScript file and name it as `jquery.counter.js`. This file will contain the code for the plugin. Put the following code for creating the plugin:

```javascript
(function( $ )
{
  $.fn.cashCounter = function(options)
  {
    return this.each(function()
    {
      settings = $.extend
      (
        {
          start: 0,
          end: 0,
          step: .5
        },
        options
      );
      var e = $(this);
      if(isNaN(settings.start) || isNaN(settings.end) ||
          ((settings.start) == (settings.end)))
      {
        return this;
      }
      settings.increasing = (settings.start < settings.end) ?
          true : false;
      if(settings.increasing)
      {
        if(settings.start >= settings.end)
```

```
          {
            return this;
          }
        }
        else
        {
          if(settings.start <= settings.end)
          {
            return this;
          }
        }
        var diff = parseInt(settings.end,10) -
            parseInt(settings.start,10);
        var changeBy;
        if(settings.increasing)
        {
          changeBy = Math.ceil(diff * settings.step);
        }
        else
        {
          changeBy = Math.floor(diff * settings.step);
        }
        settings.start = parseInt(settings.start,10) + changeBy;
        e.html(settings.start);
        setTimeout(function()
        {
          e.cashCounter(settings);
        }, 100);

    });//each
  };
})( jQuery );
```

3. Coming back to index.html again, include the jquery.js file first and then include the just created plugin file jquery.counter.js. After that write the code for the click handler for the button that will take the values from textboxes and will run the plugin.

```
<script type="text/javascript" src="../jquery.js"></script>
<script type="text/javascript" src="jquery.counter.js"></script>
<script type="text/javascript">
  $(document).ready(function()
  {
    $('#change').click(function()
    {
```

```
if($('#start').val() != ''  && $('#end').val() != '')
{
  var startVal = $('#start').val();
  var endVal = $('#end').val();
  $('#container').cashCounter
  (
    {
      start: startVal,
      end: endVal,
      step: .2
    }
  );
}
else
{
  $('#container').html('Please enter start and
    end values.');
}
});
});
</script>
```

4. Open your browser and run the index.html file. Enter the **Start** and **End** numbers in the textboxes and click on the **Change** button. The counting will start from the start value until the end value. Since it is not possible to show the animated image, the following screenshot captures the process in between. Also try changing the step value to see how fast or slow the counting happens:

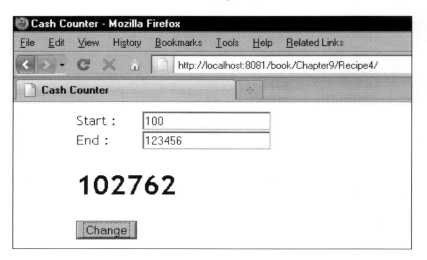

# How it works...

The `cashCounter` plugin will accept three parameters while initializing it. `start`, `end`, and `step`. While `start` and `end` values are obvious, `step` will be used to determine how fast the counting runs. Its value can vary from 0.1 to 0.9 with 0.1 being the fastest speed.

A jQuery plugin begins by extending the `jQuery.fn` object. We want to name our plugin `cashCounter`, so we wrap it in the following:

```
jQuery.fn.cashCounter = function(options)
{
};
```

All of the plugin code will go inside this block. Next is the `return this.each(function(){})` line. It ensures that a jQuery object is returned to the calling function. This will help maintain the chaining of elements as supported by jQuery.

Next is the `settings` object that defines the default values for a plugin if they are not supplied. In case these values are supplied we extend these by merging the user provided `options` object with the default settings. By default, both start and end have a zero value and the value for `step` is 5.

With all the settings in place we can now write the functionality. If `start` or `end` values are not numbers or if `start` is equal to `end` we stop the code execution by returning from the function.

Then, we set a property `increasing` for the `settings` object. If the `end` value is greater than `start` we set it to `true`, otherwise `false`. In case `increasing` is `true`, if the `start` value exceeds the `end` value we terminate further execution. Similarly, if `increasing` is `false` we terminate if the `end` value exceeds the `start` value.

Then, we find the difference of `start` and `end` values and calculate a variable `changeBy`, which will increase or decrease the `start` value depending on the variable step. The new `start` value is set and also inserted into the requesting element, `h1 container` in this case.

Finally, we call the JavaScript `setTimeout` function that calls the `cashCounter` function recursively after 100 milliseconds. On each execution, `if` conditions will be checked and once the `end` value is reached, the control will exit out of application.

# Displaying RSS feeds with jQuery and PHP

In this recipe we will fetch a **Really Simple Syndication** (**RSS**) feed of a blog using PHP and then display it in the page using jQuery. RSS is a standard format for publishing feeds and there are several formats of RSS feeds. The feed we will use is in RSS2.0 and its standard structure is shown in the following screenshot:

```
- <rss version="2.0">
  - <channel>
      <title>PHP, javascript and AJAX at vijayjoshi.org</title>
      <atom:link href="http://www.vijayjoshi.org/feed/" rel="self" type="application/rss+xml"/>
      <link>http://www.vijayjoshi.org</link>
      <description>php | javascript | ajax | and all things web</description>
      <lastBuildDate>Mon, 09 Aug 2010 12:03:19 +0000</lastBuildDate>
      <generator>http://wordpress.org/?v=2.8.4</generator>
      <language>en</language>
      <sy:updatePeriod>hourly</sy:updatePeriod>
      <sy:updateFrequency>1</sy:updateFrequency>
    - <item>
        <title>19 Things NOT To Do When Building a Website</title>
      + <link></link>
      + <comments></comments>
        <pubDate>Mon, 09 Aug 2010 12:03:19 +0000</pubDate>
        <dc:creator>Vijay Joshi</dc:creator>
        <category>Web Design</category>
        <category>Technology</category>
        <guid isPermaLink="false">http://www.vijayjoshi.org/?p=570</guid>
      - <description>
          Here is a very useful post I found today. 19 mistakes to avoid while designing websites. Although, I am no expert on designing but I have found myself making
          some of these mistakes then and now. Some of my favorites from the list are: If your website does not work in Firefox, welcome to 2007 DUMBASS. If your
          [...]
        </description>
      + <wfw:commentRss></wfw:commentRss>
        <slash:comments>1</slash:comments>
      </item>
```

## Getting ready

Create a folder named `Recipe5` inside the `Chapter9` directory.

## How to do it...

1.  Create a file `index.html` inside `Recipe5` folder. In this file, define some CSS styles for elements and create a `div` with ID `results`, which will serve as a container for displaying posts from the feed.

    ```html
    <html>
      <head>
        <title>Parse RSS Feed</title>
        <style type="text/css">
          body { font-family:"Trebuchet MS",verdana,arial;
                 width:900px;margin:0 auto; }
          ul{ border:1px solid #000;float:left;list-style:none;
              margin:0;padding:0;width:900px; }
    ```

```
      li{ padding:5px;border:1px solid #000; }
      h3 { color:brown;cursor:pointer;text-decoration:none; }
      span{ font-size: 12px;font-weight:bold;}
      .content{ display:none;}
      div { width:100%;}
      a{font-weight:bold;}
    </style>
  </head>
  <body>
    <div id="results">loading
    </div>
  </body>
</html>
```

2. Before the closing `<body>` tag, include the `jquery.js` file. Then send a get AJAX request to a PHP file `feed.php`. This file will return an XML response that will be handled by the callback function `showPosts`. Define the `showPosts` function that will parse the response XML and will create the HTML from it. The resulting HTML will be inserted inside the `results` DIV on the page.

```
<script type="text/javascript" src="../jquery.js"></script>
<script type="text/javascript">
  $(document).ready(function()
  {
    $.get(
      'feed.php',
      {},
      showPosts
    );
    function showPosts(data)
    {
      var posts = $(data).find('channel>item');
      var str = '<ul>';
      $.each(posts, function(index, value)
      {
        var title = $(value).find('title').text();
        var link = $(value).find('link').text();
        var description = $(value).find('description').text();
        var comments =
                $(value).find('slash\\:comments').text();
        var pDate = new Date($(value).find('pubDate').text());
        var day = pDate.getDate();
        var month = parseInt(pDate.getMonth(),10) + 1;
        var year = pDate.getFullYear();
        var fullDate = day + '-' + month + '-' + year;
```

```
                    str+= '<li>';
                    str+= '<div>';
                    str+= '<h3>' + title + '</h3>';
                    str+= '<div class="content">';
                    str+= '<p>';
                    str+= description;
                    str+= ' <a href="' + link + '" target="_blank">Read
                            Full Post</a>';
                    str+= '</p>';
                    str+= '<span>Published on ' + fullDate + ' with '
                            + comments + ' comments</span>';
                    str+= '</div>';
                    str+= '</div>';
                    str+= '</li>';
                });
                str+= '</ul>';
                $('#results').html(str);
                $('#results ul li:even').css({'background-color':
                        'CornflowerBlue'});
            }
            $('h3').live('click',function()
            {
                $(this).next('div').slideToggle('fast');
            });
        });
    </script>
```

3. Now create the `feed.php` file. This file will get the XML for the RSS feed from a URL and will echo it to the browser.

```php
<?php
    $feedData = file_get_contents('http://vijayjoshi.org/feed');
    header('Content-type:text/xml;');
    echo $feedData;
?>
```

4. Run the `index.html` file in the browser. You will see a loading text first. After the response is received, a list of posts will be seen initially. Clicking on a post title will expand to show its summary, publication date, and comment count. The summary will have a **Read Full Post** link that will open that post in a new window:

## How it works...

After the DOM is ready an AJAX request is sent to the PHP file `feed.php`. This file gets the contents of the RSS feed from a URL using the `file_get_contents` function. The `rss` element is the root of an XML file. `channel` is a child of the `rss` node that contains information about the blog and the ten latest entries. Each entry is represented by an `item` node in this file. We then echo the received XML to the browser.

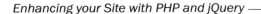

In jQuery, `showPosts` is the callback function that receives the XML in the `data` variable. jQuery can parse XML just like HTML elements. So to get the posts, we use the `find` method that gets all the item elements.

```
var posts = $(data).find('channel>item');
```

Then, we iterate over the `posts` variable and on each iteration we get the values for the title of the post, link to the post, summary of contents, number of comments, and the publishing date. Using these variables, we create a list of items inside an unordered list. The post title is given inside an `h3` element. Next is a DIV that contains the post summary, link to the post, date, and number of comments. This DIV has a class `content` assigned to it. The display property for content class is set to none. Therefore, only the post title will be visible when the posts are displayed.

After the list is complete we insert it inside a DIV with ID `results`.

We also have a click event handler function for `h3` elements. Clicking on `h3` elements gets the DIV next to it and toggles its display using `slideToggle` function. Thus, clicking the post title will show or hide its post summary. Clicking on the **Read Full Post** link will open the original post in a new window.

## See also

▶ *Adding events to elements that will be created later* from *Chapter 1*

# Firebug

In this chapter, we will cover:

- ▶ Inspecting elements
- ▶ Editing HTML and CSS
- ▶ Debugging JavaScript

## Introduction

If you are not aware of Firebug, you are missing a great web development tool. Firebug is an add-on for Firefox, which sits inside the browser and provides many tools to assist in web development. You can watch the document or HTML structure, the CSS styles applied to elements, debug JavaScript, and much more.

First of all install Firebug from its website `http://getfirebug.com/`. After installation it is ready to use in web pages. You can activate it by pressing *F12* or by clicking a bug icon in the status bar.

Firebug has six buttons on the toolbar whose names and functions are described below.

- ▶ **Console**: It shows the errors in your JavaScript in the form of friendly error messages with line numbers. Along with errors it also displays the AJAX requests. You can see the data sent with an AJAX request, request and response headers, and the response from the AJAX request itself.

  You can also log your own variables in console. `console.log()` can be used to log data in the console.

  ```
  Var x = 10;
  console.log('Value of x is: ' + x);
  ```

This code in your script will display the following in the Firebug console:

**Value of x is 10**

This is a great replacement for the ugly alert boxes, which developers use frequently to check the value of variables and so on.

▶ **HTML**: This panel shows the document structure and HTML of a page. On the right-hand side it shows the CSS styles for the selected element.

▶ **CSS:** It lists all the CSS files available to a web page. After selecting this panel, you can select the desired file from a drop down and edit it.

▶ **Script:** It lists all the JavaScript files used in the web page. You can select a file, put breakpoints on specific lines, and can watch variables.

▶ **DOM**: It lists all the DOM objects and functions. Firebug displays their values in a formatted manner. You can also edit the values of variables from here.

▶ **Net**: This panel shows all the resources or files that the page has loaded. Firebug displays the size of each file and a progress bar, which tracks how much time each file is taking to load. Using these metrics you can optimize the page performance. You can also monitor network activity by resource type. The **Net** panel has further options that allow you to group HTML, CSS, JavaScript, AJAX requests, and images together.

# Inspecting elements

This recipe will introduce the **HTML** panel of Firebug and how it can be used to inspect the document structure, select an HTML element, and watch its CSS style.

## How to do it...

1.  Open an HTML page, for example, `http://www.google.com` in your browser.

2.  Now click on the arrow icon from the Firebug bar and move your mouse pointer over any element on the page. The element will be highlighted and in the Firebug panel you will see details of that HTML element, as seen in the following screenshot:

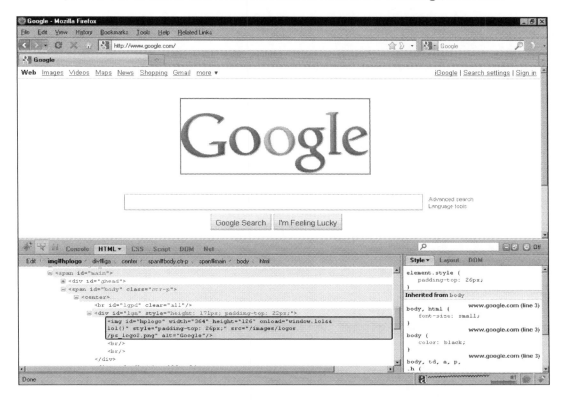

3.  Another method, which is faster and more accurate, is to right-click on an element and click on **Inspect Element** on the context menu. Firebug will set the focus on the selected element.

## How it works...

The **HTML** panel of Firebug is divided into two parts. The left panel shows the HTML whereas the right part shows the CSS styles. Clicking on the **Inspect** button allows us to inspect any element on the page. Moving the mouse pointer over any element will then display the element details in the **HTML** panel of Firebug. This panel displays the complete HTML of the document. This way we can see the complete structure of a page. There is one more advantage of inspecting elements in the **HTML** panel. It also shows the elements created after page load, that is, if you created any elements with jQuery or JavaScript, it will also show them in the **HTML** panel.

Once an element is selected, the right-hand side of Firebug shows its CSS styles whether defined in a stylesheet or created by a script.

## There's more...

### Plugins for firebug

Yes, you read that right. Firebug itself is a plugin, however, there are some other plugins that are very useful in rapid web development and are recommended to use with Firebug. Both of the tools listed next are useful in determining network activity, page performance, download time, and so on. Both of these provide a score of page performance against a set of rules and listed recommendations that can make page performance faster:

- **Google Page Speed**: It is a plugin from Google. The following is its description from the Google site:

  *Page Speed is an open-source Add-on for Firebug. Webmasters and web developers can use Page Speed to evaluate the performance of their web pages and to get suggestions on how to improve them.*

  You can download Page Speed from the following URL:
  `http://code.google.com/speed/page-speed/download.html`

- **Yahoo! YSlow**: It is a plugin from Yahoo!, and can be downloaded from `https://developer.yahoo.com/yslow/`.

## See also

- The next recipe *Editing HTML and CSS*

# Editing HTML and CSS

In a typical scenario of editing a page, you open the page in an editor, make changes in it, and then reload the web page to see the changes. If there is something wrong, or anything is not as desired, you go back to the editor and repeat the cycle.

Well, there's no need for this anymore when you have the power of Firebug. This recipe will explain how you can edit the HTML and CSS of a page or specific elements in real time using Firebug. Once all the changes are made you can implement those into your source code at once.

## How to do it...

1. Take any recipe from this book. For example *Creating an accordion style menu* from Chapter 7 and open it in the browser.

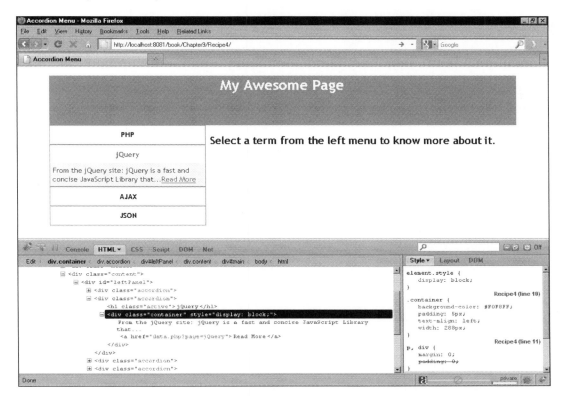

2. Now using the **Inspect** button locate the h1 element on the page, which has **jQuery** written inside it. Click on the **Edit** button beneath the **Inspect** button and you will be able to edit the HTML of the h1 element. Change the text inside it to **About jQuery**.

3. Now click on the DIV with class `container`. On the right panel you will see the container class and its CSS properties. You can edit its existing properties by clicking on the property values and then change them to the required values. For example, click on the value for `background-color` and change it from `#F0F8FF` to `#ff0000`. All elements with class `container` will now have a red background colour.

4. To add a new property, right-click on that class name and select **New Property**. It will append a new line to the existing properties where you can add new properties and their values. Add two new properties `color` and `font-weight` with values `#fff` and `bold` respectively. This change will be reflected in all elements with class `container`.

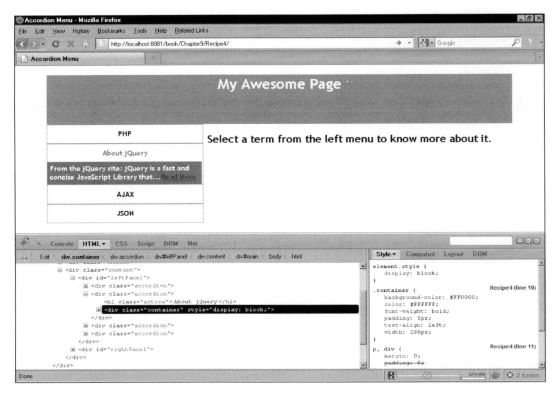

## Changing style for a specific element

Apart from changing CSS for already defined classes, you can also specify CSS properties for individual elements. For this, right-click anywhere on the right panel and select **Edit Element Style** option. This will append a new row in the right-hand column for adding CSS name values that will be applicable to only the selected element.

# Debugging JavaScript

Firebug can also be used to debug JavaScript in a browser. You can place breakpoints and debug the code line by line. In addition to it you can also watch variables and DOM elements changing in real time.

## How to do it...

1. To put breakpoints in your JavaScript code, open Firebug either by clicking the icon in the status bar or by pressing *F12*.

2. Then click on the **Script** button in the Firebug toolbar. This will show a list of all the available scripts for that page.

3. Select a script among these and that file will be displayed in the Firebug content panel.

4. After a file has been selected you can put breakpoints on a line by clicking just before the line number. A breakpoint is indicated by a dark brown colour circle.

5. Now you are ready for debugging. In the example seen in the next screenshot—the tic-tac-toe game—place a breakpoint on line **18**. It will execute whenever a column of the game is clicked upon.

6. Click on a column and you will see that the execution has halted on that line.

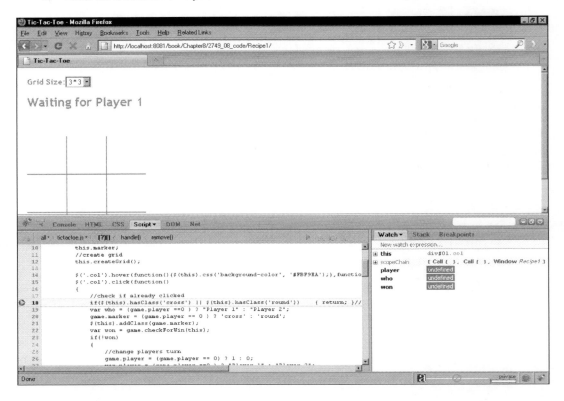

7. Now you can watch the code execution line by line. To go to the next line press *F10* on your keyboard. If you encounter a function, you can press *F11* and control step into it.

8. You can also watch variables. In the right panel there is a line called **New Watch Expression**. You can write a variable name or an expression here and Firebug will evaluate its value.

9. Pressing *F8* will continue the code execution till another breakpoint is encountered.

## There's more...

### Debugging in a nutshell

- ▶ *F8*: Continue.
- ▶ *F10*: Step Over. It takes control to next line.
- ▶ *F11*: Step Into. If you press F11 on a line where a function is defined, control will go inside the defined function.
- ▶ *F12*: Open or close Firebug on a web page.

### Inspecting AJAX requests

The console of Firebug logs all the AJAX requests sent from the browser. It also shows the response code for each request. For each request, the parameters sent, request and response headers, and server response can be seen.

### Web developer toolbar

The Web developer toolbar is another handy tool, through which you can control behaviour of various elements on the page. It also provides a large set of tools that operate on web pages.

You can disable or enable JavaScript, images, view page structure, form info, and so on. It can be obtained from `https://addons.mozilla.org/firefox/addon/60`.

# Index

# X

# Y

## Thank you for buying
## PHP jQuery Cookbook

# About Packt Publishing

Packt, pronounced 'packed', published its first book "*Mastering phpMyAdmin for Effective MySQL Management*" in April 2004 and subsequently continued to specialize in publishing highly focused books on specific technologies and solutions.

Our books and publications share the experiences of your fellow IT professionals in adapting and customizing today's systems, applications, and frameworks. Our solution based books give you the knowledge and power to customize the software and technologies you're using to get the job done. Packt books are more specific and less general than the IT books you have seen in the past. Our unique business model allows us to bring you more focused information, giving you more of what you need to know, and less of what you don't.

Packt is a modern, yet unique publishing company, which focuses on producing quality, cutting-edge books for communities of developers, administrators, and newbies alike. For more information, please visit our website: www.packtpub.com.

# About Packt Open Source

In 2010, Packt launched two new brands, Packt Open Source and Packt Enterprise, in order to continue its focus on specialization. This book is part of the Packt Open Source brand, home to books published on software built around Open Source licences, and offering information to anybody from advanced developers to budding web designers. The Open Source brand also runs Packt's Open Source Royalty Scheme, by which Packt gives a royalty to each Open Source project about whose software a book is sold.

# Writing for Packt

We welcome all inquiries from people who are interested in authoring. Book proposals should be sent to author@packtpub.com. If your book idea is still at an early stage and you would like to discuss it first before writing a formal book proposal, contact us; one of our commissioning editors will get in touch with you.

We're not just looking for published authors; if you have strong technical skills but no writing experience, our experienced editors can help you develop a writing career, or simply get some additional reward for your expertise.

# jQuery 1.4 Reference Guide

ISBN: 978-1-849510-04-2          Paperback: 336 pages

A comprehensive exploration of the popular
JavaScript library

1. Quickly look up features of the jQuery library

2. Step through each function, method, and selector
   expression in the jQuery library with an easy-to-
   follow approach

3. Understand the anatomy of a jQuery script

4. Write your own plug-ins using jQuery's powerful
   plug-in architecture

# jQuery Plugin Development Beginner's Guide

ISBN: 978-1-849512-24-4          Paperback: 288 pages

Build powerful, interactive plugins to implement jQuery
in the best way possible

1. Utilize jQuery's plugin framework to create a wide
   range of useful jQuery plugins from scratch

2. Understand development patterns and best
   practices and move up the ladder to master
   plugin development

3. Discover the ins and outs of some of the most
   popular jQuery plugins in action

4. A Beginner's Guide packed with examples and
   step-by-step instructions to quickly get your hands
   dirty in developing high quality jQuery plugins

Please check **www.PacktPub.com** for information on our titles

2288143R00177

Printed in Great Britain
by Amazon.co.uk, Ltd.,
Marston Gate.